# Introductory Java

**David Parsons**
*Senior Lecturer*
Systems Engineering Faculty, Southampton Institute

Letts Educational
Aldine Place
London W12 8AW
0181 740 2268

1998

A CIP catalogue record for this book is available from the British Library

ISBN 1-85805-366-8
Copyright David Parsons © 1998

First edition 1998

All rights reserved.
No part of this publication may be reproduced, stored in a retrieval system, or
transmitted in any form or by any means, electronic, mechanical, photocopying,
recording or otherwise, without the prior written permission of the copyright owner.

Typeset by Tech Set Limited, Gateshead, Tyne & Wear.

Printed in Great Britain by
Ashford Colour Press, Gosport, Hants.

KING ALFRED'S COLLEGE
WINCHESTER

02098124

005.133
JAV

# Introductory Java

THE LIBRARY

UNIVERSITY OF
WINCHESTER

KA 0209812 1

To my inheritance hierarchy: my parents and my children

# Contents

# Preface

Given the very large number of Java books available it might be reasonable to ask why yet another one? But if we look at the market we can see that there is a demand for many different kinds of programming book. There are readers at many different levels of skill and experience from the first-year student to the professional software developer, and each requires a different approach. With a wide-ranging language like Java that provides syntax for programming in many different contexts there are also many application areas where particular areas of the language can be explored, such as Internet programming or developing graphical user interfaces. Each area can warrant a complete book in its own right.

The approach of this book is to provide a simple introduction to the key features of Java, assuming some basic understanding of computer programming. Particular emphasis is placed on the object-oriented nature of the language, and the example programs are developed along with aspects of object-oriented design using the Unified Modeling Language to describe key features of the objects used. The book is divided into five parts:

*1. Introduction to Java*
In this section, the fundamental ideas are introduced, along with the minimum syntax required to write and run simple Java applications. Some of the objects available with Java are investigated.

*2. Building Java objects, writing Java code*
In this section, the concepts and syntax necessary to build and use our own objects are investigated. As well as the object-oriented aspects of classes, the traditional structural elements of code (namely sequence, selection and iteration) are introduced.

*3. Object and class relationships*
Having learned how to create and use objects, we then turn our attention to making collections of objects work together to produce a working application. In addition, more complex classes are investigated using inheritance and polymorphism, key features of object-oriented systems.

*4. Graphical user interfaces*
No Java book can ignore the importance of the Abstract Windowing Toolkit, a

library of classes that allows graphical user interfaces (GUIs) to be easily constructed. The most important components of a GUI are investigated, along with the necessary syntax for linking an application and an interface together.

*5. Java and the web*
The final section introduces the simplest aspects of Java and the world wide web, namely, writing applets that can be run over the Internet. It was this aspect of Java that first brought it to the attention of the computing world and it remains one of its key strengths.

The material covered in these sections is intended to cover the basic concepts and syntax upon which the reader can build. Some of the programming and design strategies employed are chosen for their simplicity and readability rather than efficiency or elegance, and the reader is encouraged to consider alternative ways of implementing some of the code. There are many features of Java either ignored completely or introduced at a very superficial level, and it is expected that readers will progress to more detailed and advanced texts once they have grasped the material in this book.

## Code and compilers

The code examples, particularly in the later chapters, assume that the reader has access to the Sun Java Development Kit version 1.1 or 1.2. It is important to note that many of the programs in this book will not work with the older version 1.0 compiler. There are also many Java programming environments available that provide more sophisticated development tools than the JDK, which does not include either an editor or a visual GUI builder. These environments can make development easier, particularly when building user interfaces, but the JDK is perfectly adequate if used in conjunction with a good text editor. The JDK itself can be easily downloaded from the Sun web site (there is a link from the Letts web page for this book) and there are many other development tools that either include it or work in conjunction with it. Chapters eight and nine assume that interfaces will be built manually, but other tools can make this process much simpler. Nevertheless the code behind the interface still needs to be written, so the examples are still valid even when the interface is automatically generated by a 'visual' programming tool.

The example code in the book has been tested on a number of different Java compilers, ranging from JDK1.1.1 to 1.1.6 and JDK1.2beta3. Given the stage of development of Java, where bug fixes have occurred on a regular basis, it is not possible to guarantee that all programs will run totally reliably on all versions of the JDK. However, none of them should cause any major problems when used on any compatible compiler.

The design notation used in this book is taken from the Unified Modeling Language, developed by Booch, Rumbaugh and Jacobson. It is a well-established standard notation for object-oriented design and is available in a number of CASE tools.

# The web site

The web page associated with the book appears on the Letts web site at the following address:

  http://www.lettsed.co.uk/parsons.htm

As well as general information about the book this page includes

- a self-extracting executable containing all the source code for the example programs and some exercises in the book. This can be downloaded and run to install the files on your machine in appropriate subdirectories
- the applets from chapter eleven of the book running in HMTL pages
- links to other web sites, including the Sun Java site ('www.javasoft.com' for the JDK and Javadoc information and other useful pages) and the Rational site ('www.rational.com' for UML information and resources).

My thanks are due to the group of students on whom I piloted most of the material in the book. They pointed out many errors and inconsistencies that I have hopefully remedied. Those that remain I have no doubt that other readers will find. If you have any comments or suggestions about the book, then you can email me at the following address:

  dave.parsons@solent.ac.uk

**Part 1**

# Introduction to Java

# 1

# Java comes to town

'We take a handful of sand from the endless landscape of awareness around us and call that handful of sand the world' – Robert Pirsig (*Zen and the Art of Motorcycle Maintenance*).

Following several years of development, Java became publicly available via the Internet in 1995 and within a year had become 'the next big thing' in software. Interest in the language was quite remarkable, considering that it existed only in 'beta' test versions. In many ways it was a question of being the right product at the right time, its popularity riding on the explosion of interest in the Internet and world wide web in the mid 1990s.

## Brief history of Java

Java was never intended to be quite what it has become. It grew out of a project at Sun Microsystems to build the 'Star7', a Personal Digital Assistant (PDA). A PDA is intended to control all the electronic devices in our homes, so needs to be driven by a language that can be used on various pieces of hardware, from televisions to toasters. The language that drove the Star7 was called 'Oak' (named after a tree outside the window of its main designer, James Gosling), but attempts to sell the technology to various potential customers, such as digital TV 'set top box' manufacturers, fell through. Eventually, it was decided to sideline the hardware development and promote the language itself on the Internet as a tool for providing on-line multimedia. This led to development of a program that would run on the Internet using the HTML (Hyper Text Markup Language) pages that provided the basis for the world wide web, which had arrived in 1993 with 'Mosaic' the first graphical web browser. This program was the 'WebRunner' web browser, later renamed 'HotJava'. Unlike the other browsers that existed at that time, HotJava was able to run small Java programs (known as 'applets') within its window, adding dynamic content to the largely static text and images that had previously been possible. The first ever applet showed 'Duke' (the Java mascot, a sort of extracted tooth with a red nose) waving, establishing a strong and abiding image of Java as a language for writing animated web pages, though in practice it is much more than that. And the Java name? It changed from 'Oak' only because there was already a registered trademark of that

3

name. Java is named after the strong Java coffee popular in the United States, though many other names were considered including 'Neon', 'Lyric', 'Pepper' and 'Silk'.

## Characteristics of Java

Java is in many ways a conservative language, in that it builds on the successes of its predecessors whilst attempting to overcome many of their limitations and problems. It was designed to be 'jargon-compatible' with a set of criteria that sum up what is 'good' in a programming language for the millennium. Its designers reasoned that such a language should be

- simple
- object-oriented
- distributed
- robust
- secure
- architecture neutral
- portable
- high performance
- multithreaded
- dynamic.

Now follows a brief outline of each of these features.

*Simple*   Nobody wants to program in a language that makes life more difficult than it already is. James Gosling is often quoted as saying that Java is 'C++ without the knives, guns and clubs'. C++, the language developed by Stroustrup in the 1980s as an object-oriented extension to the C programming language, is very popular and powerful but has many features that, like weapons, are very dangerous in the wrong hands (perhaps any hands). Java has much in common with C++, but a good deal of arms limitation has been applied. Simplicity is, however, a relative term!

*Object-oriented*   The object-oriented approach to programming has become so common that any new language must address this need. In an object-oriented language, instead of having data on one hand and processes on the other, the two are 'encapsulated' together to provide objects that have both state (data) and behaviour (processes). By tying the two together, we make it easier to model the behaviour of the real-world things that we are trying to reflect in software. Much of this book is concerned with the concepts and application of object orientation.

*Distributed*   If computing is anything these days then it is distributed since most computers are connected to a network and probably to the Internet. There is a trend towards making the machine on the desk less important and the network that it is connected to more important, by providing all software from the network rather than storing it locally on a hard disk. For companies this makes a lot of sense in terms of control, economy and organisation. Therefore any new language must provide the facilities to write systems where programs are distributed across many computers.

Java is designed for network programming and can easily work with common Internet protocols such as HTTP (Hyper Text Transfer Protocol) and FTP (File Transfer Protocol).

*Robust*   A robust program is one that does not behave unpredictably or fail due to programmer error. By automatically taking on some tasks such as memory management, Java simplifies the task of the programmer, allowing more robust code to be written. It is also very strict about using the correct 'data types', meaning that it is difficult deliberately to corrupt the data in a program to, for example, introduce a virus.

  Perhaps the most significant aspect of Java in terms of robustness is that it removes the concept of the 'pointer' from code. A pointer is a mechanism for directly accessing memory, and many languages allow a programmer to allocate and manipulate a block of memory directly. Although this is a powerful feature, it is also a dangerous one if not managed correctly. Manipulating memory that has not been correctly allocated can crash a program, whereas failing to free up memory that has been finished with leads to 'memory leaks' where a program can eventually run out of memory space to run in. Java has only 'references' to objects, not pointers to the memory they occupy. Since programmers cannot directly access memory, they cannot wrongly manipulate it. In addition, since they cannot directly allocate memory, it is not the programmers' responsibility to free it up either. That task is undertaken by the garbage collector, an aspect of the Java system that automatically recovers memory from objects that are no longer needed.

*Secure*   As well as programmer error, programs are vulnerable to deliberate sabotage. Security systems built into Java ensure that the code, once written, is not easy to tamper with. This is particularly important for a language that is used to write programs that are distributed widely over networks. There are also a number of restrictions placed on what Java programs (applets) can do when they are running on a remote machine. The detail of Java security features is beyond the scope of this book, and involves many issues including the way that browser software handles Java applets.

*Architecture neutral*   One of the most important aspects of Java (perhaps the most important) is that it is a 'write once, run anywhere' language. In other words, it does not matter which type of computer you write Java code on, or run the resulting programs on. The programs are written and run just the same. This is achieved by combining two different approaches to converting program source code into a runnable program. Most languages are either compiled or interpreted. A compiler converts the entire source code of a program into an 'executable', a program targeted to run within a specific operating system. In contrast, an interpreter converts the source code into runnable code one line at a time while the program is actually running. This is much slower than running a compiled program, but the same piece of source code can be run on different interpreters that are designed for different operating systems. Since an interpreted program can be run only when the interpreter is present, there is an extra overhead when using such programs – two pieces of software (the program and the interpreter) are needed rather than just one.

Java draws on both of these approaches by being a combination of both a compiled and an interpreted language. The Java compiler does not convert the source code into an executable for a specific environment. Rather, it compiles into 'byte code'. This byte code can then be run on any hardware that has a 'Java virtual machine', a relatively lightweight piece of software that interprets the byte code to run on a specific computer. For example the same Java byte code can be run on a PC running windows or a Sun station running Unix, with no changes to the original program. In this way the amount of interpretation required is reduced to the absolute minimum to allow the same byte code to run on different systems (Figure 1.1).

*Portable*   Part of the architecture neutrality is based on portable definitions of how big different types of data are. In many languages, there is no specific definition of how much storage, an integer, say, takes up in relation to other types such as 'short' and 'long' integers. One of these might be eight bits long on one machine and sixteen bits on another. In Java the storage sizes of all types of data are specified so an integer, for example, is always sixteen bits long. Java types are also always signed, meaning that they can contain both positive and negative numbers.

*High performance*   Execution speed can be something of a problem for Java. Because the byte code has to be interpreted, Java programs always run more slowly than programs written in languages that are compiled. To overcome this problem, a number of strategies have been adopted. Just-in-time (JIT) compilers have been developed that speed up the interpretation process, and 'native' compilers have also been written. In other words, the architecture neutrality is sacrificed in order to run the programs more quickly. A program written on a 'native' compiler works only on a specific type of machine. This can be useful for developers who want a system that

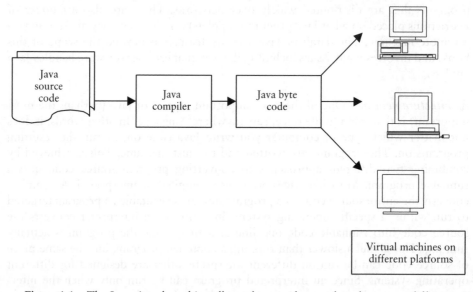

**Figure 1.1**   The Java virtual machine allows the same byte code to be run on different platforms and operating systems.

compiles and runs quickly for testing purposes. The same code can then be recompiled into portable byte code using a normal Java compiler when it is completed. Another important development has been the 'Java chip' which is a hardware virtual machine (a slightly less virtual machine perhaps) built into a chip. This is much faster than running byte code with software, and Java chips can be embedded in all kinds of electronic devices.

*Multithreaded* Since many operating systems allow multithreading (where more than one process can be going on at any one time) it is useful if a language can take advantage of this. By building syntax for multithreading into the language, Java makes it easier for programmers to write multithreaded programs that are more efficient than single-threaded programs (where only one thing can be happening at any one time). Even where the operating system itself is not multithreaded, Java code can be written that uses multiple threads of control.

*Dynamic* A Java program can dynamically change the resources it is using at run time. This is useful in a distributed environment because it means that the program can be flexible in terms of size and behaviour. It is also easy to write programs that use many different objects because it is easy for them to find each other at run time, even when they are in different places.

## Java versions

Java first appeared for public consumption as version 1.0 in 1995. There were a number of minor modifications before its first major revision to Java 1.1 in 1996. Java 1.1 has gone though a number of minor modifications and bug fixes from version 1.1.1 to 1.1.6, but is basically the same compiler and libraries. Perhaps the most significant change between these two versions is to the Abstract Windowing Toolkit (AWT) that is used to build user interfaces. In version 1.1, the way that events are handled was changed. Events are typically things that the user does such as pressing a button with the mouse or selecting an item from a menu. Java 1.2 (introduced in 1998) mainly provided extensions to Java 1.1 rather than major changes to the fundamentals of the language. The code in this book is compatible with both Java 1.1 and Java 1.2.

## Java APIs

As well as the core Java syntax, which consists of the basic keywords and some fundamental libraries, there are also a large number of Java application programming interfaces (APIs). These provide libraries to allow the development of specialised applications such as Internet programming and component-based development (using 'Java Beans'). Most of these are beyond the scope of this book, but they provide a number of powerful programming features for various types of software application.

## Learning Java

To program in Java successfully we need to understand object-oriented concepts and then apply them to Java objects, which have their own peculiarities. It is, however, worth the effort because Java can be more rewarding than any other programming language. Its rich syntax and wide-ranging APIs mean that it can be used for all kinds of programming, from simply making a web page more exciting to building a distributed client server system or a complex multithreaded real-time system. Long after the initial hype surrounding Java has died away, it will be providing programmers with the tools for coding a host of applications in all kinds of contexts.

# 2

# Learning the language of objects

'The limits of my language mean the limits of my world' – Ludwig Wittgenstein (*Tractatus Logico-Philosophicus*).

In this chapter we learn the language of objects and ask the question 'Why is Java object-oriented'?

## Objects

Object-oriented programming is based on a simple premise, that as human beings we think of the world around us as being made up of objects and that software can be made up of objects too. Of course it is not quite that simple. Although we can look at real-world objects to help us understand the key concepts of object orientation, we must also realise that objects in software have their own particular characteristics. In this chapter we will begin by looking at objects and their relationships in the real world and then see how these ideas can be applied to the task of programming.

A real-world object is something we perceive as having a unique identity (my ruler, that pencil, etc.) and an existence that can be described in terms of what it is (a blunt HB pencil with a chewed rubber on the end) and what is does (it draws and it rubs out). In *Zen and the Art of Motorcycle Maintenance*, Robert Pirsig draws a diagram of his motorcycle that includes both its components and its functions as different aspects of the same object (Figure 2.1).

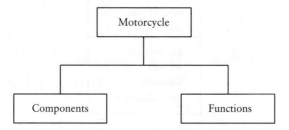

Figure 2.1    A motorcycle object includes both its components and its functions.

9

We notice some other things about objects too. We find that individual objects are not so unusual that they do not have a lot in common with other objects of a similar type. For example, we can recognise all kinds of rulers as being of type 'ruler', even though they may be different lengths, have different measuring scales and be made of different materials. We also notice that objects are not much use on their own. A ruler, to be useful, must interact with other objects (such as people and pencils) in order to measure, or to draw a line.

To explore these ideas further we will use the example of a clock, which has the advantage of being an object that spans the gap between the real world and programming. As well as being surrounded by clocks of different types in our everyday lives, we are also frequently bombarded by clocks in software, since they appear in a quiet corner of many applications. First, we will look at some aspects of 'real-world' clocks.

## A clock object

Take a particular clock and describe it. It might be a wall clock with a round face and three hands. Say it has a white face, with black hour and minute hands and a red second hand. This is all descriptive about what a clock is, or its 'state'. Some aspects of a clock's state will not be so obvious to us. In a battery-powered clock for example the level of charge in the battery does not become evident until the clock stops. The state of an object is represented by its 'attributes'.

It also has 'behaviour' which is what the clock actually does. The most important (possibly only) behaviour of a clock is to tell us the time. State and behaviour are very closely related, as we can see if we consider that the state of the clock at any one time includes the time that it is displaying. Similarly, the behaviour of an alarm clock that allows it to ring is related to its state of ringing. The behaviours that an object can perform are known as its 'methods'. Figure 2.2 shows a Unified Modeling Language (UML) diagram that shows some attributes and methods of a clock object. In this kind of diagram, a rectangle is divided into three, with the top section containing the type of the object, the middle section the names of the attributes and the bottom part the names of the methods.

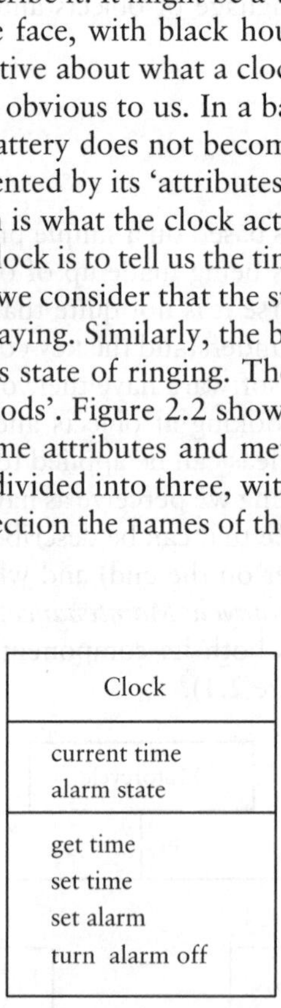

| Clock |
|---|
| current time |
| alarm state |
| get time |
| set time |
| set alarm |
| turn  alarm off |

**Figure 2.2**   UML diagram of a clock, with some attributes and methods.

## Encapsulation and information hiding

An object 'encapsulates' both state and behaviour by drawing them together into a cohesive whole. This encapsulation brings together the public interface of an object (the face it presents to the outside world) with private elements that go to make up its inner representation. Part of this drawing together of an object's state and behaviour is the ability to hide much of the inner workings of an object. We need to see the face of the clock, but we do not need to know how it works. We might need to interface with it in other ways, such as changing the battery or winding a clockwork mechanism, but we still do not need to know how it actually works to use it. This characteristic of objects is called 'information hiding' and helps to simplify the building of software systems because it hides what we do not need to know, allowing us to focus on the important aspects of an object's character. Thus an object shows the world only that which the world needs to see. This is rather like a company or other organisation that has some parts of its operation that provide its public image and other parts that provide purely internal services (Figure 2.3).

# Classifying clocks

We are able to recognise that two objects that appear the same have a different identity. If we stand next to a production line watching hundreds of identical clocks go by, we know that they are all individual objects. It may be that the internal state of all these clocks is the same. For example, analogue clocks (i.e., clocks with hands) are

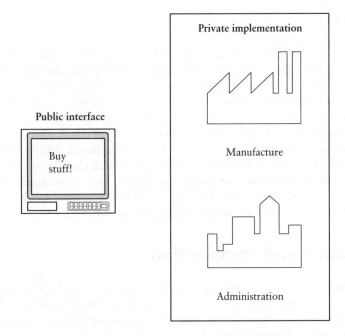

**Figure 2.3**   Information hiding means that we need to see only the public interface of an object, not its internal implementation.

typically sold with the hands pointing at ten to two to show the maker's name. Even so, we know that they are different objects because they occupy a different space at the same time. We also know, however, that all these clocks are of the same type, they belong to the same class. On one level, then, classifying objects means recognising that all identical objects belong to a single class.

## Abstraction

So we recognise that identical objects belong to the same class, but what about objects that are similar rather than identical? How do we know, for example, that a particular object is a clock rather than any other type of object? We instinctively classify objects in the world to be of a particular type, by recognising what is common between different but similar objects. A clock is anything that tells the time in some way, regardless of the technology or appearance of a particular clock. The class 'clock' encompasses all we understand about the general concept of 'clockness'. A specific type of clock belongs to a specific class, but also to higher-level abstractions.

How abstract (general) is our concept of 'clock'? In other words, how specific is our set of criteria for deciding what is or isn't a clock? Is a dandelion clock really a clock? And does it have as much 'clockness' as a wristwatch? How about a sundial? A candle clock? Stonehenge? These are not black and white questions, because there are different levels of detail that we use to classify things, from the very abstract (a clock tells the time) to the more closely defined (an examination clock starts accelerating half an hour before the end of an exam).

### Inheritance

Because we can classify objects at different levels of detail, we can put these classes into a 'classification hierarchy', with the most abstract concepts at the top and the most detailed object descriptions at the bottom. At the highest point of such a hierarchy, we might put 'object', our most abstract idea of what any object is. The term 'inheritance' is used to indicate that as we move down the hierarchy, each class inherits all the characteristics of the class above it, and then adds an extra level of detail. Every class is 'a kind of' the class above it, so that a digital clock is a kind of mechanical clock is a kind of clock is a kind of timepiece. Figure 2.4 shows a classification hierarchy of some types of clock.

We use the terms 'subclass' and 'superclass' to describe inheritance relationships. For example, 'digital clock' is a subclass of (inherits from) 'mechanical clock'. 'Mechanical clock' is therefore the superclass of 'digital clock'.

## Aggregation and composition

Many objects can be seen as aggregates of smaller objects. A clock is made up of a number of components that together combine to make the whole object. The aggregation may exist in many layers, with a larger component (such as the motor) being itself made up of a collection of smaller components. Figure 2.5 shows a clock as an aggregation of component parts.

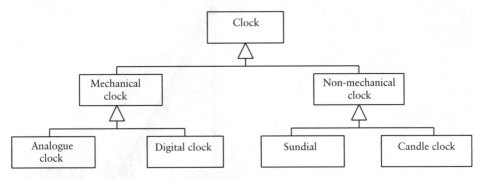

Figure 2.4 A classification hierarchy showing how each type of clock is 'a kind of' the class that it inherits from.

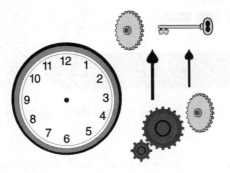

Figure 2.5 An object that is made up of smaller component objects is known as an aggregation.

Sometimes it is useful to make a distinction between aggregation and composition. This is simply a type of aggregation where the whole object and its component parts have a very close relationship such that all the objects are totally interdependent. Where the components have no role outside the aggregation, then we can describe this as a composition. In terms of the clock, we might regard the clock and its mechanical components as a composition, but the relationship between the clock and its battery is an aggregation, since although the battery is part of clock it could also exist in another context.

## Containers

Composition relationships are very stable. In contrast, we often find that some aggregated objects are gathered together in much more dynamic and unstructured collections. Traffic jams, bus queues and jumble sales are examples of situations where objects are grouped together in rather transient and informal ways. Such collections generally appear in some kind of context, a road, a bus shelter, a church hall, which act as containers for the objects. More specific examples of containers might be shopping trolleys, buses, vans etc. In the world around us, objects are frequently in some

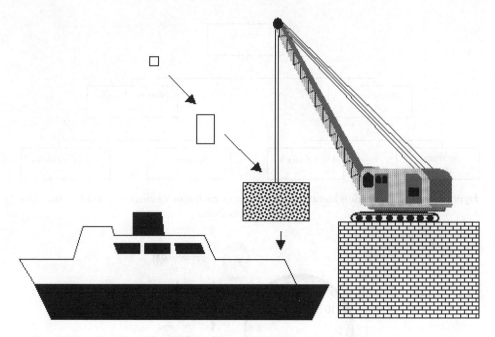

**Figure 2.6**   Containers have other objects inside them, which may in turn contain other objects.

kind of container, perhaps at more than one level. For example crisps may be put into small packets which are then put into large bags which are put into cardboard boxes which are then put into a container which is then put into the hold of a ship (Figure 2.6).

## Message passing

In the real world, people and objects constantly interact. We wind up clocks, set their alarms, change their batteries, reset their times and interact with them in many other ways. Parts of the clocks themselves also interact, for example when a mechanical alarm is triggered by the movement of the hour hand round the clock face. In object orientation, we tend to call people who interact with objects 'actors', and call the relationships between interacting objects 'associations'. We talk about objects 'passing messages' to each other. Without these kinds of connections between objects, they serve no useful purpose, like a clock in the loft.

## Objects in software

So far we have been talking about object-oriented concepts as applied to real-world objects, but there comes a point where we must start talking specifically about how objects in software work.

## Association

We noted earlier that an object alone is rather useless. In order for it to have a useful life it must interact with other objects; it must 'associate' with other objects. Associations describe the relationships between objects of different classes. In an object-oriented program we refer to objects passing messages to each other. A clock might, for example, associate with a calendar object. Messages might pass from the clock to the calendar every 24 hours, to tell the calendar to change at midnight. Other messages might pass in the opposite direction, so that the calendar might tell the clock when to move an hour forward or back when the clocks change on a particular date (Figure 2.7).

Equally importantly, people will interact with objects, to add a birthday to the calendar, for example, or to change the appearance of the clock. In object-oriented design, these 'actors' are drawn as stick people, (Figure 2.8) along with 'use cases' that are the things the actor can do with the system (in this case, the clock).

Now we will turn our attention specifically to the ways that messages are passed in a Java program. In order for an object to receive messages, it must have a set of publicly available methods that define its behaviour. When we send a message to an object, we are in fact using one of its methods. There are two general kinds of message that objects pass to each other:

- 'command' messages of the 'do this' variety
- 'query' messages that ask for information to be returned.

Messages in Java are passed by using the name of the object to receive the message, followed by the message itself. A full stop (the 'dot operator') is used to separate the object name and the message (Figure 2.9).

The general format of a message in Java is this:

```
object_name.messageName(…);
```

The brackets can contain 'parameters', which provide extra information with the message. If there is no extra information required, then the brackets can be empty.

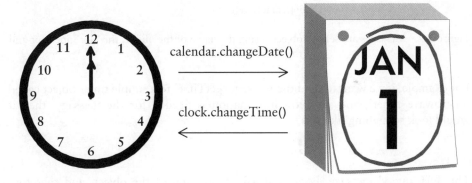

calendar.changeDate()

clock.changeTime()

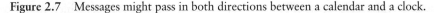

**Figure 2.7**   Messages might pass in both directions between a calendar and a clock.

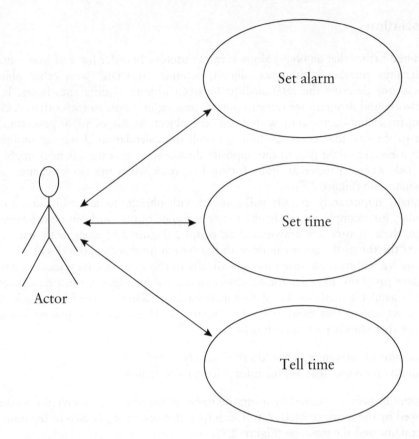

**Figure 2.8**    An 'actor' interacts with the objects in the system via 'use cases'.

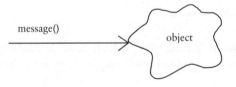

object.message();

**Figure 2.9**    Messages are sent to objects using the name of the object, the 'dot' operator and the name of the message.

For example, if we want to send the message 'getTime' to a simple timer object called 'microwave_timer', and no extra information is needed for the message, then it would look something like this

```
microwave_timer.getTime();
```

This is a 'query' message, because it asks a question of the object, and therefore expects a reply. This reply will be the 'return value' of the message, which in this case might be the number of seconds that have elapsed since the timer started (when we turned on the microwave, maybe). We might store this returned value as an integer (whole number), which would be declared as an 'int' in Java. (We will look in more detail at data types in the next chapter). The value of the message could then be assigned to this integer using the assignment operator (=):

```
int time_elapsed = microwave_timer.getTime();
```

A command message on the other hand tells an object to do something. A command message to a timer object might be:

```
microwave_timer.reset();
```

This message might set the timer back to zero. A message like this might not need a reply so might not return a value.

As described earlier, the brackets that appear after the message names are there in case we need to send any additional information (parameters) to the object as part of the message. This information takes the form of objects or variables that are listed in the brackets. For example, we may want to send a message to a timer object to stop after a specific period of time has passed. The message 'setStopTime' would need to include the information to tell the timer how many seconds should pass before the timer stops counting. This information would appear in the brackets, e.g.,

```
microwave_timer.setStopTime(120);
```

This message tells the timer to stop after 120 seconds have elapsed.

A message may have a number of parameters. A timer might be given a cooking time expressed in hours, minutes and seconds, each provided as a separate parameter, e.g.,

```
microwave_timer.setCookingTime(1, 30, 0)
```

This suggests that the cooking time is 1 hour, 30 minutes and zero seconds. Notice that we use commas to separate the different parameters.


## Class (static) methods

In the previous examples, we have been sending messages to objects. Sometimes, however, it is inappropriate for individual objects to have certain types of method because the response would always be the same regardless of which object received the message. In such cases, it is more appropriate for the class to have the method; in Java this is known as a 'static' method. An example from the clock context would be methods that contain information about time zones. Since this information is constant, and not dependent on the state of particular objects, it would reside in the class itself. Messages can be sent to classes in much the same way that they can be sent to objects, by using the dot operator. A Clock class might be able to tell us the difference between Greenwich Mean Time (GMT) and local time, e.g.,

```
int gmt_difference = Clock.getLocalTime();
```

### Polymorphism

One of the most important aspects of object-oriented programming is polymorphism, which means 'many-shaped'. Although there are a number of different types of polymorphism, the most fundamental is the ability of different objects to respond with different behaviour to the same message. For example, an Analogue Clock object and a Digital Clock object would have different ways of displaying the time. The principle of polymorphism is that the same message (e.g., showTime()) could be sent to both these objects and they would respond to it with different, class-specific behaviours. Figure 2.10 shows how these different types of clock respond to the same message.

In this book we will investigate the way that Java implements inheritance, aggregation, composition, containers and polymorphism by applying them to simple example programs.

# Why is Java object oriented?

There are a number of reasons why Java has been designed as an object-oriented language, but perhaps the most important is that objects help to reduce the complexity of software in a world where programs are expected to do increasingly complex things. Java has been developed in the context of multimedia, the Internet and powerful operating systems available on the humblest of desktop machines. Without the aid of object-oriented techniques such as encapsulation, inheritance and aggregation, it would be much more difficult to write code for these demanding contexts. A particularly important aspect of Java is that it has been designed to include a graphical user interface library as one of its standard facilities. The use of object orientation for building GUIs is now very common because it has proved an effective way to put together the components of a windowing environment. Simply by creating an object that inherits from class Frame for example we can display a graphical window on the

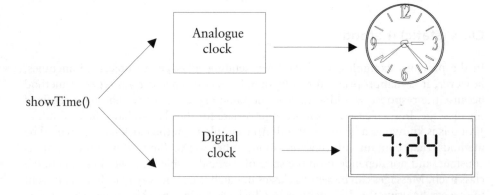

**Figure 2.10**   Polymorphism allows different types of object to respond differently to the same message.

screen. All the underlying code that allows the window to work with its surrounding operating system is encapsulated behind the public interface of the Frame class. As we look at Java syntax, we will see that much of its power comes from re-using objects that are already included in the Java system.

# Summary

This chapter provided an overview of object-oriented concepts and how some of them translate from the real world into software. It also introduced some aspects of message passing in Java. The key features covered were:

- Objects: an object encapsulates identity, state and behaviour into a single unit, hiding implementation detail behind a public interface of 'methods' that tell us what the object can do.
- Classes: objects are classified by their type. A class tells us what is common about a particular set of objects, both specifically and at more abstract levels, where we can describe similarities between types of objects that also have individual characteristics.
- Objects together: objects come together in various ways, in aggregation (an object made up of other objects), composition (a very strong form of aggregation) and containers (where one object is able to hold collections of other objects).
- Message passing: object-oriented systems rely on objects being able to communicate with each other in order to perform their tasks. Actors (people who use programs) send messages to the system to do certain things, and objects talk to each other to provide the required behaviour. Messages in Java are passed using the name of an object, the 'dot' operator and the name of a message. A message may have 'parameters' (additional information attached to a message) and may return a value (a reply to the message). Messages can sometimes be passed to classes as well as objects and messages can be 'polymorphic', where the same message gets different responses from objects of different classes.

## Implementing objects

In the next chapter we will see how a simple Java application can be written that uses a number of these concepts. Even the most basic Java program touches on issues such as classes, objects, aggregation and message passing, and we will see how objects can be created and used. We will also look at the way that a Java program is compiled and run using the Java Virtual Machine.

# 3

# Introductory Java applications

'I created for myself a creature to tell the time by' – Brian Patten (*A Creature to Tell The Time By*).

In this chapter, we meet our first Java applications. These short programs consist of classes that are used simply to test some objects provided with Java, such as strings and dates. In addition, the simple data types are introduced. These are not objects but the basic number, character and Boolean types that we need to support the nuts and bolts of programming.

## A first Java application

Like almost every other 'first program', our first Java application simply displays a message on the screen. Although it is very basic, it still introduces a number of important aspects of Java code that will be explored in detail later. It shows how to write a class in Java, the 'main' method that starts a Java program working, and a message sent to an object that is predefined in the Java system. Many of the concepts introduced in the previous chapter appear here. We will see examples of objects, class methods, aggregation, message passing, message parameters and return values.

Key aspects of this example are

- declaring a class
- the 'main' method
- displaying output with the 'System.out' object.

The source code of our first application is

```
/**
    JavaApplication.java
    a simple Java application with screen output
*/
public class JavaApplication
{
    public static void main(String args[])
    {
```

20

```
      // display a message on the screen
                System.out.println("Java Application");
          }
      }
```

## The comment heading

The class begins with a 'comment', not actual code but explanatory text. This is surrounded by the following characters:

```
    /**
          text here
    */
```

Any text between these two symbols in a Java program is treated as a comment, and ignored by the compiler. Comments are an important tool for making our program code readable, and Java provides three different types of comment syntax. As well as the previous style, there is this very similar syntax:

```
    /*
          text here
    */
```

The only difference is that the first version has two asterisks (**) after the forward slash character, whereas the second has only one. The first version is preferable in Java because it is used by 'Javadoc', the automatic class-documenting tool that works with Java code. We will look at Javadoc later in this book, but for the moment all our main comments will begin with the double asterisk.

Further down the code there is another comment, preceded by two forward slash characters:

```
    // display a message on the screen
```

This type of syntax is easier for short comments in the code, because it does not need any other character to indicate where the comment ends. The end of the comment is automatically taken to be the end of the line on which it appers. It should be noted that this kind of comment is ignored by Javadoc.

## The JavaApplication class

The first line of code (after the comment header) introduces a class.

```
    public class JavaApplication
```

No Java code can be written that does not belong to one class or another. This particular class is called 'JavaApplication' but the class name is not important here, it is something decided by the programmer. The 'public' prefix means that the class can be visible to all other classes, even those that are not in the same 'package' (a file directory or folder) and is how most of our classes are declared. If we omit this prefix, the class will be visible only within its own package. For the moment, we will assume that all our classes appear in the same package, which is the easiest way of making classes visible to each other when they are running. We will look at packages in more detail in the next chapter.

The 'JavaApplication' class must be saved in a file called 'JavaApplication.java', with exactly the same mix of upper- and lower-case letters. Calling the file by the same name as the class is required for 'public' classes, and also makes life much easier when we want to find a particular class later, since only one public class may appear in a '.java' file. It is essential that the file extension is '.java' because it is required by the Java compiler. The compiler is case-sensitive, which means that it considers the upper- and lower-case versions of a given letter to be different characters. We normally try to give our classes names that accurately describe the objects they create, but in this case the class is representing a whole program rather than a specific object. We are not actually going to create any objects of this class, just use a 'class method' that starts the program running.

The class body is surrounded by 'braces' (the curly brackets {} ). Everything between the opening and closing brace belongs to that class. This is what is described as 'scope'; the class can 'see' everything that falls within its scope (i.e., appears between the two braces). In this example, the only thing that is in the class is a method called 'main'.

## The 'main' method

The main method is always the first to be executed when a class is run on the Java virtual machine and a program must have at least one class with a main method in order to run at all. A program can have more than one class with a main method, but only one of them would actually be used to run a particular program (others might be there purely for testing purposes, not meant as part of a larger system.) The method is declared 'public', which means that it is part of the public interface of the class and also 'static' which means it belongs to the class rather than to individual objects. Its return type is 'void' meaning that it does not return any value.

```
public static void main(String args[])
```

Its parameter list ('String args[]') is always the same, and means that we can, if we wish, send one or more String objects to this method as parameters. We will investigate String objects in more detail later but they basically contain text. Although the name used to refer to these strings can be anything we like, it typically appears as 'args' or 'argv' (short for 'arguments'). The meaning of the square brackets ([]) will also be explored later. In practice, we rarely use this facility of passing String objects to the main method, but later in this chapter we will see an example of how it may be used in order to understand why it is there.

## Output with the System class

To test our programs we have to be able to output information to the screen. In Java, we can do this by sending a message to an object called 'out'. For the moment, we will not be looking at keyboard input, so all classes will be tested with 'hard-wired' data. The code that does this is this single line in 'main':

```
System.out.println("Java Application");
```

This sends a message ('println') to an object called 'out' that is aggregated inside a class called System. 'out' is a member of the 'PrintStream' class, and can be used to print text onto the screen. We can access it directly because it is part of the public interface of the System class. Public members of a class (whether methods or objects) are accessed with the dot operator, as we saw in the previous chapter. In this instance, the dot operator is used twice, first to access the 'out' object in the System class and then to call the 'println' method (Figure 3.1). This is quite unusual; most of the messages we send will go directly to a single object or class.

System.out is one of a number of Java objects that are predefined in packages provided with the language. We do not have to create the object ourselves because it is always present. The System class provides a number of other objects that have methods appropriate to input and output (among other things). It is helpful to bear in mind that the convention in Java is to start class names with an upper-case letter and object names with a lower-case letter. Therefore we can tell at a glance that System (capital S) is a class but 'out' (small 'o') is an object.

The 'println' method takes a string of characters as a parameter and prints it on the screen before adding a line feed. In fact the string of characters in speech marks is invisibly converted to an object of the String class when used with 'println' because the method expects to be passed a string object as its parameter. We will see later than a number of different things are invisibly converted to Strings when passed to 'println' for display. A similar method is 'print' which also writes text to the screen but does not add the line feed, so any subsequent output would appear on the same line:

```
System.out.print("Java Application");
```

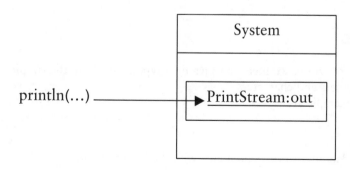

**Figure 3.1**  The 'out' object is aggregated inside the System class, so messages to it go via that class.

## Compiling and running the class

As described in Chapter one, Java code must be converted to 'byte code' by the Java compiler. This byte code is written into 'class' files, which can then be run using the Java virtual machine. If you are using an integrated development environment to write your programs, there will be various interface tools to allow you to do this. If, however, you are using a Java Development Kit (JDK) command line compiler, you can follow these steps:

1.  The source code must be compiled into a 'class' file to produce (for this example) 'JavaApplication.class'. When using the JDK, the compiler is called 'javac' so the command will be

    ```
    javac JavaApplication.java
    ```

    You must use the full filename, including the '.java' extension and the correct mix of upper and lower case. This will either compile the Java source file into byte code or, if there is some error in your program, display compiler error messages.

2.  When the file successfully compiles, it will create a class file called 'JavaApplication.class'. This class can be run on the virtual machine using 'java *classname*', in this case

    ```
    java JavaApplication
    ```

    When running a Java class you do not add a file extension, just the name of the class itself. The virtual machine is more tolerant of case than the compiler, but it is probably best to be consistent.

If you are using a different Java compiler or environment then of course the detail of the process will be different but the same things are happening, namely that the source file is compiled into a class file that is then run on the virtual machine. When run, the program displays the following on the screen:

```
Java Application
```

Control then returns to the operating system or programming environment from which the application was run.

# Java data types

In the second example program, we meet the Java data types. These are the simple types used to store numbers and characters.

Key aspects of this example are

- data types
- declaring variables
- combining output data in 'println' statements with the '+' operator.

For most of this book, we will be dealing with classes and objects. However Java, like most other programming languages, also has a set of built-in simple data types

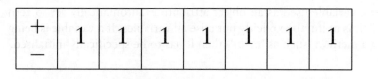

$$64 + 32 + 16 + 8 + 4 + 2 + 1 = 127$$

**Figure 3.2**   The Java 'byte' data type is eight bits long.

that represent characters and numbers. Each has a specified size in terms of bits (binary digits) and therefore a specified range of possible values. A byte, for example, is always eight bits long, so its maximum positive value is 127, which is the binary number 1111111 (seven bits) with one bit reserved for the sign (+ or –) (Figure 3.2).

Unlike some other languages Java does not have unsigned data types, which means that all of them (with the exception of 'char', which is designed to contain characters rather than numbers) can contain both positive and negative numbers. The available types are shown in Table 3.1.

In addition there is a 'Boolean' type, which can have only the values 'true' or 'false'. Its default value is 'false'.

## Declaring variables

Programs need to store data of different types and sizes in memory. To do this we must declare 'variables' of the appropriate type. A variable is simply the name of a particular memory location that stores a specific type of data. To store an integer, for example, we need to declare an 'int' with a name, e.g.,

```
int integer_value;
```

This declares 'integer_value' to be the name of a memory location that is large enough to store a 32-bit integer. A variable can also be initialised (set to an initial value) when it is declared. This is done with the = (assignment) operator

```
int integer_value = 10;
```

Table 3.1

| Data type | Stores | Can contain |
|---|---|---|
| byte | 8 bit integer | from –128 to 127 |
| char | 16 bit character | Unicode character set |
| short | 16 bit integer | from –32768 to 32767 |
| int | 32 bit integer | from –2,147,483,648 to 2,147,483,647 |
| long | 64 bit integer | big integers! |
| float | 32 bit floating-point number | big numbers with decimal points |
| double | 64 bit floating-point number | very big numbers with decimal points |

Although a numeric variable used as an object attribute is automatically set to zero when it is declared, it is useful to explicitly initialise all variables. If a variable is being locally declared in a method (such as 'main') then it has to be specifically initialised.

## Assigning characters

A 'char' variable can be assigned to a number (the character value from the Unicode table) or a specific character enclosed in single quotes, e.g.,

```
char my_letter = 'd';
```

A char may also contain one of the 'escape sequence' characters (control characters and other special characters) that are preceded by the backslash (\). Although these may appear to contain two characters, they still represent single 'chars'. This is because the escape sequences are references to numbers in the character table. For example, \n represents the newline character (Unicode number 10). The escape sequences are shown in Table 3.2.

Most of these are applicable to formatting output. Note that since the backslash is the escape character, it has to have its own escape sequence to be usable in another context.

The next example program simply shows how variables of most of the Java data types are declared and initialised.

## Combining output data with 'println'

The 'println' method is very flexible. As well as displaying a single string of characters, as it did in the first example program, it can also display any of the built-in data types in the appropriate format by automatically converting them to string objects. We do not need to know anything about string objects or the way that these conversions work to display any type of data. To format readable output we can use the addition operator ('+') to 'concatenate' (add together) different strings. This line, for example, uses the operator to display a string of characters followed by the integer variable we have already described:

```
System.out.println("Integer value is: " + integer_value);
```

Table 3.2

| backspace | \b | horizontal tab | \t |
|---|---|---|---|
| single quote | \' | double quote | \" |
| newline | \n | carriage return | \r |
| form feed | \f | backslash | \\ |
| octal character value | \xxx | Hexadecimal Unicode character number | \uxxxx |

This is the complete program, using and displaying examples of all the basic data types. Note that to put a literal value into a float variable, we have to add an 'F' to the end of the number. Otherwise, any floating-point number is assumed to be a double:

```
/**
        JavaDataTypes.java
        declares some simple Java variables
*/
public class JavaDataTypes
{
        public static void main (String args[])
        {
// declare and initialise some variables of the basic data types
                int integer_value = 10;
                long long_value = 10;
// literal numbers with a decimal fraction are assumed to be
// doubles.
// we have to specifically state that we want to treat them as
// floats by adding an 'F' to the end of the number:
                double double_value = 3.1417;
                float float_value = 3.1417F;
                char character = 'a';
// a boolean can only be 'true' or 'false'
                boolean state = false;
                System.out.println("DATA TYPES:");
                System.out.println("int value: " + integer_value);
                System.out.println("long value: " + long_value);
                System.out.println("double value: " + double_value);
                System.out.println("float value: " + float_value);
                System.out.println("char value: " + character);
                System.out.println("boolean value: " + state);

        }
}
```

The output from running this class is:

```
DATA TYPES:
int value: 10
long value: 10
double value: 3.1417
float value: 3.1417
char value: a
boolean value: false
```

We will be using a number of these data types in the chapters that follow. However, the rest of this chapter will concentrate on objects.

# Creating objects: the String class

The next example introduces objects, how to create them and how to send them messages.

Key aspects of this example are

- string objects
- constructor methods
- string object methods
- string class methods

In our first two Java applications, we sent a message (println) to an object (out) but we did not actually create any objects ourselves. In the next example, we will create objects of the String class, which we have already met indirectly, both as a parameter to the 'main' method and as the object type that is displayed with 'println'. There are many classes provided with Java for creating useful objects, some more complex than others, but perhaps the most fundamental is the string. A string is simply a string of characters (letters, numbers, spaces or other symbols) which may vary in length from no characters (a 'null string') to whole sentences.

## String constructors

To create ('instantiate') an object we call a method called the 'constructor'. The basic form of the constructor call is:

```
Classname object_reference = new Classname();
```

We use the name of the class to declare the name of an object 'reference'. A reference provides a name that we can use to refer to the object. The object is then created using the assignment operator and 'new'. For example, we can create a new (empty) string object called 'my_string' like this:

```
String my_string = new String();
```

The constructor often comes in a number of different forms using a technique known as 'overloading'. This is where more than one version of a method exists, but each version has a different list of parameters. The String class has a number of different constructors.

In this example program, we create two string objects using two different versions of the constructor. The first uses the 'default' constructor (that has no parameters):

```
String string1 = new String();
```

The second uses a different version that takes a string of characters as a parameter

```
String string2 = new String(" virtual machine");
```

One string can be made to equal another (i.e., contain the same text) by using the assignment operator (=), which can also be used with literal text inside speech marks, for example:

```
String1 = "Java";
```

There is also a special kind of constructor that uses the assignment operator called a 'copy constructor'. This allows us to create a new object that is a copy of one that already exists. In the example, object 'string2' is created as a copy of 'string1':

```
String string2 = string1;
```

Because 'string1' has the value 'Java' at this point in the program, then 'string2' will also be 'Java'. The difference between the copy constructor and simply using the assignment operator is that one creates a new object whereas the other simply changes the contents of an existing string.

## String object methods

All objects have methods to provide their behaviour. The example program shows two of the methods provided for objects of the String class:

length()        this method returns the number of characters in the string.
toUpperCase()   this method returns another string that is a copy of the existing string but with all its characters converted to upper case.

## String class methods

Many of the Java classes also have class (static) methods. One of the class methods of 'String' is 'valueOf'. This method takes a number as a parameter and returns it as a string, i.e.,

```
a_string = String.valueOf(value);
```

In fact there are many different versions of 'valueOf' because it is overloaded to work with all the basic Java data types, and is the reason we could easily display all the numbers in the previous example program. In the following program, the float version is used explicitly to show how a class method is called, using the class name rather than the name of an object, i.e.,

```
float real_number = 3.1417F;
String float_string = String.valueOf(real_number);
```

This program demonstrates some of the constructors and methods of the String class. Notice that the special escape sequence character \" is used to embed speech marks inside a string of text.

```
/**
      StringTest.java
      creates a number of String objects and tests some of their
      methods
*/
```

```
public class StringTest
{
     public static void main(String args[])
     {
// the default constructor. it creates an empty string
          String string1 = new String();
// the assignment operator can be used to assign a value to a
// string
          string1 = "Java";
// the copy constructor makes a copy of an existing object
          String string2 = string1;
// another version of the constructor takes some text as a
// parameter
          String string3 = new String(" virtual machine");
// this line outputs both strings
          System.out.println("The two strings together read \""
                    + string2 + string3 + "\"");
// the 'length' method returns the number of characters in a
// string
          int string_length = string1.length();
     System.out.println("The number of characters in \"Java\" is "
                    + string_length);
// the 'toUpperCase' method converts all the letters to capitals.
// the string 'upper_case' is created using the copy constructor
          String upper_case = string1.toUpperCase();
     System.out.println("The string converted to upper case is"
                    + upper_case);
// numbers of different types can be converted to strings using
// 'valueOf' methods. this example uses the float version
          float real_number = 3.1417F;
          String float_string = String.valueOf(real_number);
     System.out.println("The float converted to a string is "
                    + float_string);
     }
}
```

The output from running this class is:

```
The two strings together read "Java virtual machine"
The number of characters in "Java" is 4
The string converted to upper case is JAVA
The float converted to a string is 3.1417
```

## Arrays

Before leaving the String class, we will look at the parameter to 'main'. Remember that a parameter is additional information added to a message. In the case of 'main', the parameter acts as a message to the program.

Key aspects of this example are

- the parameter to 'main'
- arrays
- passing parameters to a class at run time.

You will recall that the parameter we always use with 'main' is

```
String args[]
```

The square brackets mean that 'args' is an array of strings. An array is a set of variables that all have the same name, but each has a different index number. The first element is always zero, so the first string in the 'args' array would be

```
args[0]
```

The next element would be 'args[1]', the next 'args[2]' and so on (Figure 3.3). The size of the array passed to 'main' depends entirely on how many strings are passed to it from the command line when the program is run.

This program uses the parameter to 'main' to display a string on the screen that is passed to the class when it is run on the virtual machine.

```
/**
      MainStrings.java
      this class demonstrates how the arguments to main
      can be accessed as an array of Strings
*/
public class MainStrings
{
        public static void main(String args[])
        {
                System.out.println(args[0]);
        }
}
```

How, then, do we pass the string to the class? This is done when the compiled program is run on the Java virtual machine. We must add the string after the name of the Java class, e.g.,

```
java MainStrings message
```

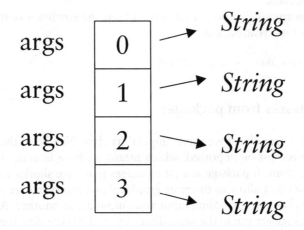

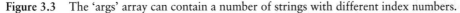

**Figure 3.3**   The 'args' array can contain a number of strings with different index numbers.

The output from this program will be simply

```
message
```

We can send several strings to main, but they cannot contain any spaces because the space character is assumed to be a gap between different strings. This is not a serious limitation since the kind of data usually sent to main tends to be single words such as file names or 'flags' that change the behaviour of a program (like the parameters to the 'Javadoc' document generator that we will look at in Chapter seven).

Of course, as it stands the program has to take it on trust that a string is supplied when it is run. Rather than trust to luck, we can find out how many arguments have been passed to main by sending a 'length' message to the array. Although arrays are not really objects, they do have the ability to tell us their size, e.g.,

```
int array_size = args.length;
```

Unlike the usual object messages, there are no brackets on 'length' since it is simply a data attribute that is publicly available.

Our example here is simply to demonstrate syntax, but in a later chapter we will see an exercise that makes more practical use of a parameter passed to 'main'.

# Date objects

Key aspects of this example are

- 'date' objects
- importing classes from packages.

There are many other useful classes provided with Java, one of the simplest of which is the Date class. In fact a date object is the nearest thing in Java to our clock object, discussed in the previous chapter, because it contains not only a date but a time as well. Although on its own it is not particularly useful it could be used as one component of a Clock class.

The date constructor has no parameters and sets the attributes of the object to the date and time of its creation, e.g.,

```
Date todays_date = new Date();
```

## Importing classes from packages

In order to use a date object we must 'import' its class. Nearly all the classes we use in Java programs must be imported, which means we have to state which 'package' the class comes from. A package is a set of classes that have similar roles. For example, all the classes that allow us to create graphical user interfaces are in one package, whereas all the classes for handling input and output are in another. All the classes in a particular package are put in the same directory, and it is the directory pathway that defines how we import the package.

The classes we have seen already, such as String, come from the default Java package 'java.lang'. Because these classes are fundamental to Java they are automatically available and do not need to be specifically imported. However, most other classes, including Date, are not part of the 'java.lang' package so we need to tell the compiler where to find them. We do this with an 'import' statement at the beginning of our code, followed by the location (subdirectory) of the package. The Date class is in 'java.util', so the import statement reads:

```
import java.util.Date;
```

If you do not put this in your Java source file, then it will not be able to find the Date class when it compiles. All the import statement does is to provide the class with a general route for locating classes so that we can, for example, simply refer to 'Date' in our class rather than 'java.util.Date' every time we want to use it.

## Displaying date objects

Date objects can easily be displayed because they have a 'toString' method that, like the built-in data types, enables them to be output as a string of characters. In this program, we once again use the '+' operator to display more than one string in a single 'println' statement:

```
/**
     Now.java
     creates a 'Date' object
*/
// import the definition of the 'Date' class from java.util
import java.util.Date;
public class Now
{
     public static void main(String args[])
     {
// the default 'Date' constructor sets the object to the current
// date and time
          Date today = new Date();
// we can display a Date object because it has a 'toString'
// method which is implicitly called here
          System.out.println("The date and time is " + today);
     }
}
```

Running the program in the early hours of 16 June 1998 produced the following output:

```
The date and time is Tue Jun 16 00:34:23 GMT+01:00 1998
```

The actual output from this program will, of course, depend on when you run it! The Date class has very little else to offer in terms of methods, but we will return to it later in this book when it is used with the rather more sophisticated 'Calendar' class.

# Summary

In this chapter, we have seen how to create a Java class, compile it using the 'javac' compiler (provided with Sun's Java Development Kit) and run it on the virtual machine. We have also seen two different types of object:

- objects that exist within the Java programming environment, such as 'System.out'
- objects of built-in Java classes that we instantiate (string and date objects).

We have also seen three different types of method being used

1. Constructors, used to create objects. These may be 'default' constructors (no parameters), e.g.,

```
Date todays_date = new Date()
```

   or they may have parameter arguments, e.g.,

```
String this_book = new String("Introductory Java");
```

2. Object methods, where the message is sent to a specific object, e.g.,

```
my_string.toUpperCase()
System.out.println()
```

3. Class methods, where a message is sent to a class rather than an object e.g.,

```
String.valueOf(value)
```

In addition, we have seen how to declare and display variables of the built in Java data types, and how to pass parameter arguments to the 'main' method of a class using an array of string objects. In the next chapter, we will see how to create objects of our own classes and send them messages.

## EXERCISES

1  Modify 'JavaApplication.java' so that the same output is achieved using two separate 'print' statements rather than one 'println'. Use the '+' operator to insert the space between the two words.

2  Test the 'MainStrings' class by running it with one, zero and two arguments. How does Java cope with the error of failing to provide the necessary arguments to 'main'?

3  Modify 'MainStrings.java' so that three strings can be passed as parameters and displayed in reverse order. Display the number of arguments passed to 'main'.

4  Write a Java class with a 'main' method that creates a date object. Create a string object that contains the same date by explicitly using the 'toString' method of the date class. Create another string object that contains the same date converted to upper case. Display the message "Today's date is...." followed by your upper-case string using a single println statement.

# Building Java objects, writing Java code

Part 2

Building Java objects,
writing Java code

# 4

# Creating objects in Java

'In creating, the only hard thing's to begin' – James Russell Lowell (*A Fable for Critics*).

'More than any other time in history, mankind faces a crossroads. One path leads to despair and utter hopelessness. The other, to total extinction. Let us pray we have the wisdom to choose correctly. ' – Woody Allen (*Side Effects*).

In this chapter we will look at writing classes that do more than just run a simple program. These classes will be able to represent our own types of object by describing both their state and their behaviour, using attributes and methods. To give our objects useful behaviour, we also introduce the Java syntax for arithmetic and making decisions. The 'random' method of the Java 'Math' class is used to provide random number data for a number of the objects. We also look at packages and how they can be used with our own classes to make them easily reusable in different programs.

## Writing classes to represent objects

In the previous chapter we saw how objects that are defined in the Java libraries can be instantiated (created) and sent messages from the main method of our own classes. In our example programs these objects were members of classes String and Date. The next step on from making objects of predefined Java classes is to describe our own types of object. To do this we must write classes that define both attributes and methods to describe object state and behaviour.

The classes that we wrote ourselves in the previous chapter only had one purpose, to provide a main method within which objects of other classes could be created. Because main is always declared 'static', it represents the behaviour of a class (being run on the virtual machine) rather than the behaviour of an object. Objects cannot be created from a class that only has static methods, so other methods must be added to a class if it is to do more than just start a program running. The classes described in this chapter have their own non-static methods so we can use them to create useful objects.

### Lift, coin and dice objects

The examples used in this chapter to explain how to create our own classes are based on very simple objects, namely a lift, a coin and a dice. Although they are simple

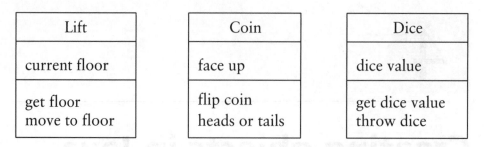

**Figure 4.1**   The Lift, Coin and Dice classes, with their attributes and methods.

objects, they also demonstrate both state and behaviour. A lift is always on a particular floor (its state), and can move between floors (behaviour). In the case of a coin, its
state is the face that it is showing, and its behaviour is to be flipped. For a dice, its
state is the number shown on its upper face, and its behaviour is to be thrown. Figure
4.1 shows the attributes and methods of the Lift, Coin and Dice classes using the
UML notation introduced in Chapter two.

## Writing a class that can make objects

Key aspects of this example are

- adding attributes to a class
- declaring object (non-static) methods
- returning values from methods
- passing parameters to methods.

This first syntax example is a program that creates and uses an object of the Lift class.
As we saw in Chapter three, a Java class is declared by using the 'class' keyword,
followed by the name of the class (which by convention begins with a capital letter)
and the opening brace of the class definition. Classes that are generally visible to
other classes are also declared 'public'. The beginning of the class definition for Lift
therefore looks like this:

```
public class Lift
{
    // class definition follows here...
```

## Adding attributes to a class

Attributes usually appear at the beginning of a class definition. In this example, the
'current_floor' attribute is an 'int' data type. A numeric attribute will have a default
value of zero, but we can assign other values if we wish or simply aid the readability
of the code by explicitly stating that the initial value of the attribute will be zero:

```
private int current_floor = 0;
```

The attribute has been declared private, because attributes are normally encapsulated inside the class and not publicly visible. A private attribute is, however, visible to any method of the class, so any method of Lift is able to access this 'current_floor' attribute.

You will see many code examples that do not include the 'private' prefix, but it is important to use it because if we do not the attribute will by default be visible to other classes in the same package. Since this breaks the principle of encapsulation, it is not an ideal object-oriented strategy.

## Adding methods to a class

After the attribute(s), the methods of a class also appear inside the class body, but these are declared public because they provide the public interface for the object. The Lift class has two object (as opposed to class) methods, the first being 'getFloor'. This is a 'query' method that asks the object to return its state to the sender of the message. We do this by using the 'return' keyword, followed by the name of the variable or object being returned, which in this case is the 'current_floor' attribute. Any method that returns a value must include the type of that returned value as part of its declaration. In this case, an 'int' is being returned, so the method definition begins with this type, followed by the name of the method and the parameter list brackets. There are no parameters to this method, so the brackets are empty:

```
public int getFloor()
{
        return current_floor;
}
```

The second method is a 'command' method that tells the lift to do something, namely move to a particular floor by changing the value of the 'current_floor' attribute. In order to do this we have to pass the number of the destination floor as a parameter, so the type and name of the parameter must be provided. In this case, it is an integer called 'floor_number'. The name of the parameter cannot be the same as the name of the attribute or the compiler cannot tell them apart. The return type of the method is 'void', meaning that it does not return any value.

```
public void moveToFloor(int floor_number)
{
        current_floor = floor_number;
}
```

These attributes and methods are those that appear in Figure 4.1. In addition, we will need a main method in order to run the program, calling the Lift constructor to make an object of the Lift class and send it messages. Notice that when we display the floor that the lift is on, the 'getFloor' method can be put into the 'println' statement:

```
System.out.println("The lift has moved to floor " +
a_lift.getFloor());
```

Any method that returns a value of any built-in type can be passed as a parameter to 'println', and the value returned will be converted to a string and displayed.

This version of the class is called 'LiftMain' since the main method is also in the class. A revised version of this class will appear in the next example.

```
/**
      LiftMain.java
      a class that represents a lift moving between
      the floors of a building
*/
public class LiftMain
{
// a private attribute to record the lift position
      private int current_floor = 0;
// this method returns the current floor
      public int getFloor()
      {
            return current_floor;
      }
// this method uses a parameter value to set the lift's position
      public void moveToFloor(int floor_number)
      {
            current_floor = floor_number;
      }
// 'main' tests an object of the 'Lift' class
      public static void main(String args[])
      {
// instantiate a 'Lift' object
            Lift a_lift = new Lift();
// get the current floor (starts at zero)
            int floor = a_lift.getFloor();
// display the current floor;
            System.out.println("The lift is on floor " + floor);
// move the lift to the third floor
            a_lift.moveToFloor(3);
// display the current floor. note that we do not have to use a
// separate variable to store the return value of 'getFloor', we
// can put the method call directly into the 'println' message
            System.out.println("The lift has moved to floor " +
                  a_lift.getFloor());
      }
}
```

The output from this program is:

```
The lift is on floor 0
The lift has moved to floor 3
```

# Adding a Controller class

Key aspect of this example are

● associated classes
● separate '.java' files for each class
● objects and their references.

**Figure 4.2**   The LiftController associates with the Lift.

You might think it strange that the Lift class creates objects of its own type in its main method. Although it is perfectly valid Java syntax, because the class exists separately from any objects, it does not really match our understanding of real objects. We might think it more appropriate if some kind of separate lift control mechanism, to model reality a little more closely, is used to operate the lift. In the next example, we will create another class, LiftController, and give it the responsibility for managing a Lift object. In design terms, we now have two classes that have an association, meaning that the objects can pass messages to one another. In the UML an association is drawn as a line between the two classes, labelled with an association name ('controls' in this example) and an arrowhead indicating the direction of the relationship, so this indicates that the LiftController controls the Lift. In this case the messages will pass in one direction only, from the lift controller to the lift, so a UML diagram indicates this with an arrowhead on the association line itself (Figure 4.2).

The code is very similar to our previous single class, except that the main method now appears in the LiftController class, not in Lift. It is not possible to have more than one public class written in a single '.java' source file, so the Lift and LiftController classes must appear in separate files. The example uses files Lift.java and LiftController.java. The requirement for keeping the file names consistent with the public class names ensures a match between the .java files in our system and the compiled .class files, and makes our classes more easily re-usable in different programs.

There is one other change to the code, a slightly different constructor. In the previous example, the Lift object was constructed like this:

```
Lift a_lift = new Lift();
```

This line actually consists of two different things, a 'reference' to an object (called 'a_lift') and a call to the constructor ('new Lift()'). These two elements can be written separately, like this:

```
// declare a reference to a 'Lift'
    Lift a_lift;
// create a 'Lift' object
    a_lift = new Lift();
```

Why would we separate the reference from the object? Although it makes no difference here, we often find that we want to separate the declaration of an object reference from the actual creation of the object, for example, when using objects as attributes of other classes. The reference to an object is all that is required to declare the attribute. The actual object can be created when it is needed. In fact a single object reference can refer to different objects at different times, so a 'person' object's

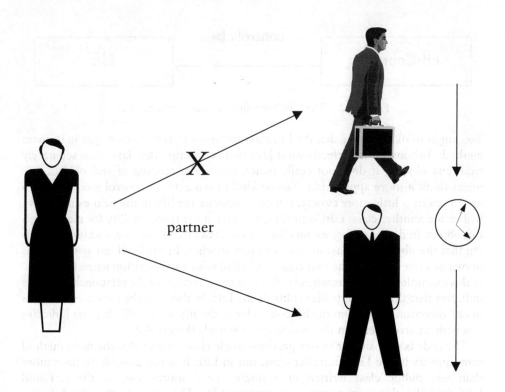

**Figure 4.3**    A reference can refer to different objects at different times.

partner (who is also a 'person') might change from one object to another over time
(Figure 4.3).

When a reference is reused to refer to a new object, any old object that was previously being referenced will be removed from memory by the garbage collector that
trawls through memory looking for unreferenced objects. It is possible to give the
garbage collector a signal that an object has been finished with by directing its reference to 'null', but this is not usually necessary.

This is the revised version of the lift class ('Lift.java') without a main method:

```
/**
      Lift.java
      a class that represents a lift moving between
      the floors of a building
*/
public class Lift
{
// a private attribute to record the lift position
      private int current_floor = 0;
// this method returns the current floor
      public int getFloor()
      {
            return current_floor;
      }
```

```
// this method uses a parameter value to set the lift's position
    public void moveToFloor(int floor_number)
    {
        current_floor = floor_number;
    }
}
```

This is the separate 'LiftController.java' file:

```
/**    LiftController.java
       the 'LiftController' controls an object of the 'Lift' class
*/
public class LiftController
{
    public static void main(String args[])
    {
// instantiate a 'Lift' object
        Lift a_lift;
        a_lift = new Lift();
// get the current floor (starts at zero)
        int floor = a_lift.getFloor();
// display the current floor;
        System.out.println("The lift is on floor " + floor);
// move the lift to the third floor
        a_lift.moveToFloor(3);
// display the current floor. note that we do not have to use a
// separate variable to store the return value of 'getFloor', we
// can put the method call directly into the 'println' message
        System.out.println("The lift has moved to floor " +
        a_lift.getFloor());
    }
}
```

The files must be compiled separately to create two '.class' files. Because Java is dynamic, the LiftController will automatically be able to access the Lift class if they are in the same 'package'. A package is a directory where '.class' files are located. If we do not specifically put our classes into named packages, they exist in a default package where they are visible to other '.class' files in the same directory. Later in this chapter we will see how to put classes into named packages to make them visible to classes in other directories.

The output from the LiftController class is exactly the same as running our previous LiftMain class. You may wonder why we bother to have two classes when the program runs exactly as it did with just one. The important point here is one of appropriate design. We can write Java programs that are just one enormous class, but then we lose many of the advantages of true object-oriented programming. We should always try to keep the responsibilities of a class limited to those that are truly behaviours of that particular type of object. Instead of classes running themselves, we should use 'controller' objects to manage other objects. LiftController is a simple version of such a controller, because it manages the application objects. Controllers are also useful for managing input and output, providing an interface between the user of a program and the underlying objects in the system. Many of the programs in this book follow the convention of using a controller object with a main method that instantiates, and sends messages to, objects of other classes. Although these are often trivial, they establish the principle of separating different responsibilities into different classes. Equally, however, all classes in a system can have their own main method for test purposes, so that their interfaces can be tested separately from their use in other programs. In some cases in this book, where 'main' is a very simple interface test, it is attached to the class itself rather than appearing in a separate file.

## Creating and controlling multiple objects

Key aspects of this example are

- declaring and using arrays of objects
- multiple objects of a single class.

In the previous chapter, we created a number of objects of the String class. Equally, we can create as many objects of our own classes as we wish. In the next example, we build on the previous LiftController by making it control a number of different lifts.

## Declaring arrays

In the previous chapter, we looked at an array of string objects. This was the array that can be passed to the main method of a class when that class is run on the Java virtual machine. You may recall that an array consists of a number of elements that all have the same name but a different index number, which appears in square brackets, e.g.,

```
args[0]
```

was the first element in the 'args' array from our example program.

The array passed to main is already defined for us as a parameter but if we want to use other arrays in our classes then we have the declare them. An array is declared like an object by using the word 'new', but we also have to put empty square brackets after the array name to indicate that this is an array rather than a single object. We must also give the size of the array that we want in square brackets after the second reference to the class name. This looks a bit convoluted, but is necessary to allow us to separate the declaration of an array from its actual creation. Like object references and constructors, it is possible to separate the two events, although in this context we declare and create the array in one statement.

This example program declares and creates an array called 'lifts' that can contain three lift objects:

```
Lift lifts[] = new Lift[3];
```

This means that the array has three elements, named 'lifts[0]', 'lifts[1]' and 'lifts[2]'.

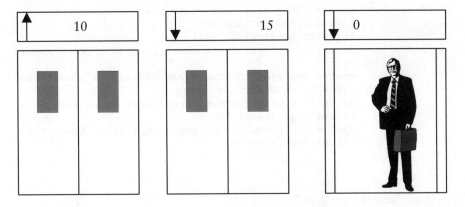

**Figure 4.4**    Different objects (e.g., lifts) may have different states (current floor, direction of travel, whether the doors are open or closed etc.).

Because the array index numbers start at zero there is, of course, no 'lifts[3]'. It is important to note that this creates an array of Lift references but does not actually create any Lift objects. Each of the array elements will be initialised as a null reference (i.e., there is no object being referenced). Trying to send a message to a null reference will result in the program stopping, so we have to make sure that the objects as well as the array are created. The objects are added to the array by calling the Lift constructor for each reference:

```
lifts[0] = new Lift();
lifts[1] = new Lift();
lifts[2] = new Lift();
```

Once the array has been created and populated with lifts by the LiftController, then messages can be sent to the different lifts. This is a good example of how objects of the same class can have different states; all three lifts may be on the same floor, but equally they may be on different floors (Figure 4.4).

This program shows our three lifts being sent to various floors by a class called 'LiftArrayController':

```
/**
        LiftArrayController.java
        the 'LiftArrayController' controls objects of the 'Lift'
        class
*/
public class LiftArrayController
{
        public static void main(String args[])
        {
// create an array of 'Lift' object references
                Lift lifts[] = new Lift[3];
// instantiate three 'Lift' objects
                lifts[0] = new Lift();
                lifts[1] = new Lift();
                lifts[2] = new Lift();
```

```
            // move two of the lifts to different floors
                    lifts[0].moveToFloor(30);
                    lifts[2].moveToFloor(10);
            // display the current floors (note the methods are put directly
            // into 'println')
                    System.out.println("The first lift is on floor " +
                    lifts[0].getFloor());
                    System.out.println("The second lift is on floor " +
                    lifts[1].getFloor());
                    System.out.println("The third lift is on floor " +
                    lifts[2].getFloor());
            }
    }
```

The output from this program is

```
The first lift is on floor 30
The second lift is on floor 0
The third lift is on floor 10
```

# Methods that make selections

The methods we have seen so far have been sequences of Java statements, but sometimes we also need to make selections, to choose between more than one possible course of action. There are two ways of making selections in Java, 'if' statements and 'switch' statements.

## 'if' statements

An 'if' statement consists of two (and only two) different courses of action and a condition. A condition in Java will always return a value of type boolean, and which of the two courses of action is taken depends on whether that boolean value is true or false. One course of action may be, in fact, to do nothing.

'if' statements look like this:

```
if(condition)
{
    // do this
}
else
{
    // do this instead
}
```

The 'else' part is optional. If the condition is false and there is no 'else' part then nothing will happen.

## Relational operators

When writing any kind of conditional statement, including both 'if' statements and the loops covered in the next chapter, we need to express conditions that compare variables using relational operators. In Java the symbols used are shown in Table 4.1.

**Table 4.1**

| Condition | Relational operator | Example |
|---|---|---|
| equal to | == | if(temperature == 100) |
| not equal to | != | if(grade != 'F' ) |
| less than | < | if(sales < target) |
| less than or equal to | <= | if(engine_size <= 2000) |
| greater than | > | if(hours_worked > 40) |
| greater than or equal to | >= | if(age >= 18) |

To evaluate more complex conditions we need to use Boolean operators to combine the simple relational operators shown in Table 4.1. There are three of these operators used for conditions in Java as shown in Table 4.2.

**Table 4.2**

| Meaning | Operator | Example |
|---|---|---|
| and | && | if(age > 4 && age < 16) |
| or | \|\| | if(time_elapsed > 60 \|\| stopped == true) |
| not | ! | if(!drawing_changed) |
| | | // assumes 'drawing_changed' is a boolean variable |

All these expressions return either false or true. The 'not' operator (!) can be confusing because it returns true if the expression is false. For example, the expression if(!drawing_changed) in the table will be true if 'drawing_changed' is false, i.e., if the current drawing has not been changed then 'not drawing changed' is true. We often find this operator being used to test Boolean 'flag' variables that indicate when something has happened. The 'not' operator is matched by the ability to do a test for true, for example 'if(drawing_changed)' is an equally valid expression.

## Using selection: the Coin class

Key aspects of this example are

- an 'if' statement
- the 'Math.random' class method.

The Coin class includes a method that makes a selection using an 'if' statement. This selection is based on using a randomly generated number to set the state of the coin to either heads or tails.

The Coin class has a 'face_up' attribute and a 'get' method ('headsOrTails') to tell us the value of this attribute. There is also a 'flipCoin' method that may or may not change the state of the coin (it may fall with the same face up as before). In this example, the 'face_up' attribute is a single 'char' data type that is initialised to the value H (to represent 'heads'). As is usual for attributes, it is declared private to encapsulate it in the class.

```
private char face_up = 'H';
```

The 'heads or tails' method, of course, is public, and allows us to find out the state of the object:

```
public char headsOrTails()
{
      return face_up;
}
```

The other method is a little more complex. In order to represent the flipping of the coin, we need to randomly generate a value. A simple way of generating a (pseudo) random number is to use a static method of the Math class called 'random' that returns a random double value between 0.0 and 1.0. In the code, we put the return value from this method into a local double variable:

```
double random_number = Math.random();
```

Having got this value from the Math class, the method then uses an 'if ' statement to choose whether the coin is showing heads or tails. If the random number is less than 0.5 then the coin is set to heads, otherwise it is set to tails. Of course, from the point of view of the program it makes no difference whether we use 'less than' or 'greater than', since either way we get a 50/50 chance (more or less).

```
if(random_number < 0.5)
{
// heads
      face_up = 'H';
}
else
{
// tails
      face_up = 'T';
}
```

Because the Math class is part of the default 'java.lang' package, we do not need to use an 'import' statement to find it. This is the complete class:

```
/**
      Coin.java
      represents a coin that can be showing either heads or tails
*/
public class Coin
{
// this private attribute maintains the state of the coin (i.e.
// which face is up). in this example the state is initialised to
```

```
// 'H' (heads)
        private char face_up = 'H';
// this method returns the current state of the coin
        public char headsOrTails()
        {
                return face_up;
        }
// the 'flipCoin' method sets the state of the coin
        public void flipCoin()
        {
// generate a random number between 0.0 and 1.0 with the
// static 'random' method of the 'Math' class
                double random_number = Math.random();
// use the random number in an 'if' statement to set the state of
// the coin
                if(random_number < 0.5)
                {
// heads
                        face_up = 'H';
                }
                else
                {
// tails
                        face_up = 'T';
                }
        }
}
```

The Thumb class provides a test main for the Coin class:

```
/**
        Thumb.java
        a 'Thumb' is used to flip a 'Coin' object
*/
public class Thumb
{
        public static void main(String args[])
        {
// construct a 'Coin' object
                Coin my_coin = new Coin();
// look at the state of the coin before flipping
                char face_up = my_coin.headsOrTails();
                System.out.println("The coin shows " + face_up);
// flip the coin
                my_coin.flipCoin();
                face_up = my_coin.headsOrTails();
                System.out.println("After flipping, it shows " +
                        face_up);
        }
}
```

One possible output from running this program is

```
The coin shows H
After flipping, it shows T
```

The other possible output is

```
The coin shows H
After flipping, it shows H
```

# Arithmetic in Java

In the previous chapter we looked at the simple data types available in Java, including several different types of number (int, float etc.) and saw a few examples of how to assign values to variables of these types and display them. Most programs use numeric variables to do some kind of arithmetic, even if this is no more complicated than keeping a count of something. Arithmetic in Java can be done with five 'operators': the four familiar arithmetic operators that are common to most programming languages, plus a remainder operator

| add | + |
| subtract | − |
| multiply | * |
| divide | / |
| remainder | % |

## Arithmetic statements

All arithmetic statements in Java have the same format, namely that a variable on the left of an assignment (=) operator is made to equal the result of an arithmetic expression on the right:

```
variable = expression;
```

Some examples might be

```
int total_bananas = my_bananas + your_bananas;
float net_pay = gross_pay - deductions;
int area = height * width;
float distance_in_km = distance_in_miles * 1.6093;
```

When writing expressions that contain more than one arithmetic operator, you need to be aware of 'order of precedence' i.e., which part of the expression will be evaluated first? There is a standard table for this that applies to virtually all languages, but the most important part is this:

( )       brackets have a higher order of precedence than

* / %     multiply, divide and remainder, which have a higher order of precedence than

+ −       add and subtract

Consider this example:

```
int x = 4 + 2 * 3;
```

Since the multiplication will be executed before the addition, the result would be 10. If this is not what we want, we can use brackets to change the order in which parts of an expression are evaluated. To force the addition to be executed first we can write

```
int x = (4 + 2) * 3;
```

As you would expect, this gives the result of 18, since the addition is now performed before the multiplication. If two operators of the same precedence (i.e., add and subtract, or multiply and divide) appear in the same expression, then they are evaluated from the left to the right. For example,

```
int x = 10 * 3 / 2
```

will evaluate the multiplication before the division, giving the answer 15. The remainder operator works quite simply, as we can see from this example,

```
int x = 5 / 3;
int y = 5 % 3;
```

While x would contain 1 (the result of dividing 5 by 3) y would contain 2 (the remainder from dividing 5 by 3). An integer remainder is usually known as a 'modulus', but since we can also use this operator with other data types it is not strictly speaking a modulus operator.

## Increment and decrement operators

There are simple operators to increment and decrement a variable by one. The most commonly used is probably the '++' operator that adds one to a variable, like this:

```
int counter = 1;
counter++;
```

In this example, the integer variable 'counter' would be incremented to hold the value 2. We can see that the increment operator is simply shorthand for the following:

```
counter = counter + 1;
```

There is also a decrement operator, which logically enough is '--'and subtracts one from a variable:

```
counter--;
```

This would subtract 1 from the current value of 'counter', and is shorthand for:

```
counter = counter - 1;
```

## Other expression shorthands

Both the increment and decrement operators are appropriate only when we need to add one or subtract one from the existing value of a variable. However, we also have shorthand for changing the value of a variable by arithmetic on its existing value. In this syntax outline, '?' means any one of the five arithmetic operators:

In general terms:         *variable_name* = *variable_name* ? n
can be replaced with:   *variable_name* ?= n

Therefore to add 5 to 'counter' we could replace

```
counter = counter + 5;
```

with

```
counter += 5;
```

Variables can be decremented similarly, so to subtract 4 from 'counter' we could write

```
counter -= 4;
```

Similar examples for the other operators might be

```
counter = counter * 2;     is equivalent to     counter *= 2;
counter = counter / 2;     is equivalent to     counter /= 2;
counter = counter % 2;     is equivalent to     counter %= 2;
```

## Prefix and postfix operators

The previous examples of the increment and decrement operators both used 'postfix' notation (i.e., the '++' or '--' appears after the variable). We may also use prefix notation (the operator appears before the variable):

```
postfix notation:    counter++    or    counter--
prefix notation:     ++counter    or    --counter
```

This makes no difference if the operator is not used as part of a larger expression, but can be significant if it is. If one of these operators is used in prefix notation, then the operator will execute before the rest of an expression, but if postfix notation is used then it will be executed afterwards. For example, if the value of our counter variable is to be assigned to another variable in the following expression:

```
int counter = 1;
int x = counter++;
```

The value of x will be 1, because the increment operator (which adds 1 to counter) will be evaluated after the assignment of the value of counter to x (postfix notation). With prefix notation, the value of x will be 2:

```
int counter = 1;
int x = ++counter;
```

To avoid confusion, the increment and decrement operators will not be used as part of larger expressions in this book, and the postfix notation will be adopted in all cases.

## Type casting

Sometimes we need a variable of one type but have something different. Values that are returned from methods are not always of the type that we want, so we sometimes have to convert them using a technique called 'type casting'. This allows us to convert from one number to another compatible type or from one object type to another. The syntax is:

```
(type we want) value we've got
```

For example, we might have a double value that we want to convert to a float. If 'double_value' is of type double, we can cast it like this

```
float float_value = (float) double_value;
```

Similarly, if we are interested only in the whole number value of a float, we could cast like this:

```
int whole_number = (int) float_value;
```

Although this might seem a bit obscure, it is actually quite a useful technique, as we will see in the next example program where the double value returned from 'Math.random' is converted to an integer.

## The Dice class

Key aspects of this example are

● arithmetic
● type casting
● packages and the 'CLASSPATH'.

This Dice class is rather similar to the Coin class, but can have six different states rather than two (the six possible values on a dice). To get a random number of the appropriate range, we use both arithmetic and type casting. First, we generate a random number between zero and one using the Math.random method as we did in the Coin class. Then we multiply it by six and add one:

```
double random_number = Math.random();
random_number *= 6;
random_number++;
```

This will give us a floating point number (a double) between one and seven. Because the number generated is a double, we must then cast it to get an integer, ignoring any fractional part of the number:

```
dice_value = (int)random_number;
```

This gives us a random number in the integer range one to six.

## Packages

Some classes are general enough in application to be easily reusable in different programs. A Dice class is a good example of this because a dice can be reused in any number of games programs that require a number of dice to be thrown. However, to successfully reuse Java classes we need to understand how packages are defined and how they relate to the 'CLASSPATH', which is set in the operating system.

Our discussion of packages so far has been that we assume all our classes are in the same package (directory) but that public classes can be visible from outside their own package. This is not, however, automatic. A class can only be seen by another class in another package if its directory is in the CLASSPATH or is specifically defined as a member of a package that is in some subdirectory of the CLASSPATH. The CLASS-PATH is a value set in the operating system that defines the pathway(s) where Java classes may be found. Exactly where it appears varies between operating systems, but in Windows systems for example it appears in the autoexec.bat file. Packages are defined in conjunction with the CLASSPATH to enable running Java programs to find the necessary classes at run time.

We will declare the Dice class public to enable it to be accessed by programs in different packages, but this on its own is not enough. We also need to add an extra clause to the code that places the Dice class in a specified package. This is done with the package statement that appears at the beginning of a class, and indicates the location of that class in terms of its directory. The directory pathway, separated by dots, then becomes the package name. If we put the Dice class into a subdirectory called 'chapter4' within a directory called 'javabook', then the package statement looks like this:

```
package javabook.chapter4;
public class Dice
{
    // etc.
```

Even this, however, is not quite the whole story, because the first directory used in the package name (in this example 'javabook') must be a subdirectory of a directory specified in the CLASSPATH. For example, if our CLASSPATH is something like the following:

```
set CLASSPATH= c:\java
```

then the package names do not include the 'java' directory, only those that are subdirectories of it. Using the package name 'javabook.chapter4' assumes that 'javabook' is a subdirectory of 'java'. In this chapter, we place the Dice class in a package, and in the next we will see how it can be imported into classes in other packages.

```java
/**
        Dice.java
        this class is similar to 'Coin', but can have six different
        states rather than two. to get a random number in the
        appropriate range, we use both arithmetic and type casting.
*/
package javabook.chapter4;
public class Dice
{
        private int dice_value;
        public void throwDice()
        {
// generate a random number in the range 0.0 to 1.0
                double random_number = Math.random();
// to get a number in the range 1 to 6, we need to multiply the
// random number by 6 and add 1
                random_number *= 6;
                random_number++;
// to convert this value into an integer, we cast it
                dice_value = (int)random_number;
        }
// 'get' method to return the dice value
        public int getDiceValue()
        {
                return dice_value;
        }
}
```

An important aspect of object orientation is that we can have many objects of a single class. In a previous example, we saw a number of lift objects created. In this program, the ThrowDice class uses two separate dice objects to simulate the throwing of two dice. Like the lifts, over time their states may be the same or they may be different (Figure 4.5).

Although ThrowDice is in the same directory as Dice, it is no longer in the same package because it occupies the default (unnamed) package rather than 'javabook.chapter4'. One solution is to give it the same package name as the Dice so the class can be successfully located.

**Figure 4.5**    The state of dice objects changes over time, and different objects may have the same state or different states.

```
/**
    ThrowDice.java
    simulates the throwing of two dice
*/
package javabook.chapter4;
public class ThrowDice
{
    public static void main(String args[])
    {
// create two dice
        Dice dice1 = new Dice();
        Dice dice2 = new Dice();
// 'throw' both of them
        dice1.throwDice();
        dice2.throwDice();
// get their values
        int dice1_score = dice1.getDiceValue();
        int dice2_score = dice2.getDiceValue();
// calculate the total score
        int total_score = dice1_score + dice2_score;
// display the dice values and the total
        System.out.println("The first dice shows " +
            dice1_score);
        System.out.println("The second dice shows " +
            dice2_score);
        System.out.println("Your total score is " +
            total_score);
    }
}
```

Here is a sample output from running the class:

```
The first dice shows 5
The second dice shows 2
Your total score is 7
```

### The Dice Man

In Luke Reinhart's book *The Dice Man*, the main character in the story begins to run his life by throwing a dice to determine his actions. In this example, we do something similar using a dice object. The dice is thrown, and then we check its value and display a message telling us what to do. Because a dice has six possible states, we would have to use six 'if' statements to decide how to respond to it. In circumstances like this, we might be better off using a 'switch' statement.

## 'switch' statements

Because an 'if' statement can only handle a maximum of two different courses of action, it can be rather ponderous to check all the possible different states of a single variable. When a selection is based on a single variable that can have many different values then a 'switch' statement can be useful. It looks like this:

```
switch(variable)
{
      case value1 : // some code here
            break;
      case value2 : // some code here
            break;
      // etc. for as many cases as need to be handled
      default:
      // default code to handle cases not already dealt with
}
```

Each case is a specific value that the variable being tested may have. The default clause is used if the value passed to the switch does not match any of the specified case values. This, like the 'else' part of the 'if' statement, is optional. The break clause is important because it sends control to the end of the switch statement without evaluating any other cases, otherwise the rest of the cases will also execute. This may seem rather odd, but allows us to use a single response to more than one possible value. For example, we could use it to check for both cases of a character:

```
switch (a_char)
{
      case 'a' :
      case 'A' : // my code here
            break;
      case 'b' // etc…
}
```

Since the case for 'a' has no break clause, if 'a_char' is an 'a' then control will drop through to the next case ('A') and that code will be executed.

This is the Dice Man program that uses a switch statement to look at the state of the dice. Note that there is no default clause in the switch statement because all six possible dice values are catered for in the case clauses:

```
/**
      DiceMan.java
      this program is a little similar to 'Coin.java', but uses a
      'switch' statement rather than an 'if' statement because
      there are more than two possible values to check.
```

```
    */
    package javabook.chapter4;
    public class DiceMan
    {
        public static void main(String args[])
        {
// throw a dice and get its value
            Dice a_dice = new Dice();
            a_dice.throwDice();
            int dice_value = a_dice.getDiceValue();
// the dice value is used to display an instruction (slightly
// modified version of the Dice Man's first throw of the dice!)
            switch(dice_value)
            {
                case 1 :

                System.out.println("forget the affair");
                    break;
                case 2 : System.out.println
("wait until the party on Saturday");
                    break;
                case 3 : System.out.println
("do what Arlene says");
                    break;
                case 4 :System.out.println
("have a platonic relationship");
                    break;
                case 5 : System.out.println
("follow your emotions");
                    break;
                case 6 : System.out.println
("go to Arlene's apartment tonight");
                    break;
            }
        }
    }
```

This is the output similar to that achieved by the Dice Man:

```
have a platonic relationship
```

Note that it would be wise to read the book before following this philosophy of deci-
sion making. It does not have a happy ending.


# Summary

In this chapter, we have seen how to create classes from which objects can be made,
and to give those objects behaviours.

- Object behaviours are defined in methods, which have included both sequence
  and selection.

- Methods are often related closely to the attributes that represent an object's state, so a method may return or change the values of object attributes.
- Many objects of a single class can be created, either with individual names or as elements in an array.

We have looked at a number of aspects of Java syntax:

1. Syntax for creating classes, particularly private attributes and public methods. e.g.,

```
private int current_floor = 0; // attribute
public int getFloor()          // method
{...}
```

2. Creating arrays of objects, e.g.,

```
Lift lifts[] = new Lift[3]; // create array of references
Lifts[0] = new Lift();     // create an object in the array
```

3. Selection in Java:
   'if' statements, e.g.,

```
if(random_number < 0.5)
```

   'switch' statements. e.g.,

```
switch(dice_value)
{
      case 1: //..etc.
```

We also looked at arithmetic in Java: operators, precedence, shorthand versions of expressions (including incrementing and decrementing) and type casting. In the next chapter we will reuse some of the classes described here, look at code that iterates (repeats) and investigate how to get input from the keyboard.

## EXERCISES

1 Create a class called 'counter' to represent the type of counter used to play board games. It should have attributes to represent its colour and the number of the square it is currently on. It should have methods to set and return its colour. It should also have a method to move to a given position on the board using an integer parameter and another method to return its current position. The counter should begin on square zero (i.e., off the board) and its default colour should be white.

2 Create a class called 'BoardGame'. This class should create two counters of different colours. For each counter, use a dice object to move it with four throws of the dice. Display the various positions of the two counters as they are moved.

3 Many games insist that the player throw a six before being allowed to start. Use an 'if' statement to write a start BoardGame class that checks if the counters have thrown a six on the dice. To avoid too much tedious code, give each counter only two throws, and display whether or not either has thrown a six (and is therefore able to start). If a counter throws a six on its first go, move the counter on its second throw.

4 'I don't believe in *I Ching*' (John Lennon)

The ancient Chinese 'book of change' (the *I Ching*, pronounced 'yee jing') describes a method of divination using 50 yarrow stalks. For those who do not have fifty yarrow stalks handy, they can also use three coins. Write a *I Ching* program that throws three coins and displays the kind of hexagram line that they represent. This will be one of the following:

| | | |
|---|---|---|
| Three heads: | Old Yang line | ---- o ---- |
| Three tails: | Old Yin line | ---- x ---- |
| Two heads and a tail | Young Yang line | ----------- |
| Two tails and a head | Young Yin line | ----    ---- |

Hold the coin objects in an array.

Use appropriate Unicode characters to display the appropriate hexagram symbol as well as the name. A hexagram consists of six of these lines, a rather tedious prospect with the code we have covered so far, so we will revisit the *I Ching* in the exercises at the end of the next chapter.

5  For reasons best known to the designers of Java, The Date class has a getTime method that returns (as a long integer) the number of milliseconds that have passed since January 1 1970. We can use this to calculate the current time by using the divide (/) and remainder (%) operators. It is not the simplest way of displaying the time (the Calendar class provides a simpler solution), but serves as a useful arithmetic exercise for these operators. To save you getting out the calculator, the following figures are required:

● there are 86,400,000 milliseconds in a day.
● there are 3,600,000 milliseconds in an hour
● there are 60,000 milliseconds in a minute

Use these to write a class that will tell you the current time (Greenwich Mean Time).

# 5

# Iteration and input

'Experience isn't interesting till it begins to repeat itself – in fact, till it does that, it hardly is experience.' – Elizabeth Bowen (*The Death of the Heart*)

In the previous chapter we saw how methods could be written that included selections between more than one possible course of action. Examples used both 'if' and 'switch' statements. In this chapter we will see how to write code that iterates, meaning that it can repeat a section of code more than once. We will also investigate how to write and call static methods for our own classes and handle various forms of keyboard input. There are not many new objects in this chapter because most of the code is based on interaction with other predefined objects, either our own (the Dice class) or various Java classes (String and Integer).

## Iteration

Iteration can be achieved in three slightly different ways

1.  'for' loops
2.  'while' loops
3.  'do...while' loops

In each case, there will be a condition that allows the loop to terminate. Which one to use depends on a number of factors and we often find that more than one will meet our requirements, but we have to be aware of their differences in order to use them correctly.

### 'for' loops

A 'for' loop has three principal elements:

1.  the start condition
2.  the terminating (while) condition
3.  the action that takes place at the end of each iteration.

The format is

```
for(start condition; 'while' condition; action)
{
    // some code here
}
```

Note that the three parts of the statement following the word 'for' are enclosed in brackets and separated by semicolons.

## A Unicode character viewer

The next example is a class that displays some characters from the Unicode character set using a 'for' loop. The Java 'char' character is big enough to represent all the international characters in the Unicode set, but for most purposes, programs written for English-language readers need only to use the basic printable characters in the ASCII (American Standard Code for Information Interchange) table. The 'UnicodeViewer' class described here has two methods, one to display a character given its Unicode number and another to display the (reliably) printable characters in the ASCII character set.

Key aspects of this example are

- declaring class (static) methods
- a 'for' loop
- casting to type 'char' for output with 'println'
- using the remainder (%) operator.

## Static (class) methods

Because the UnicodeViewer class has no attributes, and therefore no state representation, it will always behave in the same way. This being the case, we may as well interact directly with the class rather than creating objects that would all have exactly the same behaviour. To do this we declare our methods 'static', as we normally do with the 'main' method. We have seen a number of examples of calling static methods of Java classes, such as 'Math.random', where the message is sent directly to the class rather than to an object. In this example, we can send messages directly to the UnicodeViewer class, for example,

```
UnicodeViewer.showASCIITable();
```

## Iteration with a 'for' loop

The 'showASCIITable' method uses a 'for' loop to display the printable characters from the ASCII table. These fall in the range 33 to 126, so the loop looks like this:

```
for(int i = 33; i < 127; i++)
{
    // etc.
```

This means that the integer 'i' is declared with the value 33. The terminating condition is a 'while' condition; the loop continues while the value of i is less than 127. Each time round the loop, i is incremented by one (i++). This happens at the end of the loop. The output from the program shows both the ASCII value of a character and the character itself. Since the loop is counting integers, we can display this directly as the ASCII value. To display the character, we cast the integer value to type char:

```
char character = (char)i;
```

When we pass a 'char' variable to a 'println' statement, the character itself is displayed rather than its ASCII value, so the following statement displays both the value and the character:

```
System.out.print(i + ": " + character + '\t');
```

Notice that the escape sequence character \t is used to put a tab stop between each pair of values. The other method ('showCharacter') uses the same casting tetchnique on the integer value passed to it as a parameter.

Because we are displaying the output tabbed across the screen, we will soon run out of space and need to move on to the next line. In the program, this is handled by an 'if' statement that works out if there are nine number/character pairs on the current line (this value can easily be changed to give different widths). If there are, it forces a line feed. The arithmetic that calculates this uses the remainder operator. Bear in mind that the first character we are displaying has the value 33, so we ignore the first 32 characters by subtracting 32 from the current value of i (the variable that is being incremented by the 'for' loop). If the resulting number can be divided by nine with no remainder, then we must be on the ninth character of the current line, so a new line is needed:

```
if((i - 32) % 9 == 0)
{
      System.out.println('\n');
}
```

This is the complete class with its two static methods.

```
/**
      UnicodeViewer
      this class displays Unicode characters
      and the printable ASCII table
*/
public class UnicodeViewer
{
      public static void showCharacter(int value)
      {
// convert the integer parameter to a 'char' using a cast
            char character = (char)value;
```

```
// display the Unicode number along with its character
        System.out.println("Unicode character number " +
            value + " is " + character);
    }
    public static void showASCIITable()
    {
        System.out.println("ASCII character table" + '\n');
// the 'for' loop counts from 33 to 126, the range of the
// reliably printable characters in the ASCII table
        for(int i = 33; i < 127; i++)
        {
// convert the integer counter to a 'char' using a cast
            char character = (char)i;
// display the ASCII number along with its character, then add a
// tab
            System.out.print(i + ": " + character + '\t');
// if there are 9 characters on a row, add a line feed
            if((i - 32) % 9 == 0)
            {
                System.out.println('\n');
            }
        }
    }
}
```

This class (UnicodeViewerTest) simply provides a test main for the two UnicodeViewer methods. The key point about this class is that it sends messages directly to the UnicodeViewer class and does not create any objects

```
/**
    UnicodeViewerTest
    this class simply tests the methods of the UnicodeViewer
    class
*/
public class UnicodeViewerTest
{
    public static void main(String args[])
    {
// because the UnicodeViewer class only has static (class)
// methods, we send messages directly to the class and do not
// (indeed cannot) create any objects
        UnicodeViewer.showCharacter(63);
        UnicodeViewer.showASCIITable();
    }
}
```

The output from this program is:

```
Unicode character number 63 is ?
ASCII character table

33: !  34: "  35: #  36: $  37: %  38: &  39: '  40: (  41: )

42: *  43: +  44: ,  45: -  46: .  47: /  48: 0  49: 1  50: 2
```

```
51: 3  52: 4  53: 5  54: 6  55: 7  56: 8  57: 9  58: :  59: ;

60: <  61: =  62: >  63: ?  64: @  65: A  66: B  67: C  68: D

69: E  70: F  71: G  72: H  73: I  74: J  75: K  76: L  77: M

78: N  79: O  80: P  81: Q  82: R  83: S  84: T  85: U  86: V

87: W  88: X  89: Y  90: Z  91: [  92: \  93: ]  94: ^  95: _

96: `  97: a  98: b  99: c  100: d 101: e 102: f 103: g 104: h

105: i 106: j 107: k 108: l 109: m 110: n 111: o 112: p 113: q

114: r 115: s 116: t 117: u 118: v 119: w 120: x 121: y 122: z

123: { 124: | 125: } 126: ~
```

## 'while' and 'do...while' loops

These loops are very similar in that both execute until a given condition is false (i.e., while it is true), but there is one key difference between them. The 'while' loop tests for a precondition, which is to say that the condition is evaluated at the beginning of each loop. In contrast, the 'do..while' loop tests for a postcondition, where the condition is evaluated at the end of each loop. This means that the 'do..while' loop executes at least once, whereas the 'while' loop may not execute at all if the condition is already false. The 'while' loop therefore is a true iteration (i.e., it executes 0 or more times) whereas the 'do...while' loop is a repetition (it executes one or more times). Which one you choose in a particular application depends entirely on the context.

The 'while' loop has the following syntax:

```
while(condition)
{
    // statement(s) here...
}
```

Similarly, the 'do...while' loop has this syntax

```
do
{
    //  statement(s) here…
} while (condition);
```

note the semicolon that must follow a 'do..while' loop.

## Looping with a 'while' condition

The next example program uses a 'while' condition to control a loop that simulates the throwing of a dice until it shows a six.

Key aspects of this example are

- importing programmer-defined packages
- reuse of an existing class
- a 'do..while' loop.

This program uses the Dice class from the previous chapter. Reuse of existing classes is an important aspect of object-oriented programming. By using classes that already exist, we avoid the need to keep reinventing the wheel by coding everything from scratch.

## Importing our own packages

When we use classes provided with Java, we use an import statement to indicate which package they are in. We do exactly the same thing with classes that we write ourselves, so we can use an import statement to give the location of the Dice class in its package. In the GameStarter class that uses a Dice, the import statement looks like this:

```
import javabook.chapter4.Dice;
```

This, you may recall from Chapter four, indicates that the Dice class is in a package called 'javabook.chapter4'. The package name indicates the subdirectory that the class occupies relative to the CLASSPATH.

## The GameStarter class

This class consists of a 'do...while' loop that iterates until we throw a six with a Dice object, rather similar to one of the exercises from the end of Chapter four, but this time the condition is used with 'while' rather than 'if'. Although a 'do...while' loop has been used here, it could equally be written using a 'while' loop, since we set the initial dice value to zero before the first throw to ensure that it does not begin with a valid number.

The GameStarter class is just a main method containing a dice object and a loop. Because it is simply a syntax example it does not involve any new user-defined objects.

```
/**
    GameStarter.java
    a class that demonstrates a 'do..while' loop to 'throw'
    a Dice imported from another package
*/
import javabook.chapter4.Dice;
public class GameStarter
{
    public static void main(String args[])
    {
```

```
// create a 'Dice' object
          Dice a_dice = new Dice();
// set the initial 'thrown' value to zero
          int dice_value = 0;
// loop until throwing the dice gets a six
          do
          {
                  a_dice.throwDice();
                  dice_value = a_dice.getDiceValue();
                  System.out.println("You have thrown a " +
                          dice_value);
          } while(dice_value != 6);
// confirm the dice value is six
          System.out.println("Well done, you can start the
                  game);
     }
}
```

A sample test run produced this output:

```
You have thrown a 1
You have thrown a 4
You have thrown a 6
Well done, you can start the game
```

# Handling keyboard input

The next example introduces keyboard input, though it should be noted that this is a very basic approach that treats input as a stream of single characters. It is not recommended as a general approach for all occasions where input from the keyboard is required and other strategies are described later in this chapter. In the next chapter, we will build on the basic syntax and ideas introduced here to create a Keyboard class to handle various types of keyboard input.

Key aspects of this example are

- basic keyboard input using 'System.in'
- throwing IO exceptions
- a 'while' loop.

All this random number generation is all very well, but sometimes we do need to put some data into a program ourselves. In Java, we would typically do this via a graphical user interface (GUI) written using the classes in the abstract windowing toolkit (AWT) covered in Chapters eight and nine. However, it is also possible (though not always very simple) to enter data directly at the keyboard to non-graphical Java applications. There are a number of classes that may be used to handle input in Java, but at this stage we will use an approach similar to that we have used for output. All program output so far has been through the 'out' object provided by the System class. There is also an 'in' object in System, which is a member of the InputStream class. This class has a number of basic methods for handling keyboard input, including several versions of a 'read' method. The most basic version of 'read' takes a single character from the keyboard and returns its Unicode value as an integer:

```
int read();
```

We can use casting to convert this integer into a 'char' data type, as here, where 'input_char' is a char variable:

```
input_char = (char)System.in.read();
```

## Input and exceptions

When we input data from the keyboard, Java insists that we at least acknowledge that it may cause an exception. That is, there is the potential for unexpected data to be entered that cannot be handled by the existing code. Ideally, we should 'handle' all exceptions, which means writing code to intercept different kinds of exceptional input. However, we can for the moment take the path of least resistance and add a 'throws' clause to methods that handle keyboard input. In this case, the exception is an 'IOException' defined in 'java.io', so we add the following to our main method where the input takes place:

```
public static void main(String args[]) throws java.io.IOException
```

The full package name is needed in this example only because we are not specifically importing the 'java.io' package. A 'throws' clause is a way of recognising that our code may throw an exception, but we are not going to handle it ourselves. If an exception does occur, then the program will terminate with a message from the virtual machine. All methods that take keyboard input must throw or handle this exception. You will find other situations where Java insists that you at least acknowledge that some kind of exception may occur, and your code will not compile without a minimum of an appropriate throws clause.

The following example program shows how we can combine keyboard input with an iteration, in this case a 'while' loop, and a selection (an 'if'). The program counts the number of words being entered at the keyboard by using the space character to define the end of a word. This is rather crude, since it does not allow for multiple spaces, but the basic principles of a word counter are present. To indicate the end of input, the user must enter a '|' character, because the 'while' loop continues until this character is found. Again, because it is a syntax example rather than a proper class, all the code is confined to main.

```
/**
    WordCounter.java
    this class uses a 'while' loop and an 'if' to count the
    number of words input from the keyboard
*/
public class WordCounter
{
    public static void main(String args[])
```

```
// we must throw an IO exception when taking input from the
// keyboard
    throws java.io.IOException
    {
// display a message. note the use of concatenation to split a
// long string over more than one line
    System.out.println("Enter a number of words. Multiple lines"
    + "may be entered. Use the | character to terminate the
    input");
// variable to hold the current input character (initialised to a
// space)
        char input_char = ' ';
// variable to hold the word count
        int word_count = 0;
// loop that iterates until the terminating character (|) is
// input. it also requires a following carriage return or end of
// file character (e.g. ctrl-z)
        while(input_char != '|')
        {
// read a character from the keyboard, casting the returned 'int'
// to a 'char'
            input_char = (char)System.in.read();
// if the character is a space or a carriage return
// add one to the word count
            if(input_char == ' ' || input_char == '\r')
            {
                word_count++;
            }
        }
// add one to the counter for the last word
        word_count++;
// display the word count
        System.out.println("The number of words input was " +
            word_count);
    }
}
```

Here is an example test run. In run-time output examples where there is some user input, this input is shown in bold type:

```
Enter a number of words. Multiple lines may be entered. Use the
| character to terminate the input
The quick brown Java
jumped over the lazy C++|
The number of words input was 9
```

## String input from the keyboard

The previous example showed how keyboard input could be crudely handled one character at a time. We can also use the 'System.in' object to read in a series of characters (as an array of bytes) and use these to create a string object. We can then trim this string to remove any unwanted trailing spaces (Figure 5.1).

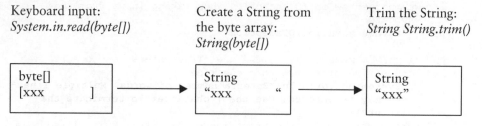

Keyboard input:
*System.in.read(byte[])*

Create a String from
the byte array:
*String(byte[])*

Trim the String:
*String String.trim()*

**Figure 5.1**   Strings can be retrieved from the keyboard by using System.in.read(byte[]),
creating a string from the byte array and then trimming it.

Although there are better ways to handle input, this method at least provides a
relatively simple approach that is adequate for simple input of ASCII characters.
Key aspects of this example are:

● keyboard input of byte arrays using 'System.in'
● creating strings from byte arrays
● trimming leading and trailing spaces from a string.

The version of 'read' we saw in the previous program took a single character from
the input stream and returned it as an integer. There is another version of 'read' that
takes an array of bytes as a parameter and uses it to store the input. It takes this
form:

```
void read(byte[]);
```

The example program declares an array of bytes called 'buffer', so the 'read' method
appears as:

```
System.in.read(buffer);
```

Once we have typed in a string of characters, we can pass the array to one of the
constructors of the String class, i.e.,

```
String(byte[]);
```

Because in our example the array of bytes is called 'buffer', the constructor call looks
like this:

```
String input_string = new String(buffer);
```

This will create a string as big as the array, which in our program is 80 bytes long. In
order to remove any unwanted spaces from the ends of the string, we can use the
'trim' method that returns another string containing only the text. Therefore we use
the copy constructor to make a trimmed string:

```
String trimmed_string = input_string.trim();
```

At this stage we have finally created a string object that matches our keyboard input. The complete program is:

```
/**
    StringInput.java
    this class demonstrates how strings of characters can be
    input from the keyboard and then put into a String object
*/
public class StringInput
{
    public static void main(String args[])
// we must throw an IO exception when taking input from the
// keyboard
    throws java.io.IOException
    {
        System.out.print("Enter a string of characters :- ");
// we need an array of bytes to hold the input characters because
// the 'read' methods of the InputStream class handle bytes, not
// characters
        byte buffer[] = new byte[80];
// get some keyboard input
        System.in.read(buffer);
// create a String using the array of bytes (the string will be
// as long as the array)
        String input_string = new String(buffer);
// create a trimmed version of the String. this String has all
// the trailing spaces removed
        String trimmed_string = input_string.trim();
// display the trimmed string
        System.out.println("you entered \"" + trimmed_string
        + "\"");
    }
}
```

A sample test run produced:

```
Enter a string of characters :- Introductory Java
You entered "Introductory Java"
```

## Input and numbers

This is the point at which Java books have to make some choices about how they discuss input of more sensitive types of data than just characters. Java, it has to be said, provides no simple mechanism for getting numeric values from the keyboard. There are good reasons for this, but nevertheless it is often useful for learning and testing purposes to be able to type in numbers. Some books leave numeric input until after the AWT graphical interface classes have been introduced, while others use file handling for input data where a number of other classes may be used. Others again hide the details of implementation in their own classes, leaving the reader to use non-standard methods. None of these approaches is ideal, but the approach used in this book draws from the best features of others. The process of getting numbers from the keyboard here is based on the string input method described earlier, with some additional steps. This approach will be refined in the next chapter to use some further Java classes and encapsulate the process in a method of a Keyboard class. To convert string data to numbers, we can take advantage of the Java wrapper classes. The specific example program used to introduce numeric input also draws together a number of other aspects of this chapter.

Key aspects of this example are:

- keyboard input of integers using 'System.in'
- using the Integer 'wrapper' class
- creating an integer from a string
- returning an int from an integer.

This program builds on the previous one in that input is taken from the keyboard not directly as a number (which 'System.in' cannot do) but rather as an array of bytes that is converted to a string and them trimmed as before. In addition, the string is then passed to an object of the integer class that is able to return an 'int' value corresponding to the numeric values originally typed in (Figure 5.2).

## Wrapper classes

Java provides a set of Wrapper classes for the built-in types. There are classes for all the types of number including Float, Integer, Double and Long. The advantage of these classes is that they allow methods to be added to the representations of the built-in data types, in particular allowing a number of conversions between various

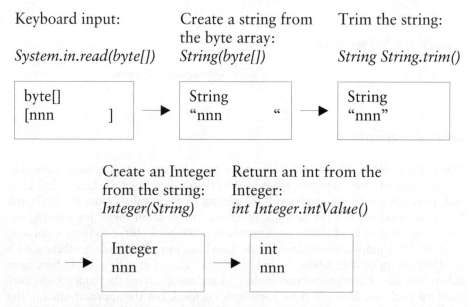

**Figure 5.2**   Using data conversion methods to get numeric data from the keyboard.

types. In our example, we use one of the Integer class constructors to create an integer object from a string, and the method 'intValue' to return a value of the 'int' data type. By this method we can indirectly convert a string to an int.

Although the exact syntax used in the example program is slightly different (because the object references are declared outside the loop and the ints are held in an array) this is how it works (assuming that 'string_object' is a string containing numeric characters):

```
// create an Integer from a String
Integer int_object = new Integer(string_object);
// return an int from the Integer
int int_value = int_object.intValue();
```

Figure 5.2 shows how we are adding another two steps to our previous process of conversion from one data representation to another.

This example uses a byte array and a 'for' loop to add two numbers together, thus demonstrating that the values derived from the input are indeed numeric values. In order for the process to work correctly, the same byte array cannot be reused for both inputs, and a new one must be declared each time round the loop. Therefore the array reference is declared outside the main loop:

```
byte buffer[];
```

Then inside the loop the array is actually created:

```
buffer = new byte[80];
```

The discarded array will be recovered by the garbage collector, so we need not be concerned with its fate.

Like the previous two examples, it is difficult to find any objects in what is simply a demonstration of syntax, so again all processes take place in main (though this will not be the case when we finally hide these processes inside a Keyboard class):

```
/**
    NumberInput.java
    this class demonstrates how numbers can be input
    from the keyboard, put into a String object and
    converted to their appropriate type using Java
    'wrapper' classes.
*/
public class NumberInput
{
    public static void main(String args[])
// we must throw an IO exception when taking input from the
// keyboard
    throws java.io.IOException
    {
// declare some useful objects and variables:
// we need an array of bytes to hold the input characters because
// the 'read' methods of the InputStream class handle bytes, not
// characters
        byte buffer[];
```

```
// a reference to a String that will contain the array data
        String input_string;
// a reference to a string that will be a trimmed version of
// 'input_string'
        String trimmed_string;
// a reference to an Integer object that will convert the string
// to an Integer
        Integer input_int;
// an array of ints to contain the actual numbers
        int int_values[] = new int[2];
// a loop to go round twice
        for(int i = 0; i < 2; i++)
        {
                System.out.print("Enter an integer :- ");
// get some keyboard input
                buffer = new byte[80];
                System.in.read(buffer);
// create a String using the array of bytes (the string will be
// as long as the array)
                input_string = new String(buffer);
// create a trimmed version of the String. this String has all
// the trailing spaces removed
                trimmed_string = input_string.trim();
// create an Integer object using the string
                input_int = new Integer(trimmed_string);
// display the Integer (converts to a String)
                System.out.println(input_int);
// convert it to an int for arithemetic
                int_values[i] = input_int.intValue();
        }
// add the numbers together
        int sum = int_values[0] + int_values[1];
// display the total
        System.out.println("The sum of these numbers is " +
                sum);
        }
}
```

Here is a test run:

```
Enter an integer :- 12
12
Enter an integer :- 18
18
The sum of these numbers is 30
```

## Summary

In this chapter we have written object methods that included both iteration (code that repeats itself) and keyboard input of various kinds. To do this we have used

- 'for', 'while' and 'do...while' loops
- 'read' methods of 'System.in'
- strings and Integers.

The syntax we have looked at has included

1.  Iteration: we have seen syntax examples of all three loops, e.g.,

```
for(int i = 33; i < 127; i++)
{…}                             // 'for' loop

do
{…} while dice_value != 6;      // 'do…while' loop

while(input_char != '|')
{…}                             // 'while' loop
```

2.  Input: we have used two versions of 'read' from the 'InputStream' class (to which 'System.in' belongs)

```
int read()
void read{byte[])
```

3.  Wrapper classes: To successfully convert input data into integers, we have used the Integer class, e.g.,

```
input_int = new Integer(trimmed_string);
int_values[i] = input_int.intValue();
```

We have now covered all the fundamental aspects of syntax for building Java classes. In the next chapter we will look at how various objects can work together to provide more complex programs.

### EXERCISES

**1** Put the Coin class from Chapter four into a named package that you can import into classes in other packages. Using this imported class, write a class that flips a coin until ten heads have appeared. Keep a count of how many times the coin has been flipped in total and display this at the end.

**2** Modify the *I Ching* class from Chapter 4, Exercise 4, importing the Coin class and using 'for' loops to check the lines and create a full hexagram.

**3** Add another class method to the UnicodeViewer class that takes a single character as a parameter and displays its Unicode value on the screen. Modify the 'UnicodeViewerTest' class to test this method, taking a character from keyboard input.

**4** Write a class that creates two string objects using keyboard input. Use the string method 'compareTo' to display the string that comes first alphabetically. The format of the method is:

```
int compareTo(String);
```

It returns a negative number if the string using the method is less (i.e., earlier in the alphabet) than the parameter string. It returns zero if they contain the same text and a positive number if the parameter is earlier in the alphabet than the string using the method.

**5** Write a class to take a float value from the keyboard, square it and display the result. You can use the Float class and its 'floatValue' method.

**Part 3**

# Object and class relationships

# 6

# Objects working together: association, aggregation and composition

'The medium is the message' – Marshall McLuhan (*Understanding Media*).

Objects that work alone do not produce very useful systems. An object-oriented program consists of many objects collaborating to produce the required system behaviour. In the preceding chapters we saw how programs can be written that use more than one programmer-defined class. When objects of different classes communicate with one another they are said to 'associate'. Examples so far have consisted only of two classes, one of which was a 'controller' that did not represent an object because it consisted only of a 'main' method. In this chapter we will see how a system can be made up of a number of different objects that associate with one another.

One particular kind of association is known as 'aggregation', where groups of objects are used as components to make some larger object. You may recall some discussion of associations and aggregations in Chapter two, when Calendar and Clock objects associated, and Clocks were aggregations of components. In this chapter we will look at both ordinary associations and some examples of what might be considered aggregations. Where aggregated objects are very tightly bound together, we refer to this as 'composition'. In a later example we will see how objects representing simple digital electronic components ('gates') are used in a composition to produce a larger component (a 'half adder').

In addition, this chapter touches once again on the issue of exceptions. Some basic exception handling is introduced that allows a program to continue running after an exception has occurred. Along the way, we encapsulate some of our keyboard handling code into a reusable 'Keyboard' class.

## Associating objects: snakes and ladders

Our first example is a game of snakes and ladders. It shows how various objects (board, snakes, ladders, dice, etc.) come together to produce a program. Snakes and

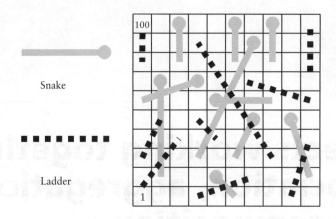

**Figure 6.1**   A snakes and ladders board.

ladders is a traditional British game based on a board of 100 squares, some of which are connected by snakes or ladders (see Figure 6.1).

Players throw dice to move counters in a snake-like fashion along each row of the board, moving up when they reach the end of a line. If they land on the head of a snake, then they must move down to its tail, and if they land at the foot of a ladder they can move to its head. The first player to land exactly on square 100 is the winner. (This may be obvious to you, but using this example with a multi-cultural class proved to me that it is not obvious to everyone!)

Key aspects of this example are:

- several classes in one program
- reuse of existing objects (importing 'Dice')
- writing constructors
- multiple (non-public) classes in a single file.

The most important aspect of this example is that it is the first program we have seen that includes several types of object that we define ourselves. In previous examples we have seen programs that used various Java classes (String, Date) etc., but in each case only one object of our own making. Although we have also had our controller classes, these have not had any methods other than 'main'. In snakes and ladders we will write a number of classes and again reuse the 'Dice' class. Figure 6.2 shows the classes in the snakes and ladders game with their associations and public methods.

You may notice that in this example we have no Counter class (refer to Chapter 4 Exercise 1), but we could quite easily use one. The diagram shows that the SnakesAndLadders class associates with a Dice and a Board. The Board is an aggregation of squares, and each square may associate with a snake or a ladder object. The diagram also shows some of the 'multiplicity' of the associations, which indicate how many objects are involved in each association. The multiplicity '0..1' means that there can be either zero or one objects in the association. Where no number is shown, the multiplicity is always assumed to be '1'. The 'or' constraint, indicated by a dashed line across the two associations from square to snake and square to ladder, means that we cannot have both a snake and a ladder on any one square.

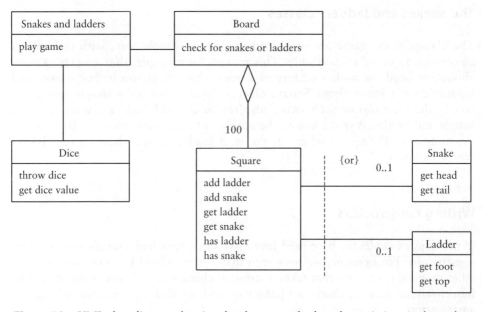

**Figure 6.2**    UML class diagram showing the classes, methods and associations in the snakes and ladders program.

## Classes that are not 'public'

In Chapter four, we saw that there can be only one public class in a given Java source file. However, classes that are not declared public (and therefore are only visible to other classes in the same package) can share the same file. This is appropriate where these classes do not have any role beyond the specific programming context in which they are being used. Consider the difference between the Dice and Snake classes. A dice may be used in any number of game programs, so it is useful to make the class public and put it into a named package so that it can be easily reused by other classes. In contrast, the Snake class is totally tied to the game of snakes and ladders. It has no realistic chance of reuse outside this specific program so there is no need to make it a public class. In fact none of the classes that are part of the snakes and ladders game is reusable in other contexts, so none needs to be made public and all can appear in the same file. The only public class is SnakesAndLadders so that it can be accessed and played from other places. The file name is therefore SnakesAndLadders.java because the file name must always match the name of the public class (assuming there is one). The other class the game uses is the Dice that we previously declared as a public class, accessible from outside its own package. Putting closely related classes into one file can make it easier to manage our code. It does, however, cause potential confusion because we cannot tell from the file name what '.class' files it will generate when compiled. Indeed, we are also unable to tell from a class file generated for a non-public class which '.java' file that class comes from.

## The snakes and ladders classes

The classes in the game are organised in a rather simple way, with the objects associating in one direction only. This means, for example, that a square knows about any heads of snakes or feet of ladders that appear on it, but snakes and ladders do not know about Square objects. Instead, we use a simple integer to record the locations of their two ends. The Snake and Ladder classes are both simple and similar. A snake knows the number of the square where its head is and the number of the square where its tail is. A ladder knows where its foot is and where its top is.

## Writing constructors

In previous examples we have used Java classes that have had a number of different constructors. For example, we have seen that a string object has a constructor that takes no parameters, one that takes a string of characters enclosed in speech marks (effectively, an array of chars) as a parameter and one that takes an array of bytes as a parameter:

```
String()          // no parameters
String(char[])    // array of chars
String(byte[])    // array of bytes
```

It is often useful to write constructors for our own classes to initialise objects appropriately. Although we can set attributes to an initial value when we declare them in the class, it is sometimes useful to create objects with different initial states. The Snake and Ladder classes are good examples of this because every snake and ladder needs to be created at a different position on the board. To set the position of a snake, a parameterised constructor is provided that takes the head and tail positions as parameters. A ladder has a similar constructor that takes the positions of the foot and head of the ladder.

To create our own constructors, we declare them in a similar way to any other method, except that constructors have two unusual features:

- They have the same name as the class.
- They do not have a return type because they cannot return a value.

The constructor for the 'Snake' class therefore looks like this:

```
public Snake(int h, int t)
{
    head = h;
    tail = t;
}
```

Where h and t are used to pass the head and tail positions respectively. The head and tail attributes (integers) are made to equal the parameter values so that when the object is created the head and tail positions are already set. Similarly, the Ladder constructor positions the top and the foot:

```
public Ladder(int t, int f)
{
        top = t;
        foot = f;
}
```

In both cases we could omit the 'public' prefix because the class itself is not public, so the constructor could not be called from outside its package anyway. However, since nearly all of the constructors we will use will be public, it is more consistent to introduce these constructors in this way.

The 'Board' constructor is rather different in that it does not have any parameters. However, it does perform a number of initialisation processes, namely to

- create all the 'Square' objects (using their default constructor)
- add all the snakes to the appropriate squares
- add all the ladders to the appropriate squares

The 'SnakesAndLadders' class also has a constructor with no parameters, and simply creates the Board and Dice objects:

```
public SnakesAndLadders()
{
        board = new Board();
        dice = new Dice();
}
```

We could have created these objects where they are declared as attributes, for example

```
private Board board = new Board();
private Dice dice = new Dice();
```

Given that this is possible, why might we choose to only declare references as private attributes and create the objects in the constructor? There are two common reasons why we might do this:

1.  When objects are not fixed attributes of the class but associations that might change over time; in this case the reference might not always need to point to the same object (or indeed any object). Separating the reference from the creation of the object gives us more flexibility.
2.  When objects being created have parameterised constructors, and the parameters are being passed down from the constructor of one object to the constructor of another; we might, for example, change the board class so that it could have different numbers of squares for different games, and pass this value to the board via the game constructor.

## The Snake and Ladder classes

Apart from their constructors, the only other methods of snakes and ladders are simple 'get' methods to return the positions of the head/top or tail/foot. Note that the classes have not been declared 'public' so they cannot be made visible outside their own package, but can appear in the same source file as other classes. Like the constructors, the methods here have been declared public for consistency with other examples, though for visibility within a single package this is not essential. In any case it makes sense to declare the public interface of a class to be explicitly public. This is the complete Snake class:

```
class Snake
{
        private int head;
        private int tail;
        public Snake(int h, int t)
        {
                head = h;
                tail = t;
        }
        public int getHead()
        {
                return head;
        }
        public int getTail()
        {
                return tail;
        }
}
```

The Ladder class is very similar, again with a parameterised constructor:

```
class Ladder
{
        private int top;
        private int foot;
        public Ladder(int t, int f)
        {
                top = t;
                foot = f;
        }
        public int getTop()
        {
                return top;
        }
        public int getFoot()
        {
                return foot;
        }
}
```

## The Square class

The Square class might look rather odd as it stands. This is because it is a class that has to represent three different types of square:

1.  a square with a snake's head
2.  a square with a ladder's foot
3.  a square with no snakes or ladders.

So that it can fulfil all three roles, each square object contains references to both a snake and a ladder so that either can be used for a particular square. As we discussed in the context of the SnakesAndLadders constructor, the attributes are references rather than objects since no square will hold both a snake and a ladder at the same time. There are also methods to add snakes or ladders and methods to check if a snake or a ladder is present. In the next chapter, we will see how inheritance provides an alternative approach for designing classes that represent different (but similar) types of object. However, for the moment, this is the complete class:

```
class Square
{
// by default, a square has neither a snake nor a ladder
      private boolean has_snake = false;
      private boolean has_ladder = false;
// we may use one or neither of these references for a particular
// square
      private Snake a_snake;
      private Ladder a_ladder;
// we may want to add a snake head
      public void addSnake(Snake s)
      {
            a_snake = s;
            has_snake = true;
      }
// or add the foot of a ladder
      public void addLadder(Ladder l)
      {
            a_ladder = l;
            has_ladder = true;
      }
// methods to find out if the square has a snake or a ladder
      public boolean hasSnake()
      {
            return has_snake;
      }
      public boolean hasLadder()
      {
            return has_ladder;
      }
// methods to return either a snake or a ladder (if present)
// otherwise they will return null
      public Snake getSnake()
      {
            return a_snake;
      }
```

```
public Ladder getLadder()
{
        return a_ladder;
}
}
```

You will notice that there is no error check here to ensure that a given square does not have both a snake and a ladder. This could be easily remedied but will not be necessary if the classes are re-engineered to use inheritance so is not included here.

## The Board class

The board has two major responsibilities:

1.  To set up the squares that make up the board by creating them and adding snakes and ladders as appropriate. This is done according to the following board layout:

| Ladders: | from: | 1  | 4  | 9  | 21 | 28 | 36 | 51 | 71 | 80  |    |
|----------|-------|----|----|----|----|----|----|----|----|-----|----|
|          | to:   | 38 | 14 | 31 | 42 | 84 | 44 | 67 | 91 | 100 |    |
| Snakes:  | from: | 16 | 47 | 49 | 56 | 62 | 64 | 87 | 93 | 95  | 98 |
|          | to:   | 6  | 26 | 11 | 53 | 19 | 60 | 24 | 73 | 75  | 78 |

2.  To move counters appropriately by checking if they have landed on squares with snakes or ladders, and displaying appropriate messages.

When the board is moving a counter, some of the code looks rather clumsy. For example the game must check a square for a snake or a ladder and, if there is one, get the snake or ladder object from the square to find out where it goes. Figure 6.3 shows a UML 'collaboration diagram' that indicates the sequence of message passing between objects. An object can be indicated by underlining the class name and preceding it with a colon. If the object has a specific name it will appear before the colon, but since this applies to all squares with ladders a specific name is not required here.

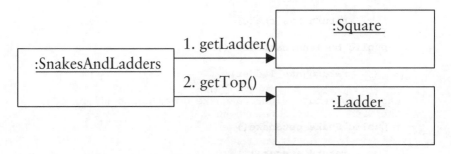

Figure 6.3   Message passing between objects in the snakes and ladders game.

In the code, a message is passed to the square to return a ladder that we then send another message to:

```
counter = squares[counter].getLadder().getTop();
```

A similar chain of events takes place when we communicate with snakes. Although this is perfectly acceptable code, it is not a very clean design. Again, this can be refined somewhat by using inheritance (Chapter seven).

## Creating new objects as parameters

Sometimes a method expects to be passed an object. Where does this object come from? In many cases, the object will exist in another part of a program, so its reference can simply be passed to the method. In other cases, the object will not necessarily need to exist anywhere else before it is needed by the method. The 'addLadder' and 'addSnake' methods of the Board class are a case in point – the snakes and ladders do not exist anywhere except on the board, so will not need to be created elsewhere. In such cases, we can create the object directly as the parameter to the method, using 'new' without a separate object reference. For example:

```
squares[1].addLadder(new Ladder(38,1));
```

In this case, the new Ladder object is created when the method needs it by calling the constructor within the parameter brackets of 'addLadder'. This uses the reference declared for the 'addLadder' parameter to create the object. All the snakes and ladders are instantiated this way. This is the complete Board class:

```
// the board consists of 100 squares
class Board
{
        private Square squares []
// the constructor creates the squares and adds the snakes and
// ladders
        public Board()
        {
// the array will be one square bigger than needed so that we can
// start from array element 1, ignoring element 0
        squares = new Square[101];
        for(int i = 1; i < 101; i++)
        {
// add the next Square object to the board
                squares[i] = new Square();
        }
// add the ladders
        squares[1].addLadder(new Ladder(38,1));
        squares[4].addLadder(new Ladder(14,4));
        squares[9].addLadder(new Ladder(31,9));
        squares[21].addLadder(new Ladder(42,21));
        squares[28].addLadder(new Ladder(84,28));
        squares[36].addLadder(new Ladder(44,36));
        squares[51].addLadder(new Ladder(67,51));
        squares[71].addLadder(new Ladder(91,71));
        squares[80].addLadder(new Ladder(10,80));
```

```
// add the snakes
       squares[16].addSnake(new Snake(16,6));
       squares[47].addSnake(new Snake(47,26));
       squares[49].addSnake(new Snake(49,11));
       squares[56].addSnake(new Snake(56,53));
       squares[62].addSnake(new Snake(62,19));
       squares[64].addSnake(new Snake(64,60));
       squares[87].addSnake(new Snake(87,24));
       squares[93].addSnake(new Snake(93,73));
       squares[95].addSnake(new Snake(95,75));
       squares[98].addSnake(new Snake(98,78));
       }
// this method checks the counter position to see if it matches
// the head of a snake or the foot of a ladder, and adjusts the
// counter position accordingly
       int checkForSnakesOrLadders(int counter)
       {
// if the square has the foot of a ladder
          if(squares[counter].hasLadder())
          {
// move to the top of the ladder
             System.out.println("On " + counter + ", up the
             ladder :-)");
             counter = squares[counter].getLadder().getTop();
          }
// if the square has the head of a snake
          if(squares[counter].hasSnake())
          {
// move to the tail of the snake
             System.out.println("On " + counter +
             ", down the snake :-(");
             counter = squares[counter].getSnake().getTail();
          }
// return the counter position. this will be unchanged unless the
// square had a snake's head or the foot of a ladder
          return counter;
       }
}
```

## The SnakesAndLadders class

This class simulates the playing of the game, and in this example is confined to moving a single counter (represented by an 'int' variable) around the board. It is responsible for throwing the dice, telling the counter where to move to and asking the square to check for snakes or ladders. It checks to see where the counter is and stops the game when it throws the dice to land exactly on square 100.

Remember that in this example we have put all the classes in a single file. Only the SnakesAndLadders class is public and can therefore be visible outside its own package ('javabook.chapter6'). The Dice class is not redefined here since it has already been written. If we are both naming a package and importing other packages, the package name must come before the 'import' statement, i.e.,

```
package javabook.chapter6;
import javabook.chapter4.Dice;
```

These appear right at the beginning of the file before any classes. The SnakesAndLadders class itself is as follows:

```
public class SnakesAndLadders
{
        private int counter = 0;
// references to Board and Dice objects
        private Board board;
        private Dice dice;
// the constructor creates the Board and Dice objects
        public SnakesAndLadders()
        {
                board = new Board();
                dice = new Dice();
        }
// this method acts as a controller for playing the game
        public void playGame()
        {
// iterate until we reach the end (square 100)
                while(counter != 100)
                {
// throw the dice
                        dice.throwDice();
// see what square it will take us to
                        int next_square = counter + dice.getDiceValue();
// we only use the throw if it does not take us beyond square 100
// (i.e. we need an exact number to win)
                        if(next_square <= 100)
                        {
                            counter = next_square;
                        }
// if we have not finished, we check the board to see if we have
// to go up a ladder or down a snake
                        if(counter < 100)
                        {
// calling this method will change the value of 'counter' only if
// it goes up a ladder or down a snake
                                counter = board.checkForSnakesOrLadders(counter);
                                System.out.println("On square " + counter);
                        }
                }
                System.out.println("counter finished on " + counter);
        }
// 'main' creates a 'SnakesAndLadders' object and starts the game
        public static void main(String args[])
        {
                SnakesAndLadders my_game = new SnakesAndLadders();
                my_game.playGame();
        }
}
```

Of course, every time we play the game the output will be different. Here are two sample test runs:

First test run

```
On square 3
On square 8
On square 10
On 16, down the snake :-(
On square 6
On square 8
On square 14
On square 19
On square 23
On square 27
On square 30
On square 32
On square 34
On 36, up the ladder :-)
On square 44
On square 48
On 51, up the ladder :-)
On square 67
On 71, up the ladder :-)
On square 91
On square 97
On square 99
counter finished on 100
```

Second test run

```
On 1, up the ladder :-)
On square 38
On square 41
On square 46
On 49, down the snake :-(
On square 11
On square 15
On square 20
On square 23
On square 25
On square 30
On square 34
On 36, up the ladder :-)
On square 44
On square 50
On 56, down the snake :-(
On square 53
On square 55
On square 61
On square 63
On square 66
On square 72
On square 78
On square 84
On square 89
```

```
On 95, down the snake :-(
On square 75
On square 79
On square 82
On 87, down the snake :-(
On square 24
On square 30
On square 32
On square 37
On square 40
On square 42
On square 44
On square 50
On square 54
On square 59
On square 61
On square 66
On square 69
On 71, up the ladder :-)
On square 91
On square 96
On square 96
On square 99
On square 99
counter finished on 100
```

## Association, aggregation or composition?

In the snakes and ladders game, there are a number of associations between classes and an aggregation between Board and Square. This means that the Board object is made up of a number of Square objects. Given that the board and its squares are tightly related, we might realistically regard this as a composition relationship. How, then, do we draw a distinction between the two? Although the lines between association, aggregation and composition may sometimes be blurred, we can say in general that the most important characteristic is ownership. In an association objects do not own each other, only communicate. In aggregation, one object may own other objects but they may also have an independent lifetime and other associations. In composition, the whole owns its parts, and their lifetimes are probably identical. It is unlikely that the parts have any relationships with other objects outside the composition.

The remaining two examples in this chapter may help to demonstrate some of the differences between aggregation and composition. First, we look at the relationship between a course of studies and the modules (subject areas) that it contains. For example, a degree course in computer studies may contain modules in programming, analysis and design, operating systems, mathematics, etc. Although a course is made up of modules, these modules may also appear in other courses and the modules in a course may be replaced by others. Therefore we can regard this as an aggregation relationship (see Figure 6.4). The second example mimics computer hardware components being composed of other pieces of hardware, where the larger component depends entirely on its parts and they have no separate existence. This can be seen as an example of composition (see Figure 6.9).

# Aggregation

Key aspects of this example are

- aggregation of objects
- exception handling: 'try' and 'catch'.

The classes in this example are Module and Course. A module represents a particular subject being taught as part of a course. A module has three attributes:

1. the name of the module (e.g., 'Java Programming')
2. a credit point rating (e.g., 20 credit points for a full module or 10 credit points for a half module)
3. an assessment method (e.g., 'exam', 'assignment', etc.).

To keep things simple, modules only have a constructor to set their attributes and 'get' methods to return them:

```java
/**
      Module.java
      a module represents an element of a course
*/
public class Module
{
// attributes
      private String module_name;
      private int credit_points;
      private String assessment;
// constructor
      public Module(String name, int points, String assess)
      {
            module_name = name;
            credit_points = points;
            assessment = assess;
      }
// 'get' methods
      public String getModuleName()
      {
            return module_name;
      }
      public int getCreditPoints()
      {
            return credit_points;
      }
      public String getAssessment()
      {
            return assessment;
      }
}
```

Course objects are aggregations of modules, shown in a UML diagram by adding a diamond shape to the containing end of the association. Figure 6.4 shows how the two classes relate. The '*' multiplicity means 'zero to many', so the number of modules in a course can vary.

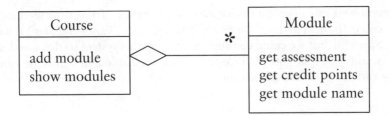

**Figure 6.4**    Course is an aggregation of Module objects.

A course object has a course title and is able to display the details of its modules, which are stored in an array.

```
/**
      Course.java
      the 'Course' class is an aggregation of 'Module'
      objects
*/
public class Course
{
// the name of the course
      private String course_name;
// an array of modules
      private Module modules[];
// a count of how many objects are in the module array
      private int module_count = 0;
// the constructor sets the course name and the array size from
// its parameter list
      public Course(String name, int number_of_modules)
      {
            course_name = name;
            modules = new Module[number_of_modules];
      }
// 'addModule' adds a parameter module to the array.
      public void addModule(Module new_module)
      {
            modules[module_count] = new_module;
            module_count++;
      }
// this method shows the modules aggregated inside the course
// object
      public void showModules()
      {
            System.out.println(course_name +
              " contains the following modules:");
            System.out.println
            ("Module name \t credit points \t assessment");
            for(int i = 0; i < module_count; i++)
            {
            System.out.println(modules[i].getModuleName() +
                  '\t' + modules[i].getCreditPoints() +
                  '\t' + modules[i].getAssessment());
            }
      }
}
```

Having assembled our aggregation we can make objects of the Course class, add Module objects to them and see the result. The test class ('CourseBuilder') does not do anything useful, but we could continue to develop this system so that a collection of courses could be put into a 'Prospectus', or timetabled into 'Room' objects, providing various levels of aggregation.

```
/**
        CourseBuilder.java
        this class simply acts as a test for the 'Module'
        constructor and the methods of the 'Course' class
*/
public class CourseBuilder
{
        public static void main(String args[])
        {
// create a Course
        Course degree = new Course("Computer Studies", 3);
// create the Module objects
        Module module1 = new Module("Operating Systems", 10,
                "Exam");
        Module module2 = new Module("Java Programming", 20,
                "Coursework");
        Module module3 = new Module("Intelligent Systems", 20,
                "Vulcan Mind Meld");
// add the modules to the course
                degree.addModule(module1);
                degree.addModule(module2);
                degree.addModule(module3);
// display the course details
                degree.showModules();
        }
}
```

The output from the CourseBuilder class is:

```
Computer Studies contains the following modules:
Module name      credit points  assessment
Operating Systems      10        Exam
Java Programming       20        Coursework
Intelligent Systems    20        Vulcan Mind Meld
```

## Exception handling

In Chapter five, we introduced the idea of exceptions by using the 'throws' clause on a method that used an input stream. Because there are some circumstances where Java anticipates the possibility of an exception, we sometimes have to deal with this. The minimum response is to simply acknowledge that an exception may occur, as we did with the possibility of an 'IOException' when using 'System.in.read'. Our 'WordCounter' class, for example, had a 'throws' clause:

```
public static void main(String args[])throws java.io.IOException
```

This allowed the class to compile without actually dealing with any exception that might be thrown at run time. If an exception did occur, the program would terminate with an exception message.

## Catching exceptions – 'try' and 'catch'

Instead of simply throwing an exception, we can do something to catch it ourselves. This has the benefit of allowing a program to continue running even if an exception has occurred. The syntax for doing this is based on the 'try' and 'catch' keywords:

```
try
{
        // do this
}
catch (aJavaException obj)
{
        // if it all went horribly wrong, do this
}
```

'aJavaException' must be one of the predefined exception classes that exist in Java or an object of an exception class we have written ourselves, though in this book we will only be concerned with the Java exception classes. We have already seen that 'IOException' is one of them, and another is the 'ArrayIndexOutOfBoundsException' that occurs if we try to access an array element that has not been declared. In the 'Course' class, we declare an array of a size provided as a parameter to the constructor and then add Module objects to it. What happens if we try to add too many Modules? If we take our 'ClassBuilder' example, it creates a 'Course' with only three modules. If we attempt to add a further module to the course, when we run the class it will crash (well, crash land) with the following message:

```
java.lang.ArrayIndexOutOfBoundsException:
        at Course.addModule(Course.java:26)
        at CourseBuilder.main(CourseBuilder.java:17)
```

As you can see, the virtual machine does furnish us with some useful information, including the type of exception, the classes and methods where the exception occurred and the line numbers from the relevant source files. However, we are still in the position of having a terminated program. To stop this happening, we can explicitly catch the exception in the 'addModule' method, so that if it is thrown we handle it inside the method. This is a modified version of 'addModule' that catches the exception and displays a message. It also shows that the 'catch' clause is provided with an object of the appropriate exception type that we can output using 'System.out.println':

```
// 'addModule' adds a parameter module to the array.
// if the array is full then we catch the exception
        void addModule(Module new_module)
        {
```

```
try
{
        modules[module_count] = new_module;
        module_count++;
}
catch(ArrayIndexOutOfBoundsException exception)
{
        System.out.println("Exception thrown:");
        System.out.println(exception);
}
}
```

If we use our CourseBuilder that adds too many modules with this version of Course, then the exception is handled without the program stopping, and the output is:

```
Exception thrown:
java.lang.ArrayIndexOutOfBoundsException:
Computer Studies contains the following modules:
Module name       credit points assessment
Operating Systems       10      Exam
Java Programming        20      Coursework
Intelligent Systems     20      Vulcan Mind Meld
```

Clearly, once the exception has been thrown and caught, the program carries on executing as it did before.

## A Keyboard class with exception handling

In the previous chapter, we looked at some aspects of handling keyboard input in Java. Given that this is not particularly simple, it is helpful to encapsulate the code that handles input inside a class. Building a reusable 'Keyboard' class means that we do not have to write the same code over and over again every time we want to get some data from the keyboard. While we are writing this class we can also add in some exception handling.

### 'char' and 'String' input methods

In Chapter five, we used two different 'read' methods of 'System.in' to get data from the keyboard, one for single characters (by reading an int and casting it to type char) and another for strings (by reading an array of bytes and creating a string from it). In this class, we use the latter version for all types of input. When reading a single character from the keyboard in the 'getChar' method, we read it into a byte array, create a string from it and then take the first character of the string using the 'charAt' method. This method returns a character from a string when passed an index number as a parameter, the first character having the index number zero. This line assigns the first character in 'temp_string' to 'read_char'

```
read_char = temp_string.charAt(0);
```

This is a little more robust than using the other version of 'read' since it does not matter if too many characters are entered. Any extra characters are simply discarded.

One other minor change is the way that 'trim' is used when entering strings. In the first version of the code, the trim method was used to create a new (trimmed) string from an existing string. However, it is possible to assign a string to the return value of its own trim method, i.e.

```
temp_string = temp_string.trim();
```

This means we have one fewer object to deal with.

## Catching IOExceptions

When we wrote methods with keyboard input in Chapter five, we simply added the 'throws java.io.IOException' clause to the method declaration. This meant that any exceptions that arose would cause the program to terminate but it might to better to use 'try' and 'catch' to handle this exception, i.e.,

```
try
{
        // input handling code here
}
catch(java.io.IOException e)
{
        // exception handling code here
}
```

The full package name (java.io.IOException) is only necessary if there is no import statement for that particular package. Otherwise 'IOException' is enough. This example from the 'getString' method shows that the read is enclosed in a try block

```
try
{
        System.in.read(buffer);
// create a string from the characters
        temp_string = new String(buffer);
// trim the string
        temp_string = temp_string.trim();
}
catch(IOException e)
{
        System.out.println(e);
}
```

This ensures that any exception will cause a message to be displayed but will not terminate the program. The other methods have similar try and catch blocks for IO exceptions.

## The 'getInt' method

This method of the Keyboard class is not very different from the integer input code in Chapter five, but is slightly modified. Previously, we created an Object of the 'Integer' class, passed it a string object and converted it to an int using the 'intValue' method. An alternative approach is to use a class method of 'Integer' called 'parseInt'. By using a class method we do not need to create an object, just pass the string to the class and get the resulting int:

```
temp_int = Integer.parseInt(temp_string);
```

There is also an added exception hander, to deal with data that does not have the correct format for a number, the 'NumberFormatException':

```
catch(NumberFormatException e)
```

This exception class is in the standard 'java.lang' package so we never need to use the full package name. This is the class, encapsulating the input of characters, strings and integers inside three methods.

```
/**
    Keyboard.java
    this class encapsulates some aspects of keyboard input
*/
// make the class reusable by putting it into a named package
package javabook.chapter6;
import java.io.*;
public class Keyboard
{
// getString reads a string from the keyboard
    public String getString()
    {
// byte array for input characters
        byte buffer[] = new byte[80];
// declare a String reference with a default value (null)
        String temp_string = null;
// read characters into the byte array, handling
// IOExceptions if necessary
        try
        {
            System.in.read(buffer);
// create a string from the characters
            temp_string = new String(buffer);
// trim the string
            temp_string = temp_string.trim();
        }
        catch(IOException e)
        {
            System.out.println(e);
        }
// return the string
        return temp_string;
    }
```

```java
// this method gets a single char by reading a string
// and using only the first character
    public char getChar()
    {
// byte array for input characters
        byte buffer[] = new byte[80];
// declare a 'char' with a default value (space)
        char read_char = ' ';
// read characters into the byte array, handling
// IOExceptions if necessary
        try
        {
            System.in.read(buffer);
// create a string from the byte array
            String temp_string = new String(buffer);
// take the first character of the string and
// put it into 'read_char'
            read_char = temp_string.charAt(0);
        }
        catch(IOException e)
        {
            System.out.println(e);
        }
// return the character
        return read_char;
    }
// the getInt method gets an integer by converting a string
    public int getInt()
    {
// byte array for input characters
        byte buffer[] = new byte[80];
// declare an int with a default value of zero
        int temp_int = 0;
// read characters into the byte array, handling
// IOExceptions if necessary
        try
        {
            System.in.read(buffer);
// create a string from the byte array
            String temp_string = new String(buffer);
// trim the string
            temp_string = temp_string.trim();
// use the static 'parseInt' method of Integer to convert the String
            temp_int = Integer.parseInt(temp_string);
        }
        catch(IOException e)
        {
            System.out.println(e);
        }
// if the characters are not numeric, catch the exception
        catch(NumberFormatException e)
        {
            System.out.println(e);
            temp_int = 0;
        }
// return the int value
```

```
                    return temp_int;
            }
    }
```

There are many more sophisticated keyboard classes around, but this one is reasonably simple and robust as a tool for testing programs with interactive input.

We will use this class for keyboard input in some later programs. For the moment, however, this is simply a test class that demonstrates the three keyboard methods:

```
/**
        KeyboardTest.java
        this class provides a basic test of the methods
        of the Keyboard class
*/
import javabook.chapter6.Keyboard;
public class KeyboardTest
{
        public static void main(String args[])
        {
// create a 'Keyboard' object
                Keyboard keyboard = new Keyboard();
// test the 'getString' method
                System.out.print("Enter a string ");
                String string = keyboard.getString();
// test the 'getChar' method
                System.out.print("enter a character ");
                char character = keyboard.getChar();
// test the 'getInt' method by getting two integers
// and adding them together
                System.out.print("enter an integer ");
                int int1 = keyboard.getInt();
                System.out.print("enter another integer ");
                int int2 = keyboard.getInt();
// display the results
                System.out.println("String is: " + string);
                System.out.println("Character is: " + character);
                System.out.println("First integer is: " + int1);
                System.out.println("Second integer is: " + int2);
                int sum = int1 + int2;
                System.out.println("The sum of the integers is " +
                        sum);
        }
}
```

This is the output from a test run (user input in bold):

```
Enter a string Introductory Java
enter a character J
enter an integer 100
enter another integer 250
String is: Introductory Java
Character is: J
First integer is: 100
Second integer is: 250
The sum of the integers is 350
```

# Composition

The next example shows how object composition can be used to create objects from components that are tightly bound together. Real-world objects are often clear examples of composition, because many objects are composed of smaller objects. Electronic devices are very much of this type, and provide the context for this example.

Key aspects of this example are

- logic with AND, OR, NOT
- composition.

## What is a gate?

A gate is a fundamental component of digital electronics, and the behaviour of some types of gate will be very familiar to anyone who has used a programming language. In Chapter one we looked at how Boolean operators can be used as part of the conditions used with selections (if statements) and iterations (while or do...while statements). These Boolean operators were:

| && | AND | are both conditions true? |
| &#124;&#124; | OR | is either of the conditions true? |
| ! | NOT | is the condition false? |

In electronics, these Boolean operators are applied to components known as gates, which compare binary digits rather than conditions. For example, an AND gate has two or more inputs, each of which may have the value zero or one. It has a single output that will have the value one if, and only if, all the inputs are also one, otherwise the output will be zero (Figure 6.5). To keep things simple our examples will assume that AND gates and OR gates have only two inputs.

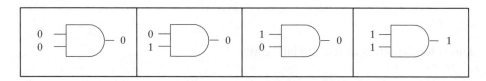

**Figure 6.5**    The possible inputs and outputs from AND gates.

An OR gate will again have two or more inputs and a single output, but in this case will output a one if any of the inputs have the value one. If all the inputs are zero then the output will be zero (Figure 6.6).

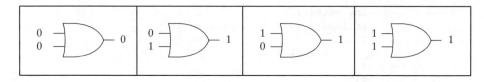

**Figure 6.6**    The possible inputs and outputs from OR gates.

A NOT gate has a single input and a single output. All it does is convert an input of zero to an output of one, or an input of one to an output of zero (Figure 6.7).

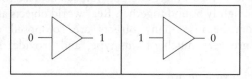

**Figure 6.7**     The possible inputs and outputs from NOT gates.

To model these three types of gate, we will have three classes. They are very simple, and indeed in this implementation they have no attributes and consist only of a single method. These are the three classes, starting with the 'AndGate' class:

```java
/**
    AndGate.java
    the And gate will output 1 only if both inputs are 1
*/
public class AndGate
{
    public int generateOutput(int input1, int input2)
    {
        int output;
        if(input1 == 1 && input2 == 1)
        {
            output = 1;
        }
        else
        {
            output = 0;
        }
        return output;
    }
}
```

This is the definition of the 'OrGate' class

```java
/**
    OrGate.java
    the Or gate will output a 1 if either or both inputs is 1
*/
public class OrGate
{
    public int generateOutput(int input1, int input2)
    {
        int output;
        if(input1 == 1 || input2 == 1)
        {
            output = 1;
        }
        else
        {
```

```
                        output = 0;
                    }
                return output;
            }
    }
```

Finally, the definition of the 'NotGate'

```
/**
        NotGate.java
        this class represents a Not gate that takes a single
        digital input and outputs the opposite signal, i.e. if
        1 is input then the output is 0, and if the input is 0
        then the output is 1
*/
public class NotGate
{
        public int generateOutput(int input1)
        {
                int output;
                if(input1 == 1)
                {
                        output = 0;
                }
                else
                {
                        output = 1;
                }
                return output;
        }
}
```

This test class shows how the gates respond to different combinations of input by displaying their output in a simple 'truth table' format. Truth tables are often used to show the result of Boolean logic, and for numbers alone the order of the values is unimportant. For the gates with two inputs (AND gates and OR gates) a two-dimensional grid can be used to show the output for each pair of values, showing the physical as well as the logical combinations of inputs possible. For the single input NOT gate only one row is required. The code is a bit laborious, since it is mostly 'println' statements. The tab stop characters (\t) have to be treated as strings rather than chars (i.e., put in double quotes rather than single) or the compiler insists on doing arithmetic on them instead of concatenating them as strings. This happens because we are concatenating the chars (which have numeric values) with integers, so it looks to the compiler as if we are trying to do an arithemetic expression.

```
/**
        TruthTable.java
        test class for the three Gate classes: AndGate, OrGate and
        NotGate
*/
public class TruthTable
{
        public static void main(String args[])
        {
```

```
// create objects of the three classes
            AndGate and_gate = new AndGate();
            OrGate or_gate = new OrGate();
            NotGate not_gate = new NotGate();
// variables to hold output from gates
            int output1 = 0;
            int output2 = 0;
            int output3 = 0;
// output the column headings for the AND gate truth table
            System.out.println("Truth table for AND gate");
            System.out.println("\t0\t1");
// generate outputs for the three possible input combinations
            output1 = and_gate.generateOutput(0,0);
            output2 = and_gate.generateOutput(1,0);
            output3 = and_gate.generateOutput(1,1);
// output the rows of the truth table
            System.out.println("0\t" + output1 + "\t" + output2);
            System.out.println("1\t" + output2 + "\t" + output3);
// output the column headings for the OR gate truth table
            System.out.println("Truth table for OR gate");
            System.out.println("\t0\t1");
// generate outputs for the three possible input combinations
            output1 = or_gate.generateOutput(0,0);
            output2 = or_gate.generateOutput(1,0);
            output3 = or_gate.generateOutput(1,1);
// output the rows of the truth table
            System.out.println("0\t" + output1 + "\t" + output2);
            System.out.println("1\t" + output2 + "\t" + output3);
// output the column headings for the NOT gate truth table
            System.out.println("Truth table for NOT gate");
            System.out.println("\t0\t1");
// generate outputs for the two possible inputs
            output1 = not_gate.generateOutput(0);
            output2 = not_gate.generateOutput(1);
// output the row of the truth table
            System.out.println("\t" + output1 + "\t" + output2);
        }
    }
```

This is the output:

```
Truth table for AND gate
        0       1
0       0       0
1       0       1
Truth table for OR gate
        0       1
0       0       1
1       1       1
Truth table for NOT gate
        0       1
        1       0
```

On their own, gates are fairly useless, but put them together into an aggregation and we can build a useful component. One very simple component is the half adder.

## What is a half adder?

One of the fundamental operations of a computer is to perform arithmetic on binary numbers. It can do this by using collections of gates put together in particular ways. One component that we can build simply from gates is the 'half adder', a component that is able to add two binary digits, producing a result and a carry. There are only four possible combinations of input bits to a half adder, and only three possible results (Figure 6.8)

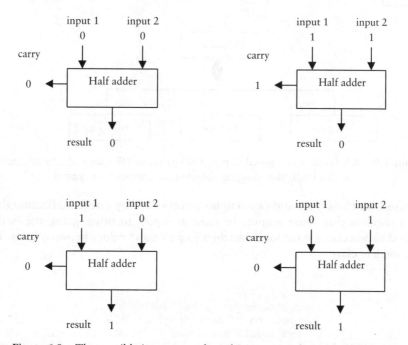

**Figure 6.8**  The possible inputs to and resulting outputs from a half adder.

There are a number of ways of using gates of different types to build half adders, but a simple and useful example (which comes from *Illustrating Computers* by Day and Alcock) is one that uses the three types of gate we have looked at, namely the AND, OR and NOT gates. A half adder built from these components is shown in Figure 6.9, along with a UML diagram of the classes. Because this is an example of the very strong form of aggregation known as 'composition', we use a filled diamond to indicate the relationship between the half adder and its component gates.

We can create a 'HalfAdder' class in Java by making it a composition of objects of the various Gate classes. Returning to our previous discussion of whether we create objects when they are declared or in the constructor, given that in a composition relationship the lifetime of the components and the composition is the same, it makes sense to create the gate objects when they are declared:

```
private AndGate and_gate1 = new AndGate();
private AndGate and_gate2 = new AndGate();
private OrGate or_gate = new OrGate();
private NotGate not_gate = new NotGate();
```

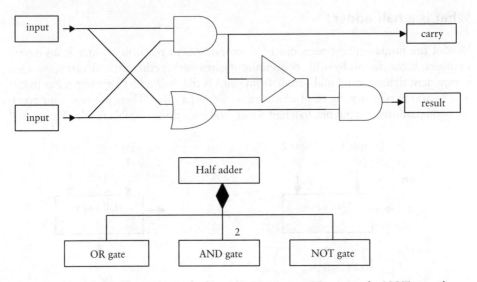

**Figure 6.9**    A half adder composed of two AND gates, an OR gate and a NOT gate along with a UML class diagram showing the composition symbol.

We also have two inputs and two outputs (represented by integers). Because the half adder requires that some outputs be used as inputs to other gates, the 'setInput' method also declares some local variables to pass these values between gates. This is the complete class:

```
/**
          HalfAdder.java
          demonstrates how a half adder object is an
          aggregation of gate objects. this half adder consists
          of two inputs connected to an AND gate and an OR
          gate. the output from the AND age provides the carry
          bit and the input to a NOT gate. The output from this
          gate is fed into a second AND gate along with the
          output from the OR gate. the output from this gate is
          the result bit.
*/
public class HalfAdder
{
// components of the half adder
     private AndGate and_gate1 = new AndGate();
     private AndGate and_gate2 = new AndGate();
     private OrGate or_gate = new OrGate();
     private NotGate not_gate = new NotGate();
// inputs to the half adder
     private int input1;
     private int input2;
// outputs from the half adder
     private int result;
     private int carry;
// set the values of the input bits
     public void setInput(int in1, int in2)
     {
```

```
                input1 = in1;
                input2 = in2;
// producing the output involves storing some intermediate
// results in local variables. first, feed the inputs into the
// AND and OR gates, resulting in the carry value and an
// intermediate result
                carry = and_gate1.generateOutput(input1, input2);
                int temp1 = or_gate.generateOutput(input1, input2);
// feed the carry value into the NOT gate
                int temp2 = not_gate.generateOutput(carry);
// use the two intermediate results as input to the second AND
// gate, producing the result bit
                result = and_gate2.generateOutput(temp1, temp2);
        }
// return the result bit
        public int getResult()
        {
                return result;
        }
// return the carry bit
        public int getCarry()
        {
                return carry;
        }

}
```

Finally, we can test our 'HalfAdder' class by making an object and sending data to the 'setInput' method. This class tests the three possible combinations of input, 1 + 1, 1 + 0 and 0 + 0. Note that 1 + 0 means exactly the same as 0 + 1 so will produce the same result.

```
/**
        Computer.java
        this class tests the behaviour of a half adder using the
        three possible input combinations:
                1,1
                1,0
                0,0
*/
public class Computer
{
        public static void main(String args[])
        {
// declare  a half adder
                HalfAdder half_adder = new HalfAdder();
// set the input to the half adder
                half_adder.setInput(1, 0);
// display the resulting output from the half adder
                System.out.println("Input to the half adder is 1, 0");
                System.out.println("Result from half adder is "
                        + half_adder.getResult());
                System.out.println("Carry value from half adder is "
                        + half_adder.getCarry());
// set the input to the half adder
                half_adder.setInput(0, 0);
```

```
      // display the resulting output from the half adder
            System.out.println("Input to the half adder is 0, 0");
            System.out.println("Result from half adder is "
                + half_adder.getResult());;
            System.out.println("Carry value from half adder is "
                + half_adder.getCarry());
      // set the input to the half adder
            half_adder.setInput(1, 1);
      // display the resulting output from the half adder
            System.out.println("Input to the half adder is  1, 1");

            System.out.println("Result from half adder is "
                + half_adder.getResult());
            System.out.println("Carry value from half adder is "
                + half_adder.getCarry());
      }
}
```

Our test class produces the following results:

```
Input to the half adder is 1, 0
Result from half adder is 1
Carry value from half adder is 0
Input to the half adder is 0, 0
Result from half adder is 0
Carry value from half adder is 0
Input to the half adder is 1, 1
Result from half adder is 0
Carry value from half adder is 1
```

## Summary

In this chapter we have built on our knowledge of classes and objects to create larger programs based on different objects communicating with one another. We have also encapsulated our keyboard handling code into a reusable class. In particular we have seen different examples of the way that objects can work together.

- association: where independent objects talk to each other
- aggregation: where an object is made up of other objects that can vary
- composition: a very strong form of aggregation where the component objects are fixed.

We have seen several new aspects of Java syntax.

1. Writing our own constructors so that we can pass parameters to them, e.g.,

   ```
   public Snake(int h, int t)
   {...}
   ```

2. Declaring references to objects as attributes and creating the objects within a method, e.g.,

   ```
   private Dice dice; // reference declared as an attribute
   dice = new Dice(); // reference used to create the object
   ```

3.  Creating objects without names by using 'new' in the parameters of methods, e.g.,

```
squares[1].addLadder(new Ladder(38,1));
```

4.  Catching exceptions; instead of simply using a 'throws' clause to ignore exceptions, we can use 'try' and 'catch' to manage exceptions without the program terminating, e.g.,

```
try
{…}
catch(ArrayIndexOutOfBoundsException exception)
{…}
```

5.  Modifying the code for keyboard input, including the use of a character input stream rather than a byte input stream:

```
InputStreamReader reader = new InputStreamReader(System.in);
```

Also using a class method of Integer to convert a string to an int:

```
temp_int = Integer.parseInt(temp_string);
```

In the next chapter we will look at some more relationships between classes and objects, including containers (a very loose form of aggregation where one object contains other objects) and inheritance, where classes can build upon existing classes to extend and refine their behaviours.

### EXERCISES

**1** Add another counter to the snakes and ladders game, and indicate which counter reaches the finish first.

**2** Replace the 'int' representation of the counters with your Counter class from Chapter four, Exercise one.

**3** Create a Prospectus class that is an aggregation of many courses. It should allow courses to be added and viewed. Write a test class that creates a Prospectus object and tests its methods.

**4** Replace the 'Computer.java' test class with one that takes two binary digits (1 or 0) from the keyboard (using the Keyboard class) to test the half adder.

**5** Using the existing HalfAdder and OrGate classes, write a FullAdder class that simulates the following diagram of a 4-bit full adder (Figure 6.10, from Alcock and Day, 1982).

Test the FullAdder by using it to add various combinations of four-bit numbers.

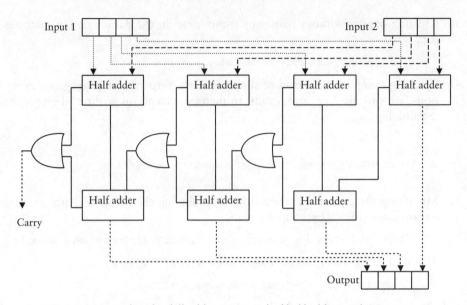

**Figure 6.10**    A four-bit full adder composed of half adders and OR gates.

# 7

# Containers, inheritance and polymorphism

'All the teachers in the pub, passing round the ready rubbed' – Madness (*Baggy Trousers*).

'They f___ you up, your mum and dad. They may not mean to, but they do. They fill you with the faults they had and add some extra, just for you' – Philip Larkin (*This Be The Verse*).

In this chapter we will look at some Java classes that can be used as containers for other objects. Java containers work by using inheritance, an important object-oriented concept that we will also use to build some of our own classes. Part of this chapter investigates the 'Javadoc' document generator. Although not actually a part of the Java language, 'Javadoc' is a useful tool provided with the JDK that, among other things, can tell us about the inheritance structures used with our classes.

## Inheritance and polymorphism

All Java classes use inheritance because they automatically inherit from the Object class. They can also easily exhibit polymorphism by providing their own implementations for the 'toString' method. Our first example introduces a class that will be developed throughout this chapter to demonstrate various aspects of containers, inheritance and polymorphism.
Key aspects of this example are

- providing a 'toString' method
- including comments for the 'Javadoc' document generator.

The main example used in this chapter is an identification card class, similar in concept to those that many organisations use to identify individuals for security purposes. Figure 7.1 shows the attributes and methods of the 'IDCard' class, which is very simple. It has three attributes and a 'get' method for each one, along with a constructor that is used to initialise them. In addition there is a 'toString' method that provides a simple way of displaying the object.

111

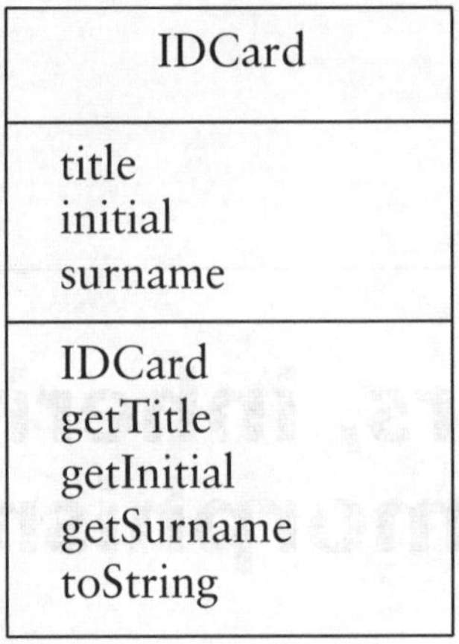

**Figure 7.1**    The attributes and methods of the 'IDCard' class.

## The attributes of the class

The IDCard attributes are 'title' and 'surname' (instances of class String) and 'initial', represented by a single 'char' data type. This, then, is the beginning of the class:

```
public class IDCard
{
        private String title;
        private char initial;
        private String surname;
```

## The methods of the class

The IDCard class has a constructor with three parameters. As we discussed in the context of some of the snakes and ladders classes, adding a constructor method can be a useful addition to a class. It allows us to initialise the state of an object when it is created, rather than having a separate initialisation method that would have to be explicitly called. The 'IDCard' constructor takes the title, initial and surname of a person as its parameters and sets the attributes accordingly:

```
public IDCard(String title_in, char initial_in, String
surname_in)
{
        title = title_in;
        initial = initial_in;
        surname = surname_in;
}
```

The class also has 'get' methods to return the attribute values.

```
public String getTitle()
{
      return title;
}
public char getInitial()
{
      return initial;
}
public String getSurname()
{
      return surname;
}
```

## The 'toString' method

We have seen a number of Java classes that have a 'toString' method, used by 'println' when displaying objects, and in fact all Java objects have a 'toString' method by default. Even our own objects are automatically provided with a default 'toString' method but it does not usually produce very helpful output. Fortunately, we are able to provide versions of 'toString' for our own classes by writing a method (called 'toString') that returns a string object. Here, we provide our own version of the method for 'IDCard' objects. It works by concatenating the title, initial (plus a full stop) and surname attributes into a single string object and then returning that string from the method:

```
public String toString()
{
      String temp_string = new String(title + initial + "."
            + surname);
      return temp_string;
}
```

## Polymorphism

When we provide our own versions of methods that already exist in other classes we are using 'polymorphism'. This simply means that different classes can respond differently when receiving the same message. In this example, the message being received is 'toString', and different classes of object can respond differently by returning string objects created specifically by that class. Polymorphism, like Java containers, works because of inheritance. Classes inherit the 'toString' method from class Object so they can all receive the same message. Their individual response to that message can then be specifically tailored for that class. Later in this chapter we will see further examples of polymorphism.

## Testing the IDCard class

The SecurityDesk1 class is used to test objects of the IDCard class. It comprises a 'main' method that calls the IDCard constructor to make two objects of the IDCard class, then tests the 'get' methods and the polymorphic 'toString' method by using 'println' directly on an IDCard object.

```
/**
        SecurityDesk1.java
        the 'SecurityDesk1' class is used to create objects of
        the IDCard class and send messages to them
*/
public class SecurityDesk1
{
// 'main' calls the constructor and then tests the methods of the
// class
    public static void main(String args[])
    {
// call the constructor to create two IDCard objects. note that
// the string parameters appear in double quotes, but the char
// parameter appears in single quotes
        IDCard id_card1 = new IDCard("Dr.",'J',"Ava");
        IDCard id_card2 = new IDCard("Ms.",'B',"Rowser");
// test the three 'get' methods by calling them with 'println'
        System.out.println(id_card1.getTitle() +
        id_card1.getInitial() + "." + id_card1.getSurname());
// get much the same result (much more easily) by just displaying
// the object. this implicitly uses the 'toString' method
        System.out.println(id_card2);
    }
}
```

When we run the SecurityDesk1 class, the output is the two names of the ID card holders:

```
Dr.J.Ava
Ms.B.Rowser
```

# Javadoc and code comments

Javadoc is a class-documenting tool provided with the JDK that is able to create HTML pages from Java classes. This is useful because Java classes can become quite large and difficult to read. Javadoc filters out the basic information about classes such as the names of their attributes and methods and the classes they inherit from (all classes will at least inherit from the Java class Object). Our code examples so far have all begun with a comment header similar to this:

```
/**
        some comment here
*/
```

This is because this type of comment is recognised by Javadoc. There are a number of symbols that we can use inside these comment blocks to help Javadoc, for example, some HTML tags (such as the simple <BR> for a line break) and certain keywords preceded by an @ character, including:

@author (to show the author's name)
@version (to show the version number of the class)
@param (to give an opportunity to explain the meanings of the parameters to a method)

There are many other aspects to Javadoc not covered here, but there is complete information available on the Sun web site (you will find a link to this at the Letts site). This shows the complete IDCard class, including a number of Javadoc style comments:

```java
/**
        IDCard.java <BR>
        This class is a simple ID card class that contains <BR>
        only the title, initial and surname of a person.
        @author David Parsons
        @version 1.0
*/
public class IDCard
{
/** the private attributes. note that the initial is represented
    by a single 'char' rather than by a string of characters
*/
        private String title;
        private char initial;
        private String surname;
/** the constructor sets all three attributes from the parameter
    list
        @param title_in is the title of the person
        @param initial_in is their first initial
        @param surname_in is their surname
*/
        public IDCard(String title_in, char initial_in, String
            surname_in)
        {
            title = title_in;
            initial = initial_in;
            surname = surname_in;
        }
/** the three 'get' methods return the values of the three
    attributes
*/
        public String getTitle()
        {
            return title;
        }
        public char getInitial()
        {
            return initial;
        }
```

```
      public String getSurname()
      {
            return surname;
      }
/** to enable easy display of the object, we provide our own
    version of the 'toString' method. this means that using
    'println' with IDCard objects displays useful information
*/
      public String toString()
      {
            String temp_string = new String(title + initial
                  + ". " + surname);
            return temp_string;
      }
}
```

We invoke Javadoc simply by typing 'Javadoc' at the command line followed by the name of a Java file, e.g.,

```
Javadoc IDCard.java
```

This produces a number of HTML pages that tell us about the class. To get the fullest information possible written by Javadoc, we can add a number of flags to the 'Javadoc' command preceded by hyphens, e.g.

```
Javadoc -private -author -version IDCard.java
```

The first flag (-private) ensures that all attributes and methods, whether private or public, are written to the output files. The other flags (-author and -version) ensure that our '@author' and '@version' entries also appear in the file. Figure 7.2 shows how part of one of the generated pages ('idcard.html') looks in the HotJava browser. If you use a different browser you will still get the same information, and the graphical titles and bullets can be copied from the Sun web site (for some reason they are not automatically included with HotJava or the JDK).

The detailed Javadoc style of commenting is not used beyond this chapter (apart from the file headings) though, of course, you can use it in all your code if you wish. Even without any of this syntax, Javadoc is able to create some useful documentation from your classes such as superclass, attribute and method names

# Containers

Java has a number of container classes. As we discussed in Chapter two, a container is an object that exists purely to hold a collection of other objects. Different types of container vary in the way that they hold and index the objects and the public methods they provide to access them. In addition to having a number of public methods themselves, containers are also able to return an 'Enumeration' object. Enumerations can scan over the contents of a container one object at a time. They provide a simple mechanism for looking through any type

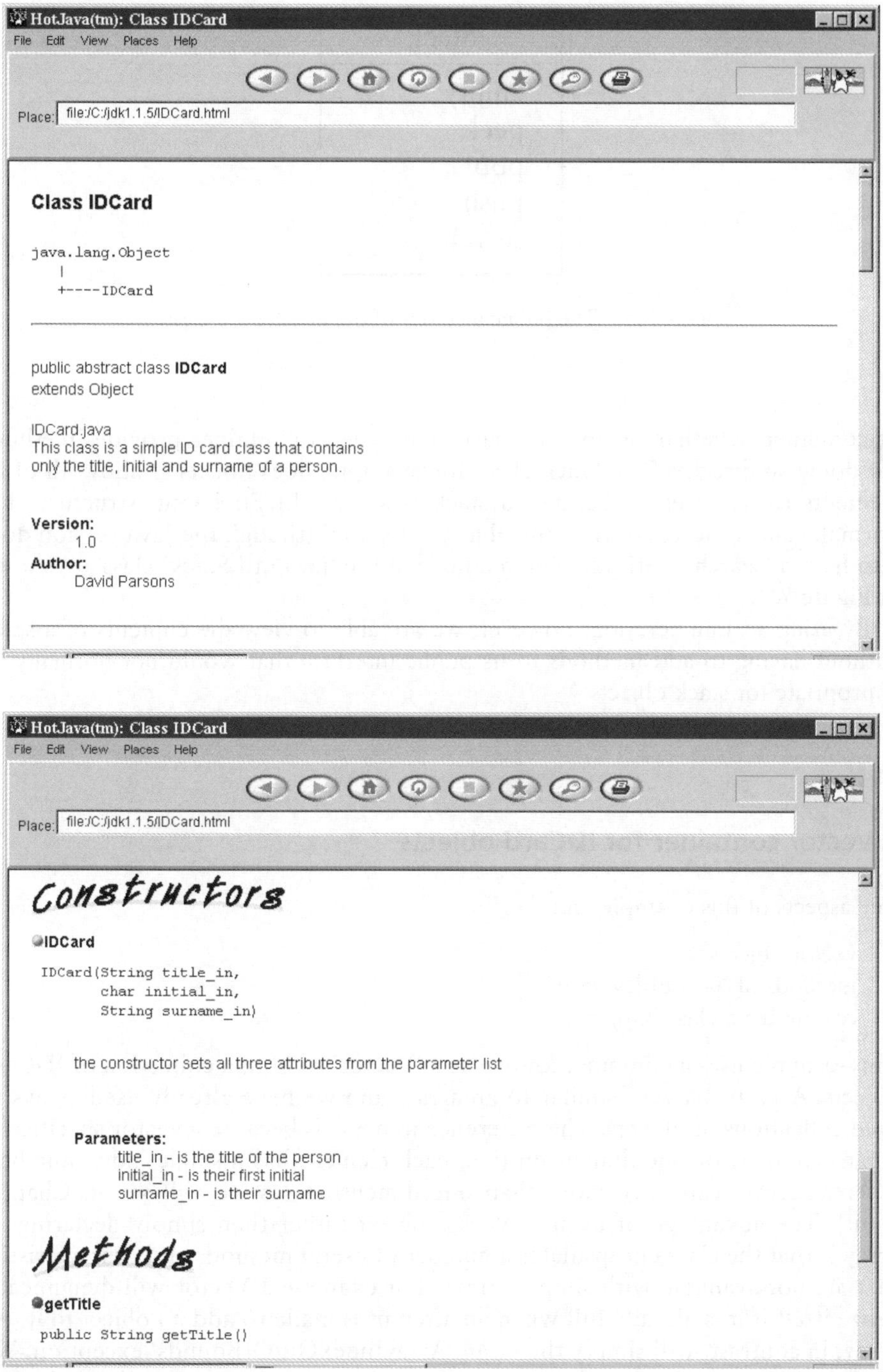

**HotJava(tm): Class IDCard**

File    Edit    View    Places    Help

Place: file:/C:/jdk1.1.5/IDCard.html

### Class IDCard

```
java.lang.Object
   |
   +----IDCard
```

public abstract class **IDCard**
extends Object

IDCard.java
This class is a simple ID card class that contains
only the title, initial and surname of a person.

**Version:**
    1.0
**Author:**
    David Parsons

---

**HotJava(tm): Class IDCard**

File    Edit    View    Places    Help

Place: file:/C:/jdk1.1.5/IDCard.html

## Constructors

●IDCard

```
IDCard(String title_in,
       char initial_in,
       String surname_in)
```

the constructor sets all three attributes from the parameter list

**Parameters:**
    title_in - is the title of the person
    initial_in - is their first initial
    surname_in - is their surname

## Methods

●getTitle

```
public String getTitle()
```

**Figure 7.2** Sections of one of the HTML pages generated by Javadoc being viewed in the 'HotJava' browser. The inheritance from class 'Object' is indicated, as well as some other information clearly related to the Javadoc keywords.

KING ALFRED'S COLLEGE
LIBRARY

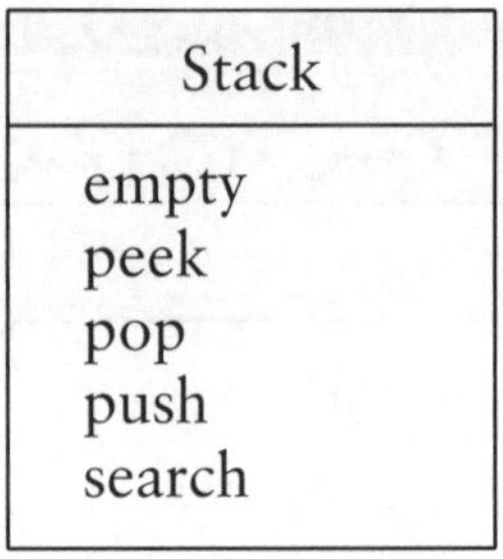

```
            Stack

      empty
      peek
      pop
      push
      search
```

**Figure 7.3**    The public methods of the Java 'Stack' class.

of container, whether or not that particular type of container provides methods for doing so directly. The Stack class, for example, does not itself allow all of its elements to be accessed because a stack is a 'Last In First Out' structure that normally allows access only to the object at its 'top' (though the Java version does also have a 'search' method). The methods of the 'java.util.Stack' class are shown in Figure 7.3.

By using an Enumeration, however, we are able to view the contents of a stack without having to add methods to its public interface that would not normally be appropriate for stack objects.

## A Vector container for IDCard objects

Key aspects of this example are:

● vector objects
● methods of 'java.util.Vector'
● casting from class 'Object'.

This example uses a container known as a 'Vector' to hold a collection of IDCard objects. A vector is very similar to an array, and we have already used arrays to hold collections of objects. The difference in name is because a vector specifically means an array of one dimension (i.e., each element has a single index number) whereas arrays can have more than one dimension (as we will see in Chapter eight). The advantage of using a Vector object rather than simply declaring an array is that the class encapsulates a number of useful methods and characteristics that are not available with simple arrays. For example a Vector will dynamically resize itself if it is already full when an attempt is made to add an object to it. An array, in contrast, will simply throw an 'ArrayIndexOutOfBounds' exception. We find the 'Vector' class in the 'java.util' package, so we can use the following 'import' statement:

```
import java.util.Vector;
```

## Vector constructors

The Vector class has three constructors:

1. `public Vector (int initial_capacity, int capacity_increment)`

This version allows us to set the initial capacity of the vector and also to define by how much it will grow if it needs to.

2. `public Vector (int initial_capacity)`

This version allows the initial capacity to be set but uses a default value for the increment.

3. `public Vector ()`

This version uses defaults for both values, and is the one used in the example program.

## The 'CardVector' class

In this example the 'CardVector' class provides a simple container class for managing a collection of IDCards based on a Vector object. It has four simple methods:

```
addCard(IDCard)
removeCardAt(int)
getCardAt(int)
showCards()
```

These are implemented by using some methods of the Vector class, namely:

```
addElement(Object)
removeElementAt(int)
elementAt(int)
toString()
```

You can see that the CardVector class is providing a simple 'wrapper' around the vector object, providing similar methods but ones that are specifically tailored to IDCard objects rather than simply the Java class Object (Figure 7.4).

Part of the role of the CardVector class is to convert (by casting) objects from the Object class to the IDCard class.

## Casting from class 'Object'

Earlier in this chapter, it was stated that the Java container classes work because of inheritance. We have also seen that all Java classes, including those we write ourselves, inherit from class Object. Java containers are basically containers of

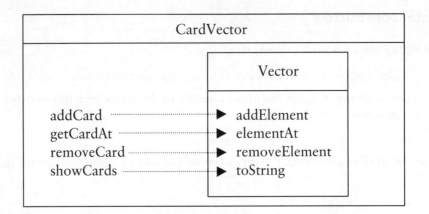

**Figure 7.4**   CardVector acts as a wrapper around the vector object inside it, and is primarily responsible for converting the general methods of vector into methods suitable for the IDCard application.

objects, regardless of their actual class, so whenever we return an object from a container it must be cast from class Object to the appropriate class. In this case, we know that we have put IDCard objects into the container, so we cast to class IDCard whenever we get objects from the Vector, e.g., in the 'getCardAt' method:

```
public IDCard getCardAt(int position)
{
        return (IDCard)card_list.elementAt(position);
}
```

To display the contents of the container, we call the Vector class version of toString via println. This in turn implicitly uses the toString method we defined for the IDCard objects themselves.

```
public void showCards()
{
        System.out.println(card_list);
}
```

This is the complete class:

```
/**
        CardVector.java
        a class that contains a number of IDCard objects in a
        Vector container
*/
import java.util.Vector;
public class CardVector
{
/** the Vector is aggregated inside the class as an attribute
*/
        private Vector card_list = new Vector();
```

```
/** 'addCard' adds an IDCard to the vector at the next position
*/
     public void addCard(IDCard add_it)
     {
          card_list.addElement(add_it);
     }
/** 'removeCard' removes a card from the given index. note that
this version does not handle the exception of providing an
invalid index
*/
     public void removeCardAt(int position)
     {
          card_list.removeElementAt(position);
     }
/** 'getObjectAt' returns the object at the given position.
because vectors contain only instances of class 'Object', we must
cast to 'IDCard'
*/
     public IDCard getCardAt(int position)
     {
          return (IDCard)card_list.elementAt(position);
     }
/** 'showCards' uses the provided 'toString' method
*/
     public void showCards()
     {
          System.out.println(card_list);
     }
}
```

To test this class, the VectorTest creates a CardVector object and adds three IDCard objects to it. The program also demonstrates that removeCardAt removes an IDCard object from the container, but in contrast getCardAt returns a reference to one of the cards without actually removing it.

```
/**
     VectorTest.java
     this class simply tests the vector container of IDCard
     objects by adding cards to it, removing cards and looking
     at its contents
*/
public class VectorTest
{
     public static void main(String args[])
     {
// create a 'CardVector' object to contain IDCards
     CardVector cards = new CardVector();
// adds three ID cards to the container
     IDCard card = new IDCard("Mr.", 'I', "Am");
     cards.addCard(card);
     card = new IDCard("Mr.", 'U', "Are");
     cards.addCard(card);
     card = new IDCard("Ms.", 'X', "Not");
     cards.addCard(card);
```

```
// show the contents of the container
    System.out.println
        ("The vector after adding three IDCards contains:");
    cards.showCards();
// remove the second card (index 1)
    cards.removeCardAt(1);
// show the cards again (one card has been removed)
    System.out.println
        ("The vector after removing the second element contains:");
    cards.showCards();
// get a reference to the card at index 0 without removing it
    card = cards.getCardAt(0);
// display the card
    System.out.println
        ("The card returned from the first element of the vector is "
        + card);
// show the cards again (getting the reference has not removed
// the card)
    System.out.println
        ("The vector after returning a reference is unchanged:");
    cards.showCards();
    }
}
```

The following output is produced. Notice how the toString method of the Vector class displays the collection of objects inside square brackets, separated by commas:

*The vector after adding three IDCards contains:*

*[Mr.I. Am, Mr.U. Are, Ms.X. Not]*
*The vector after removing the second element contains:*
*[Mr.I. Am, Ms.X. Not]*
*The card returned from the first element of the vector is Mr.I. Am*
*The vector after returning a reference is unchanged:*
*[Mr.I. Am, Ms.X. Not]*

We will return to the IDCard class later in this chapter to see how it might provide the basis for an application that uses inheritance and polymorphism.

## An indexed container using a Hashtable

In the previous example we saw that the Vector class allows access to objects by using an index number. Another type of Java container is the Hashtable that allows a stored object to be accessed by using another object as a key. A hash table therefore consists of a series of 'key' objects, each associated with a single 'value' object. The next example uses a Hashtable to implement a simple appointment diary, using dates as the keys and names (strings) as the values (Figure 7.5).

Key aspects of this example are

- Calendar objects
- factory methods
- DateFormat objects
- Hashtable objects.

Name

Date

**Figure 7.5**   The appointment diary program uses a Hashtable, with dates acting as the keys to the names (strings) stored in the table.

We looked at the Date class in Chapter three, but unfortunately on its own it does not have enough functionality to act successfully as a key object for our appointment diary because it can contain only the date and time of its creation. It also lacks formatting methods to improve its display layout. To overcome these problems, we can use the Calendar class that allows dates to be specifically set, and the DateFormat class that allows a Date object to be formatted for output.

## The Calendar class and factory methods

The Calendar class is unusual in that it does not have a constructor, which means that we cannot directly create a Calendar object. Instead, it has a number of 'factory' methods. A factory method is one that returns a new object to us by encapsulating the constructor call inside the class. This is often done where the class knows more about the type of object that we want to create than we know ourselves. When it comes to dates, their format and content can vary depending on the international 'locale' in which the date is being used. The Calendar class is able to use the default locale for the current system and create a Calendar object appropriate to that locale (in practice this is usually an object of the 'GregorianCalendar' class, which applies to most of the world). The 'Calendar' factory methods are called 'getInstance', so we can create a new Calendar object like this:

```
Calendar key = Calendar.getInstance();
```

This will return a new calendar object to the reference 'key'. By default, this will contain the current date, but we can then change this date using the 'set' method:

```
key.set(year, month, day);
```

In the program, the parameters 'year', 'month' and 'day' are passed to this object from another class. It is important to provide a full four-digit year and also to be aware that Java uses zero to eleven as the range of month values, not one to twelve.

## Creating a Hashtable object

To create a Hashtable we can call the constructor with an initial size for the table, though like the vector there is also a constructor with no parameters that provides a default initial capacity. In this example a Hashtable is included as a private attribute of the Diary class (called 'slots') with an initial capacity of ten:

```
private Hashtable slots = new Hashtable(10);
```

Entries are made into this Hashtable using the 'put' method, which adds the key and its associated value (where 'key' in this case is a Calendar object and 'value' is a string):

```
slots.put(key, value);
```

## Returning an enumeration from a container

Java containers can provide us with enumeration objects to scan through their contents. A Hashtable can provide us with two different enumerations, one to scan the keys and another to scan their values, In this example we use an enumeration to scan the keys and retrieve their associated values using the 'get' method. A key enumeration can be returned from a Hashtable using the 'keys' method:

```
Enumeration key_scanner = slots.keys();
```

If we wanted an enumeration for the values we would similarly use the 'elements' method to return an appropriate enumeration object, e.g.,

```
Enumeration element_scanner = slots.elements();
```

All Java containers have an 'elements' method to return an enumeration able to scan their contents in sequence, but only the Hashtable has a 'keys' method. An enumeration itself has only two methods:

```
hasMoreElements()  (which returns true or false)
nextElement()      (which returns the next object from the container)
```

We can use a 'while' loop to iterate through the Hashtable and return each object in turn using these two methods. Because nextElement returns an object we must cast it to class Calendar, the actual class of the key object:

```
        while(key_scanner.hasMoreElements())
        {
// 'nextElement' returns the next key, which we cast to 'Calendar'
    current_key = (Calendar)key_scanner.nextElement();
// etc..
```

Once an enumeration has reached the last object in a container, it cannot be reset. To scan the container again, a new enumeration must be created.

## Displaying a calendar date with the DateFormat class

The showAppointments method displays both the keys and the values in the table. We could simply display the Calendar object, but this is not very helpful. Getting a Date object from the Calendar and displaying that would be an improvement, but still not ideal. One possibility is to format the date using a DateFormat object. The DateFormat class appears in 'java.text' and allows us to improve the output format of Date objects. Like the Calendar class, and for similar reasons, it has a factory method rather than a constructor, in this case called 'getDateInstance':

```
    DateFormat date = DateFormat.getDateInstance();
```

Using the 'getTime' method of the Calendar class, which (rather strangely) returns a Date object, can make the relationship between a DateFormat and a Calendar. This Date can be formatted by passing it as a parameter to the 'format' method of DateFormat, which returns a string containing the formatted date. In the example class, 'appointment_string' is a string object and 'appointment_time' is a date object.

```
    appointment_string = date.format(appointment_time);
```

This is the complete class:

```
/**
      Diary.java
      this class uses a Hashtable to represent a simple
      appointment diary. each entry in the table consists of a
      Calendar date as the key and a name (String) as its
      associated value
*/
/** java.util contains the Hashtable, Calendar and Date classes
*/
import java.util.*;
/** the DateFormat class, used to improve the output format of a
date object, is in java.text
```

```
 */
import java.text.DateFormat;
public class Diary
{
// declare and initialise a Hashtable object initially with
// 10 slots
      private Hashtable slots = new Hashtable(10);
/** the 'makeAppointment' method assembles the parameter
information into appropriate String and Calendar objects
*/
      public void makeAppointment(String name, int day, int
            month, int year)
            {
// use the Calendar factory method 'getInstance' to create a
// Calendar object
            Calendar key = Calendar.getInstance();
// subtract 1 from the month because Java counts months from
// 0 to 11!
            month--;;
// set the Calendar date using the method's parameters
            key.set(year, month, day);
// create a String object from the name parameter
            String value = new String(name);
// add the date and name to the hash table as key and value
// respectively
            slots.put(key, value);
}
/**
      the 'showAppointments' method uses an Enumeration object to
      iterate through the hash table returning each key in turn.
      the keys are then used to get the values (names). to
      improve output format, we get a 'Date' object from our
      'Calendar' and format it using a 'DateFormat' object
*/
      public void showAppointments()
            {
// declare some local references to objects returned from the
// hash table
            Calendar current_key;
            Date appointment_time;
            String current_name;
            String appointment_string;
// create a 'DateFormat' object using the 'getDateInstance'
// factory method
            DateFormat date = DateFormat.getDateInstance();
// get an Enumeration object returned from the hash table 'keys'
// method
            Enumeration key_scanner = slots.keys();
// loop while the Enumeration finds more keys
            while(key_scanner.hasMoreElements())
                  {
// 'nextElement' returns the next key, which we cast to
// 'Calendar'
                  current_key = (Calendar)key_scanner.nextElement();
// having got the key, we can return its associated value with
// 'get', which we cast to 'String'
```

```
                current_name = (String)slots.get(current_key);
// we can return a Date object from the Calendar key using
// 'getTime'
                appointment_time = current_key.getTime();
// to format our date, we pass it to the DateFormat object that
// returns a String containing a formatted date
                appointment_string = date.format(appointment_time);
// finally we can display a reasonably readable message
            System.out.println(current_name +
            " has an appointment on " + appointment_string);
        }
    }
}
```

The Appointments class tests an object of the Diary class by making three appointments and displaying the contents of the diary.

```
/**
    Appointments.java
    this class tests an object of the Diary class by making
    some appointments and displaying them
*/
public class Appointments
{
    public static void main(String args[])
    {
// create a Diary object
        Diary diary = new Diary();
// add three appointments to the diary
        diary.makeAppointment("Neville Chamberlain", 28, 9, 1938);
        diary.makeAppointment("Beast 666", 31, 12, 1999);
        diary.makeAppointment("Santa Claus", 24, 12, 1998);
// display the appointments in the diary
        diary.showAppointments();
    }
}
```

The output from Appointments shows that the sequence of the Enumeration is not the same as the original sequence of entry. There is no way to guarantee the sequence of objects returned by an enumeration.

```
Santa Claus has an appointment on 24-Dec-98
Beast 666 has an appointment on 31-Dec-99
Neville Chamberlain has an appointment on 28-Sep-38
```

# Inheritance

In this chapter we have looked at how all Java classes, whether provided in a Java package or written by ourselves, inherit from the base class 'Object'. We can also inherit from our own classes to add extra functionality to an existing class and implement polymorphic methods. In the next example, we will create two derived classes of 'IDCard' (Figure 7.6).

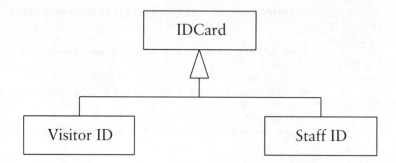

**Figure 7.6**    IDCard is the superclass of VisitorID and StaffID, which both inherit from it.

Key aspects of this example are

- creating subclasses using 'extends'
- calling superclass methods using 'super'.

The IDCard class encapsulates some basic behaviours of an identity card, but perhaps we need to model some more specific objects, for example, ID cards appropriate to both visitors and employees. These cards, while having a number of similarities, will also have some different functionality. We can inherit from an existing class by using the keyword 'extends', i.e.,

```
public class class_name extends superclass_name
{
// etc..
```

In this example there are two derived classes of 'IDCard', namely 'StaffID' and 'VisitorID', so they inherit like this:

```
public class StaffID extends IDCard
{
// etc..

public class VisitorID extends IDCard
{
// etc..
```

A 'StaffID' object has an additional attribute (the name of a department) along with 'set' and 'get' methods. An interesting piece of syntax is used to implement the constructor. The question arises, how do we pass the other parameters (title, initial, surname) from the constructor of 'StaffID' to the constructor of 'IDCard' that actually uses them? The answer is to use the keyword 'super'. This allows us to call the constructor of the superclass from within the constructor of the subclass, e.g.,

```
public StaffID(String title, char initial, String surname)
{
     super(title, initial, surname);
}
```

In addition, the class also implements its own version of toString that again uses a call to the 'super' version of the same method. This is an example of a polymorphic method that extends, rather than replaces, the inherited version. When we provided a version of toString for the IDCard class, we replaced the default version that was inherited from class Object. In this case we are using the existing method but adding some more functionality to it, namely, the output of the department name. This is achieved by concatenating the string returned by the 'super' version of toString with the information about the staff member's department:

```
public String toString()
{
     return super.toString() + " of the " + department + "
         department";
}
```

This is the complete StaffID class:

```
/**
     StaffID.java
     this file contains a derived 'IDCard' class called
     'StaffID' that adds methods to get and set the name of the
     staff member's department and extends the superclass
     version of 'toString'
*/
public class StaffID extends IDCard
{
// an extra attribute is added
     private String department;
// the constructor passes its parameters to the superclass
     public StaffID(String title, char initial, String surname)
     {
          super(title, initial, surname);
     }
// additional 'set' and 'get' methods
     public void setDepartment(String dept_in)
     {
          department = dept_in;
     }
     public String getDepartment()
     {
          return department;
     }
// a version of 'toString' that extends the superclass version
     public String toString()
     {
          return super.toString() + " of the " + department +
              " department";
     }
}
```

The VisitorID class makes some different extensions to IDCard. The extra attribute added here is a contact name (i.e., the person who is being visited). Again, the constructor and toString methods make calls to the superclass to implement their behaviour.

```
/**
        VisitorID.java
        this file contains 'VisitorID', a derived class of
        'IDCard'.it adds methods related to a contact name
*/
public class VisitorID extends IDCard
{
// an extra attribute is added
        private String contact_name;
// the constructor passes its parameters to the superclass
        public VisitorID(String title, char initial, String
                surname)
        {
                super(title, initial, surname);
        }
// additional 'set' and 'get' methods
        public void setContactName(String contact)
        {
                contact_name = contact;
        }
        public String getContactName()
        {
                return contact_name;
        }
// a version of 'toString' that extends the superclass version
        public String toString()
        {
                return super.toString() + " visiting " +
                        contact_name;
        }
}
```

These classes are tested by the SecurityDesk2 class:

```
/**
        SecurityDesk2.java
        in this version of the 'SecurityDesk' class, objects of the
        two derived classes of 'IDCardClass', 'StaffID' and
        'VisitorID', are created and tested
*/
        public class SecurityDesk2
        {
// 'main' calls the constructor and then tests the methods of the
// derived classes of 'IDCard'
        public static void main(String args[])
        {
// call the constructor of the StaffID class. note that the
string
// parameters appear in double quotes, but the char parameter
// appears in single quotes
                StaffID staff_id = new StaffID("Dr.",'J',"Ava");
                staff_id.setDepartment("Research and Development");
// construct a VisitorID object
                VisitorID visitor_id = new
                        VisitorID("Ms.",'H',"Otjva-browser");
                visitor_id.setContactName("Doctor J. Ava");
```

```
// test the 'get' methods of the classes by calling them with
'println'
            System.out.println(staff_id);
            System.out.println(visitor_id);
        }
    }
```

Running this class produces:

```
Dr.J. Ava of the Research and Development department
Ms.H. Otjva-browser visiting Doctor J. Ava
```

## An interactive test program

All the programs seen so far in this chapter have been simple test classes that do not do anything interactive. In contrast, this program (SecurityDesk3) also uses objects of the IDCard subclasses but in a rather more interactive way. It uses an object of the Keyboard class to get input from the keyboard for the constructors and methods of the StaffID and VisitorID objects, allowing security cards to be issued and listed dynamically.

```
/**
        SecurityDesk3.java
        in this version of the 'SecurityDesk' class, a menu is used
        to interactively manage objects of the two
        derived classes of 'IDCardClass', 'StaffID' and
        'VisitorID'.
*/
import javabook.chapter6.Keyboard;
public class SecurityDesk3
{
// 'main' calls the constructor and then tests the methods of the
// derived classes of 'IDCard'
    public static void main(String args[])
    {
// create a CardVector object
        CardVector cards = new CardVector();
        int menu_choice = 0;
        while(menu_choice != 4)
        {
          System.out.println("menu");
          System.out.println("1: list security cards");
          System.out.println("2: add a member of staff");
          System.out.println("3: add a visitor");
          System.out.println("4: quit");
          System.out.println("please enter a choice");
// create a Keyboard object
          Keyboard keyboard = new Keyboard();
          menu_choice = keyboard.getInt();
// list cards
          if(menu_choice == 1)
          {
                cards.showCards();
          }
```

```
// add a member of staff
            if(menu_choice == 2)
            {
            System.out.print("Enter title of staff member ");
            String title_string = keyboard.getString();
            System.out.print("Enter initial of staff member ");
            char initial = keyboard.getChar();
            System.out.print("Enter surname of staff member ");
            String surname_string = keyboard.getString();
            StaffID staff_id = new
                 StaffID(title_string,initial,surname_string);
            System.out.print("Enter department ");
            String dept_string = keyboard.getString();
            staff_id.setDepartment(dept_string);
            cards.addCard(staff_id);
            }
// add a visitor
            if(menu_choice == 3)
            {
                System.out.print("Enter title of visitor ");
                String title_string = keyboard.getString();
                System.out.print("Enter initial of visitor ");
                char initial = keyboard.getChar();
                System.out.print("Enter surname of visitor ");
                String surname_string = keyboard.getString();
                VisitorID visitor_id = new
            VisitorID(title_string,initial,surname_string);
                System.out.print("Enter contact name ");
                String contact_string = keyboard.getString();
                visitor_id.setContactName(contact_string);
                cards.addCard(visitor_id);
            }
        }
    }
}
```

A brief interactive run follows. The format of the output is rather poor, since it simply uses the 'toString' methods of both the Vector and the IDCard classes. This could be improved with a little work:

```
menu
1: list security cards
2: add a member of staff
3: add a visitor
4: quit
please enter a choice 1
[]
menu
1: list security cards
2: add a member of staff
3: add a visitor
4: quit
please enter a choice 2
Enter title of staff member Mr.
Enter initial of staff member J
```

```
Enter surname of staff member Beans
Enter department Research
menu
1: list security cards
2: add a member of staff
3: add a visitor
4: quit
please enter a choice 1
[Mr.J. Beans of the Research department]
menu
1: list security cards
2: add a member of staff
3: add a visitor
4: quit
please enter a choice 4
```

# Polymorphic methods in user defined classes

So far our discussion of polymorphism has centred on the toString method that is inherited from the Object class. We can also use polymorphism with methods written specifically for our own classes. In the next example we modify the various ID card classes to provide a polymorphic method called 'showSecurityClearance' (Figure 7.7).

Key aspects of this example are

- abstract classes and methods
- polymorphic methods.

## Declaring methods and classes abstract

Sometimes we use superclasses as a way of sending messages to objects of subclasses. We can do this because a reference can be used for objects of subclasses as well as those of the class of the reference itself. For example, we could use references of the IDCard class with objects of both the StaffID and VisitorID classes:

```
IDCard staff_id = new StaffID("Dr.",'J',"Ava");
IDCard visitor_id = new VisitorID("Ms.",'H',"Otjva-browser");
```

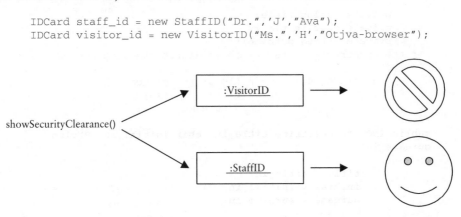

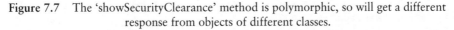

**Figure 7.7**   The 'showSecurityClearance' method is polymorphic, so will get a different response from objects of different classes.

This allows us to send messages to the subclasses via the superclass reference but only if those messages appear as methods in the public interface of the superclass. For example, we could not send the message 'setDepartment' to the StaffID object declared above, since that method is not a member of 'IDCard'. In this modified version of IDCard (called 'IDCardBase') we add a method called 'showSecurityClearance' so that this message can be sent to subclass objects declared using a reference of this class. However, it has no implementation in the superclass because all the behaviour will be written into the methods of the subclasses. Where a method has no implementation in a superclass, it can be declared 'abstract':

```
public abstract void showSecurityClearance();
```

This has a significant effect on the class itself. Once a class has one or more abstract methods, it must itself be declared 'abstract':

```
public abstract class IDCardBase
```

The reason for this is that the class now has a method that cannot directly be used, so the class is incomplete. Its only role is to be the superclass for other classes that complete the interface by providing an implementation for the abstract method:

```
/**
        IDCardBase.java <BR>
        this class is an abstract superclass for the subclasses
        <BR> 'StaffID2' and 'VisitorID2'. these classes implement
        the <BR> abstract 'showSecurityClearance' method
        @author David Parsons
        @version 1.0
*/
public abstract class IDCardBase
{
/** the private attributes. note that the initial is represented
    by a single 'char' rather than by a string of characters
*/
        private String title;
        private char initial;
        private String surname;
/** the constructor sets all three attributes from the parameter
    list
        @param title_in is the title of the person
        @param initial_in is their first initial
        @param surname_in is their surname
*/
public IDCardBase(String title_in, char initial_in, String
surname_in)
        {
                title = title_in;
                initial = initial_in;
                surname = surname_in;
        }
/** the three 'get' methods return the values of the three
    attributes
```

```
*/
        public String getTitle()
        {
            return title;
        }
        public char getInitial()
        {
            return initial;
        }
        public String getSurname()
        {
            return surname;
        }
/** to enable easy display of the object, we provide our own
    version of the 'toString' method. this means that using
    'println' with IDCard objects displays useful information
*/
        public String toString()
        {
            String temp_string = new String(title + initial + ". "
                + surname);
            return temp_string;
        }
/** 'showSecurityClearance' has no implementation in this class.
    it exists purely to allow the message to be passed to
    subclasses
*/
        public abstract void showSecurityClearance();
}
```

## Implementing the abstract method in subclasses

The derived class 'StaffID2' has a modified constructor that sets the date that the employee started work. This is stored in a 'Calendar' attribute called 'date_started'. The class implements the 'showSecurityClearance' method by comparing a Date object returned from 'date_started' (using the 'getTime' method of the 'Calendar' class) with the current date. The 'getTime' method of the 'Date' class returns the number of milliseconds that have passed in the current epoch, so we can use some simple arithmetic to find out how many milliseconds have passed since the person was employed (clock watching gone mad, perhaps?). If the person has been employed less than 6 months (15,768,000,000 milliseconds!) then their security clearance is displayed as 'provisional', otherwise it is 'full'. Using milliseconds to compare the dates may seem rather peculiar but, in fact, it is easier than handling separate days, months and years in Calendar objects. This is the full method implementation:

```
public void showSecurityClearance()
{
// get today's date
        Date now = new Date();
// return a date object from the 'date_started' attribute
        Date then = date_started.getTime();
// calculate the number of milliseconds between the two dates
        long time_worked = now.getTime() - then.getTime();
```

```
// if the period is less than 6 months, clearance is provisional.
// we have to put 'L' on the end of the number to make it a long,
// since an int is not big enough
      if(time_worked < 15768000000L)
      {
            System.out.println("Provisional security clearance");
      }
// otherwise it is full security clearance
      else
      {
            System.out.println("Full security clearance");
      }
}
```

This is the complete class:

```
/**
      StaffID2.java
      this file contains a derived 'IDCard' class called
      'StaffID' that adds methods to get and set the name of the
      staff member's department, extends the superclass version
      of 'toString' and provides an implementation for
      'showSecurityClearance'
*/
import java.util.*;
public class StaffID2 extends IDCardBase
{
      private String department;
      private Calendar date_started;
      public StaffID2(String title, char initial, String surname,
            int day_started, int month_started, int year_started)
      {
            super(title, initial, surname);
            date_started = Calendar.getInstance();
            date_started.set(year_started, month_started,
                  day_started);
      }
      public void setDepartment(String dept_in)
      {
            department = dept_in;
      }
      public String getDepartment()
      {
            return department;
      }
      public String toString()
      {
            return super.toString() + " of the " + department
                  + " department";
      }
      public void showSecurityClearance()
      {
// get today's date
            Date now = new Date();
// return a date object from the 'date_started' attribute
            Date then = date_started.getTime();
```

```
// calculate the number of milliseconds between the two dates
        long time_worked = now.getTime() - then.getTime();
// if the period is less than 6 months, clearance is provisional.
// we have to put 'L' on the end of the number to make it a long,
// since an int is not big enough
        if(time_worked < 15768000000L)
        {
                System.out.println("Provisional security
                        clearance");
        }
// otherwise it is full security clearance
        else
        {
                System.out.println("Full security clearance");
        }
    }
}
```

Like the modified staff ID class, the modified Visitor ID ('VisitorID2') provides its own implementation of 'showSecurityClearance'. This method is rather more straightforward than that for 'StaffID2' because it simply displays a message and today's date, on the assumption that visitors are given temporary clearance for one day only.

```
/**
    VisitorID2.java
    this file contains 'VisitorID2', a derived class of
    'IDCardBase'. it adds methods related to a contact name,
    extends the superclass version of 'toString' and provides
    an implementation for 'showSecurityClearance'
*/
import java.util.Date;
public class VisitorID2 extends IDCardBase
{
    private String contact_name;
    public VisitorID2(String title, char initial, String
        surname)
    {
            super(title, initial, surname);
    }
    public void setContactName(String contact)
    {
            contact_name = contact;
    }
    public String getContactName()
    {
            return contact_name;
    }
    public String toString()
    {
            return super.toString() + " visiting " +
                contact_name;
    }
    public void showSecurityClearance()
    {
```

```
                    Date today = new Date();
                    System.out.println
                    ("Temporary security clearance only for today " +
                        today);
                }
        }
```

This final version of the SecurityDesk class tests the 'showSecurityClearance' polymorphic method by creating employees that will have two different types of security
clearance. Of course, the output from this program is dependent not only on the
dates entered but also the date on which the program is run!

```
/**
        SecurityDesk4.java
        in this version of the 'SecurityDesk' class, objects of the
        two derived classes of 'IDCardClass', 'StaffID' and
        'VisitorID', are created and their 'showSecurityClearance'
        methods tested
*/
public class SecurityDesk4
{
// 'main' calls the constructor and then tests the methods of the
// subclasses of 'IDCardBase'
        public static void main(String args[])
            {
// call the constructor of the StaffID2 class.
// the date must include the four-digit year.
        IDCardBase staff_id = new StaffID2("Dr.",'J',"Ava",
                1,1,1997);
// the start date for this object will need to be less than six
// months ago to get the appropriate test result of 'provisional
// security clearance'
        IDCardBase new_staff_id = new StaffID2("Mr.",'W',"Page",
                29,4,1998);
// construct a VisitorID2 object
        IDCardBase visitor_id = new VisitorID2("Ms.",'H',
                "Otjva-browser");
// display the names and security clearances from the three ID
// cards
                System.out.println(staff_id.getTitle() +
                staff_id.getSurname());
                staff_id.showSecurityClearance();
                System.out.println(new_staff_id.getTitle() +
                new_staff_id.getSurname());
                new_staff_id.showSecurityClearance();
                System.out.println(visitor_id.getTitle() +
                visitor_id.getSurname());
                visitor_id.showSecurityClearance();
            }
        }
```

This was the output from running the class on a particular date, but of course the
results will vary over time:

```
Dr.Ava
Full security clearance
Mr.Page
Provisional security clearance
Ms.Otjva-browser
Temporary security clearance only for today Tue May 26 11:18:02
GMT+01:00 1998
```

## Summary

In this chapter we have looked at some aspects of the Java container classes and used them to manage collections of objects. To write closely related classes that have some attributes and methods in common we have used inheritance. This has also enabled us to write polymorphic methods that allow objects of different classes to respond differently to the same messages. Javadoc has been used to document the important aspects of our classes. We have looked at two sets of classes:

- Containers: classes from 'java.util' that enable us to create vectors, stacks and hash tables, along with Enumerations that can scan their contents.
- An inheritance hierarchy: Our own classes have been put into a hierarchy of super and sub classes and been given polymorphic behaviour.

Important aspects of Java syntax have been introduced:

1. methods of 'java.util.Vector', including:

   ```
   addElement(Object), removeElementAt(int), elementAt(int)
   ```

   Casting from class Object is also important when using containers, e.g.,

   ```
   return (IDCard)card_list.elementAt(position);
   ```

2. Factory methods, where we do not call the constructor for a class but call some kind of method that returns an object to us, e.g.,

   ```
   Calendar key = Calendar.getInstance();
   ```

3. Enumerations to iterate through a container e.g.

   ```
   Enumeration key_scanner = slots.keys();
   ```

   These objects have methods to move on the next element in the container and tell us when we have reached the last element:

   ```
   while(key_scanner.hasMoreElements())
   {
           //…
           current_key = (Calendar)key_scanner.nextElement();
   ```

4. Inheriting from a superclass with the 'extends' keyword, e.g.,

   ```
   public class StaffID extends IDCard
   {
   // etc..
   ```

   Calling superclass methods from subclass methods, for example calling the superclass constructor from within the subclass constructor:

   ```
   super(title, initial, surname);
   ```

Also making superclasses and their methods 'abstract':

```
public abstract class IDCardBase
{...
public abstract void showSecurityClearance();
```

In the next chapter we will look at how we can build a graphical user interface (GUI) using Java's Abstract Windowing Toolkit (AWT). Inheritance plays a particularly important role in the AWT classes and we will see a different type of container that contains graphical components rather than the 'Objects' handled by the containers in the java.util package.

## EXERCISES

**1**  If you have access to 'Javadoc', use it to document the snakes and ladders classes from Chapter six. Make appropriate changes to the comments in the code. Note that all the classes will be integrated into the same set of pages.

**2**  Add a 'showStatistics' method to the 'CardVector' class that tells us about the object using these methods of 'Vector':

```
int capacity()      // tells us the size of the vector
boolean isEmpty()   // tells us if there are any objects
int size()          // tells us how many objects there are
```

Modify 'VectorTest' to test this method.

**3**  Use a vector to implement a 'StringSet' class that can contain a set of string objects and has the methods 'addString' and 'showStrings'. A set does not allow duplicates, so should allow strings to be added to the container only if they are unique. You can use the 'contains' method of Vector that takes an object as a parameter and returns a Boolean value to implement this.

**4**  Create a Stack object and add string objects to it. Remove and display each one in turn. Since a stack is a 'last in first out' structure the strings should appear in reverse order.

**5**  Add a method to the Diary class called 'removeAppointment' that, given a date, will remove any appointment on that date. This can be implemented using the 'containsKey' (that returns a Boolean value) and 'remove' (that returns an object) methods of Hashtable that both take an object of the appropriate key class as a parameter.

**6**  Modify the Appointments class to test your 'removeAppointment' method.

**7**  Extend the 'SecurityDesk3' class so that cards can be removed from the system as well as being issued and viewed.

**8**  Modify the snakes and ladders game so that 'Snake' and 'Ladder' are subclasses of a superclass called Mover. Modify the Square class so that it has one reference to a Mover object rather than references to both a snake and a ladder. Use this reference to create the appropriate type of derived class object (snake or ladder) in the correct squares. You will need to modify the Snake and Ladder classes to inherit commonly named methods from 'mover'. Add a polymorphic method called 'getMessage' that returns a string containing either 'up the ladder' or 'down the snake' depending on the class.

**9**  Once the Square class has been modified, you can change the message-passing mechanism described in Figure 6.2 to one that uses the polymorphic methods of Mover to move the counter to the correct square. Ensure that the whole game still works!

**Part 4**

# Graphical user interfaces

# 8

# The Abstract Windowing Toolkit

'It is only shallow people who do not judge by appearances. The true mystery of the world is the visible, not the invisible' – Oscar Wilde (*The Picture of Dorian Gray*).

The AWT (Abstract Windowing Toolkit) is a collection of classes that allows simple graphical user interfaces to be developed in Java. The 'java.awt' package contains classes of four basic types:

*1   Component classes*
These are the objects that allow the user to interact with a graphical user interface. These include a number of different 'controls' (buttons, menus, list boxes, text boxes, etc.).

*2   Containers*
Components can be put into graphical 'containers', such as class 'Frame' (which displays a standard window with title bar, frame and buttons) and 'Panel' (which is just an area without any frame or buttons). These containers are not unlike the container classes used in Chapter 7, except that they contain visual components rather than application-level objects.

*3   Layout managers*
These classes give some simple frameworks that manage the layout of a collection of controls within a container. Rather than having to position each component individually in a window, we can use a layout manager to apply a general pattern to the layout of the components.

*4   Graphics classes*
These allow you to draw shapes and graphical text, also to change colours and fonts and load image files.

In this chapter we will look at some of the simpler AWT component classes and use them to build graphical user interfaces by adding them to 'Frame' windows using layout managers. In the following chapter we will look at using panels and graphics classes.

# Creating a main window

Most graphical user interfaces are based on a main window within which other objects appear. In Java, a window is described by a 'Frame' object, from which we inherit to create our own window classes. In the first example program, we create a simple window.

Key aspects of this example are

- inheriting from 'Frame'
- displaying a window
- event listeners
- implementing an interface.

In order to use AWT classes, we import the 'java.awt' package, so our own window class might begin like this:

```
import java.awt.*;
```

Although for very simple programs we could import the specific classes we require, most programs will use a number of AWT classes, so the * makes life easier by providing the pathway to all the classes in the package. The first example class consists only of a constructor that creates a window on the screen without adding any functionality. Since the class is so small, the test 'main' method has been put inside it. Notice that we can pass the window title to the constructor, which passes it on to the super class ('super'). The 'show' method makes the window appear on the screen.

```
/**
      FirstWindow.java
      this class displays a window
*/
import java.awt.*;
// the 'Frame' class provides a basic window with a title bar
public class FirstWindow extends Frame
{
// the constructor passes a window frame title to the superclass
// (otherwise the title bar will be blank)
      public FirstWindow(String title)
      {
            super(title);
      }
      public static void main(String args[])
      {
// create the window
            FirstWindow window = new FirstWindow("window");
// display the window
            window.show();
      }
}
```

The window will appear at first just as a title bar because it does not contain any other objects and we have not explicitly set its size (Figure 8.1).

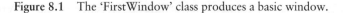

**Figure 8.1**   The 'FirstWindow' class produces a basic window.

Although we have not added any methods the window can be moved, resized, minimised and maximised. It cannot, however, be closed! The only way to close this particular window is to interrupt the program.

## Event listener interfaces

To close the window, we have to add an event listener that will respond to the mouse being clicked on the close button. Event listeners are used with all AWT components to allow us to respond to events such as windows being closed, buttons being pressed, etc. Event listener classes are contained in the 'java.awt.event' package, so as well as importing classes from the 'java.awt' package, all our event-handling examples will also import this package:

```
import java.awt.*;
import java.awt.event.*;
```

The event listener classes in this package are examples of 'interfaces'. An interface is a class that provides a number of method declarations, but does not provide any implementations of these methods. Therefore any class that uses the interface must provide definitions for all the methods that have been declared. In this case, we want to add a listener that will respond to a window event, so we will provide implementations for the methods of the 'WindowListener' interface. This interface declares the following methods:

```
public void windowClosed(WindowEvent e)
public void windowActivated(WindowEvent e)
public void windowClosing(WindowEvent e)
public void windowDeactivated(WindowEvent e)
public void windowIconified(WindowEvent e)
public void windowDeiconified(WindowEvent e)
public void windowOpened(WindowEvent e)
```

If we want to add a window listener to one of our classes we must provide implementations for all these methods. However, we can easily provide 'empty' implementations for those methods that we do not want to use by simply leaving the braces around the method definition empty. For example, to provide a 'do nothing' version of 'windowOpened' we can write:

```
public void windowOpened(WindowEvent e) {}
```

Our method implementations must, of course,  appear in a class. An interface is implemented by another class rather like inheritance, but instead of 'extends' we use the keyword 'implements'. In this example, the WindowEventListener class implements the WindowListener interface:

```
public class WindowEventListener implements WindowListener
```

Within the body of this listener definition, the method we need to provide a useful definition for is 'windowClosing'. To close the window properly, we must get a reference to the window (this can be done by using the 'getWindow' method with the event object passed as a parameter, returning a reference of class 'Window', the superclass of 'Frame') and send the 'dispose' message. Then the 'exit' method of 'System' is used to shut down the program itself (a zero parameter value is used to indicate an orderly exit):

```
public void windowClosing(WindowEvent e)
{
// get a reference to the window from the event object
    Window window = e.getWindow();
// dispose of the window resource
    window.dispose();
// exit the program
    System.exit(0);
}
```

This is the complete Listener class:

```
/**
    WindowEventListener.java
    this class implements the WindowListener interface
    so that the main window of an application can be closed
*/
import java.awt.*;
import java.awt.event.*;
public class WindowEventListener implements WindowListener
{
// allow the window to close and terminate the program
    public void windowClosing(WindowEvent e)
    {
// get a reference to the window from the event object
        Window window = e.getWindow();
// dispose of the window resource
        window.dispose();
// exit the program
        System.exit(0);
    }
// empty methods for events we do not handle
    public void windowClosed(WindowEvent e){}
    public void windowActivated(WindowEvent e) {}
    public void windowDeactivated(WindowEvent e) {}
    public void windowIconified(WindowEvent e) {}
    public void windowDeiconified(WindowEvent e) {}
    public void windowOpened(WindowEvent e) {}
}
```

Java includes a number of interface definitions, and it is also possible to write our own interfaces, as we will see in Chapter ten.

To add the window listener to our main window, we use the 'addWindowListener' method that takes a 'WindowListener' object as a parameter. Rather than declare the object separately and then pass it to the method, we can simply use 'new' with the class name within the parameter brackets (as we did with the Snake and Ladder classes):

```
        addWindowListener(new WindowEventListener());
```

This is the code for a window that can be closed. It is basically the same as 'FirstWindow' but with the window listener added and 'java.awt.event.*' imported. 'Main' has now been removed to another class

```
/**
        MainWindow.java
        this class shows a window can be displayed with a given
        size. it also shows how a 'WindowListener' object can be
        used to allow it to close
*/
import java.awt.*;
import java.awt.event.*;
// the 'Frame' class provides a basic window with a title bar
public class MainWindow extends Frame
{
// the constructor passes a window frame title to the superclass
// (otherwise the title bar will be 'blank')
        public MainWindow(String title)
        {
                super(title);
// add a window listener so the window can be closed
                addWindowListener(new WindowEventListener());
        }
}
```

This class contains a test 'main' method that displays a 'MainWindow' object on the screen. This time, the 'setBounds' method has been added to set the initial position and size of the window so that when it appears it is not just a title bar and buttons. Setting the first two parameters to zero means that the window will appear in the top left hand corner of the screen. The other parameters define the initial width and height of the window respectively.

```
/**
        ShowMainWindow.java
        creates and displays a 'MainWindow' object
*/
public class ShowMainWindow
{
        public static void main(String args[])
        {
// call the 'MainWindow' constructor with the window title as the
// parameter
                MainWindow window = new MainWindow("Main Window");
// set the initial location and size of the window
                window.setBounds(0, 0, 200, 100);
// display the window
                window.show();
        }
}
```

Figure 8.2 shows what the window looks like when the class is run.

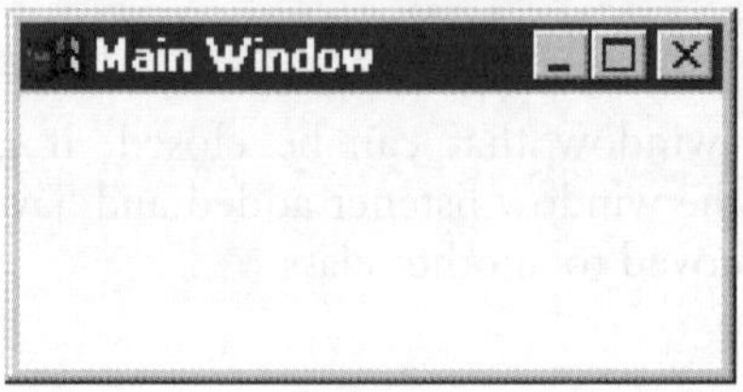

**Figure 8.2**    The Main Window class provides a sized window that can be properly closed.

## AWT component classes

A window on its own is of little use, so we need to add components to it to provide some functionality. These are perhaps the most commonly used components:

- Label
- TextField (single line of text that can be edited)

    enter text here

- TextArea (multiple lines of text that can be edited)

- Button

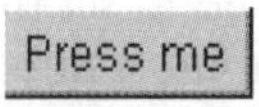

    Press me

- Checkbox (individual)

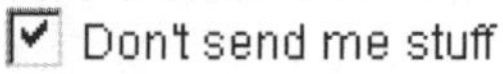

    ☑ Don't send me stuff

- Checkbox (as part of a CheckBoxGroup, also known as a 'radio button')

    ⦿ Male    ○ Female

- List

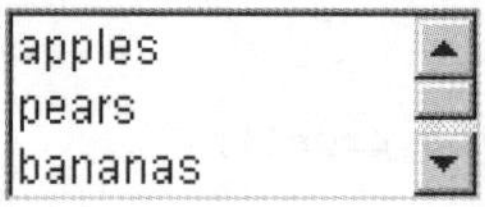

    apples
    pears
    bananas

- Choice

    cucumbers ▼

### The Label class

Labels are very simple because they are just text labels used to assist the readability of a GUI. Although an empty label can be constructed, the most commonly used form of the constructor sets the text of the label:

```
Label text_label = new Label("Component label");
```

The default alignment for the text is left aligned. Another version of the constructor can set the alignment as the second parameter. The alignment values are defined as public attributes of the Label class, and can be 'Label.LEFT', 'Label.RIGHT' or 'Label.CENTER'. For example, to create a centred label we would declare it like this:

```
Label centred_label = new Label("centred text", Label.CENTER);
```

## 'final' attributes

The Label alignment values, as well as being declared 'public' and 'static', are also declared 'final'. Any attribute that is declared final is a constant, which means that it cannot be changed. Many Java classes have final attributes, generally used to make it easier to pass parameters to objects of the class by using text names rather than numeric values. The label alignment values are in fact integers, declared in the class like this:

```
public static final int CENTER;
public static final int LEFT;
public static final int RIGHT;
```

Because they are static we must, of course, always refer to these attribute names using the class name, e.g., Label.LEFT.

## The TextField class

A TextField allows text to be typed in and edited. There is a default constructor with no parameters that will set the TextField's initial width relative to the layout of the window it appears in:

```
TextField text_field = new TextField();
```

More usefully, perhaps, we can also specify a width (in columns) for the text field and/or some initial text, using one of the three parameterised constructors:

```
public TextField(int  cols)
e.g. TextField text_field = new TextField(10);

public TextField(String  text)
e.g. TextField text_field = new TextField("enter text here");

public TextField(String  text, int  cols)
e.g. TextField text_field = new TextField("enter text here", 30);
```

## The TextArea class

A TextArea is similar to a TextField except that it can have multiple rows and columns. There are a number of constructors, but probably the most useful allows you to set the number of rows and columns:

```
public TextArea(int rows, int columns)
```

By default, TextAreas have both horizontal and vertical scrollbars. However, these can be set differently by using an alternative constructor, namely:

```
public TextArea(String text, int rows, int columns, int scrollbars)
```

The 'scrollbars' attribute can be set to any one of the following four constants ('final' attributes) declared in the class:

```
SCROLLBARS_BOTH
SCROLLBARS_HORIZONTAL_ONLY
SCROLLBARS_NONE
SCROLLBARS_VERTICAL_ONLY
```

Like the 'Label' constants, they must be preceded by the name of the class when used, for example:

```
TextArea text = new TextArea(" ", 2, 10,
        TextArea.SCROLLBARS_VERTICAL_ONLY);
```

## The Button class

Buttons are very simple objects because their only behaviour is to be pressed. The Button class has two constructors, one that creates a blank button and another one that creates a button with a text label. This, for example, instantiates two buttons, one labelled 'On' and the other labelled 'Off':

```
Button on_button = new Button("On");
Button off_button = new Button("Off");
```

## The CheckBox class

CheckBoxes are interesting in that they take different forms depending on whether they appear individually or as part of a group. An individual check box can be checked or unchecked regardless of the state of other check boxes. However, if a number of check boxes appear as part of a CheckBoxGroup object, then only one of these can be checked at any one time, and their appearance also changes from a square check box to a round radio button. The idea of a radio button is that a radio can be tuned only to one wavelength/station at a time so it does not make sense for the user to be allowed to check more than one of these buttons. In contrast, check boxes are used where the user can choose a selection of possibilities in combination. To stretch the radio metaphor further, we might select any combination of 'stereo', 'spatial' and 'bass boost' simultaneously.

Check boxes are usually instantiated with text labels as parameters, because it is not very helpful to have an unlabelled check box:

```
CheckBox check = new Checkbox("Tick me");
```

We might use an alternative constructor that also initialises the state of the checkbox using a boolean parameter after the text label. This example would initially check the box:

```
CheckBox mail_check = new CheckBox("Don't send me stuff", true);
```

Using a 'false' parameter would create an unchecked box.

To put check boxes into a group (and turn them into radio buttons) we must create a 'CheckBoxGroup' object:

```
CheckBoxGroup radio_buttons = new CheckBoxGroup();
```

We can then create CheckBox objects using another form of the constructor that takes its group object as a parameter, either between or following the label and the state:

```
CheckBox radio_1 = new CheckBox("Radio 1"' true, radio_buttons);
```

Alternatively, CheckBoxes created using the other constructors may be added to a group using the 'setCheckboxGroup' method:

```
CheckBox radio_2 = new CheckBox("Radio 2");
radio_2.setCheckboxGroup(radio_buttons);
```

## The List class

A List displays a list of strings that can be selected with the mouse. Strings can easily be added to or removed from a list. Perhaps the most useful constructor is one that lets us specify how many visible rows there will be in the list, with scroll bars automatically added where necessary

```
List list_box = new List(3);
```

There are many methods in the List class, but perhaps the most fundamental are these:

```
public void addItem(String);
// adds a String to the list

public int getSelectedIndex();
// returns the position in the list of the currently selected
// string

public String getItem(int);
// returns the String at the specified position

public void remove(String);
// removes the specified String

public void remove(int);
//removes the string at the specified index.
```

For example, to add a string to our list box we would write:

```
list_box.addItem("apples");
```

## The Choice class

This class is similar to the List except that it displays only a single line of text (the currently selected item) with a button that allows us to drop down the list and see its contents. A Choice has a single, simple constructor that takes no parameters:

```
Choice drop_down_list = new Choice();
```

Once a Choice object has been created, it has a similar set of methods to a List. All the methods described above for Lists also work with Choices, so we could, for example, add strings to it using the 'addItem' method:

```
drop_down_list.addItem("cucumber");
```

We will investigate Choice objects in more detail later in this chapter.

## Adding components to the window

Creating component objects is all very well, but they need to be added to the window. This is done in a method of the Window class (usually the constructor) with the 'add' method, which takes as its parameter any component object. For example, this creates a label and adds it to the window

```
Label my_label = new Label ("Hello");
add(my_label);
```

The 'add' method sometimes takes a slightly different form, depending on the 'layout manager' being used to format the components on the screen.

# Layout managers

If we are going to add component objects to a window, we need some way of arranging them. We can do this manually, but Java also provides a number of 'layout managers' that automate (to some extent) the arrangement of components within a window. These are the available layout managers.

*FlowLayout*
The simplest layout manager is the FlowLayout that lays the components out like text: left to right, wrapping onto the next line where necessary. Like text, the layout can be left, right or centre justified.

*GridLayout*
Rather like FlowLayout in that the components are laid out left to right and top to bottom in the sequence that they are added to the container. However, we can specify the number of rows and/or columns that we want to have.

*BorderLayout*
The default layout manager for Frame objects, this is a good manager for a small number of components, laying out up to five components at the points of a compass (North, South, East, West and Center).

*GridBagLayout*
The most sophisticated of the layout managers, it is used in conjunction with 'GridBagConstraints' objects to give maximum control over how components are arranged.

*CardLayout*
Lays out components rather like a card index box. At any one time, only one of the components is visible.

The following example programs use some of these layout managers with several different types of component. At this stage, none of these classes actually do anything. We are treating the components simply as building blocks assembled inside the frame of a main window. Later, we will begin to handle some events from these components and send them messages to write useful programs.

# The FlowLayout

Key aspects of this example are

- setting the layout manager of a window
- a FlowLayout
- adding components to a container
- the 'setTitle' method of 'Frame'.

This class ('FlowLayoutWindow') adds a 'FlowLayout' at the beginning of the constructor using the 'setLayout' method. Like the WindowListener object in the previous examples, the layout is not named here but created within the method's parameter brackets.

```
setLayout(new FlowLayout());
```

Then a number of component objects are declared and added to the window: a label,
buttons, check boxes, grouped check boxes and a text field. Note that in this
constructor, the window title is not being passed to the superclass. By default, this
would leave the window's title bar blank, but in fact the window title is passed to it
by the test program using the 'setTitle' method.

```
/**
      FlowLayoutWindow.java
      demonstrates adding components to a window with a FlowLayout
*/
import java.awt.*;
import java.awt.event.*;
public class FlowLayoutWindow extends Frame
{
        public FlowLayoutWindow()
        {
// set the layout manager of the window
                setLayout(new FlowLayout());
// instantiate and display the components
// a text label
                Label text_label = new Label("My Java Radio  ");
// a text field (editable)
                TextField text_field = new TextField("JAVA FM", 30);
// two buttons
                Button on_button = new Button("On");
                Button off_button = new Button("Off");
// two independent check boxes
                Checkbox stereo_check = new Checkbox("Stereo");
                Checkbox spatial_check = new Checkbox("Spatial");
// two checkboxes in a group (radio buttons) using the two
// different ways of grouping check boxes
                CheckboxGroup radio_buttons = new CheckboxGroup();
                Checkbox radio_1 = new Checkbox("radio 1",
                        radio_buttons, true);
                Checkbox radio_2 = new Checkbox("radio 2");
                radio_2.setCheckboxGroup(radio_buttons);
// add all the components to the window
                add(text_label);
                add(text_field);
                add(on_button);
                add(off_button);
                add(stereo_check);
                add(spatial_check);
                add(radio_1);
                add(radio_2);
// add a window listener
                addWindowListener(new WindowEventListener());
        }
}
```

The 'ShowFlowWindow' class creates and displays an object of the FlowLayoutWindow class. It also sets the window title with the 'setTitle' method, since in this case there is no constructor parameter to do this. Note that the default FlowLayout uses centred justification for the components:

```
/**
        ShowFlowWindow.java
        displays a 'FlowLayoutWindow' object
*/
public class ShowFlowWindow
{
        public static void main(String args[])
        {
// make a FlowLayoutWindow object and set its title
                FlowLayoutWindow window = new FlowLayoutWindow();
                window.setTitle("AWT FlowLayout example");
// set the window size
                window.setBounds(0,0,500,200);
// display the window
                window.show();
        }
}
```

The output is shown in Figure 8.3.

Figure 8.3    Components in a FlowLayout (centre justified).

# The GridLayout

The next class uses the same components as the FlowLayout example, but in this case uses the GridLayout layout manager. It also shows a different way of handling the main window events by using an 'adapter' class.

Key aspects of this example are

- the GridLayout class
- handling events with an 'Adapter'
- the 'pack' method of 'Frame'.

Using a GridLayout is very simple. The constructor has two integer parameters that allow us to provide the number of rows and/or columns we want. If we leave one of the parameters as zero, then the appropriate value will be calculated automatically from the other parameter. This example will use two columns with an automatic setting for the number of rows:

```
setLayout(new GridLayout(0,2));
```

## Adapters

When we use the WindowListener interface, we have to provide versions of all the window event methods even when all we want to do is close the window. An alternative approach is to use an adapter, which acts as a mediator between the full listener interface and our own classes. To use an adapter we must inherit our own class from it, in this case from the WindowAdapter class. We need then provide only the methods that we actually want to implement (just windowClosing, with exactly the same implementation as before). Because we will be using this window listener with a number of different applications, we will put it into a named package so that it can be imported by other classes. We assume here that the package is called 'javabook.chapter8', though this would be dependent on the class being resident in a directory of that name relative to the CLASSPATH. Although the rest of the examples in this chapter are assumed to be in the same package, and therefore do not need to import the WindowListener, classes in subsequent chapters will need to use an import statement.

```
/**
        MainWindowListener.java
        a class that inherits from the WindowAdapter class to
        provide a definition for the 'windowClosing' method
*/
package javabook.chapter8;
import java.awt.*;
import java.awt.event.*;
// inherit from 'WindowAdapter'
public class MainWindowListener extends WindowAdapter
{
        public void windowClosing(WindowEvent e)
        {
// get a reference to the window from the event object
                Window window = e.getWindow();
// free the window resource
                window.dispose();
// exit the program
                System.exit(0);
        }
}
```

The empty bodies for the other window event methods are defined for us in the WindowAdapter class, and because we inherit these we do not need to define them again. In the constructor, we create an object of our own class as the parameter to 'addWindowListener' in the same way that we previously provided an object of our 'WindowEventListener' class:

```
addWindowListener(new MainWindowListener());
```

This window listener class will be used for all the AWT example classes that follow.

Adapters are useful when we need to handle events but do not want to implement many of the methods demanded by the necessary interface. An adapter simply saves us from having to implement a large number of methods with empty definitions. This is the complete GridLayoutWindow class:

```
/**
        GridLayoutWindow.java
        demonstrates adding components to a window using a
        GridLayout and handling window events with an adapter
*/
import java.awt.*;
import java.awt.event.*;
public class GridLayoutWindow extends Frame
{
        public GridLayoutWindow()
        {
// set the layout of the window using a 'GridLayout'. this
// constructor is passed the number of rows and columns. passing
// '0' for the number of rows means that it will be automatically
// calculated from the number of columns and components
                setLayout(new GridLayout(0,2));
// instantiate and add the components
// a text field (editable)
                TextField text_field = new TextField("JAVA FM");
// a text label
                Label text_label = new Label("My Java Radio  ");
// two buttons
                Button on_button = new Button("On");
                Button off_button = new Button("Off");
// two independent check boxes
                Checkbox stereo_check = new Checkbox("Stereo");
                Checkbox spatial_check = new Checkbox("Spatial");
// two checkboxes in a group (radio buttons)
                CheckboxGroup radio_buttons = new CheckboxGroup();
                Checkbox radio_1 = new Checkbox("radio 1",
                        radio_buttons, true);
                Checkbox radio_2 = new Checkbox("radio 2");
                radio_2.setCheckboxGroup(radio_buttons);
// add all the components to the window
                add(text_field);
                add(text_label);
                add(on_button);
                add(off_button);
                add(stereo_check);
                add(spatial_check);
                add(radio_1);
                add(radio_2);
// add a window listener to close the window using an adapter
                addWindowListener(new MainWindowListener());
        }
}
```

This simple test class is very similar to the one that displays the FlowLayout example. However, rather than using 'setBounds', 'main' uses the 'pack' method to set the initial window size to match the components that it contains.

```
/**
        ShowGridWindow.java
        creates and displays an object of the 'GridLayoutWindow'
        class
*/
public class ShowGridWindow
{
        public static void main(String args[])
        {
// make a GridLayoutWindow object and set its title
                GridLayoutWindow window = new GridLayoutWindow();
                window.setTitle("GridLayout example");
// the 'pack' method (inherited by Frame from Window) sets the
// window size to the size of the components within the window
                window.pack();
// display the window
                window.show();
        }
}
```

The window will look something like the one in Figure 8.4.

**Figure 8.4**    Components in a GridLayout with two columns.

## The BorderLayout

The next example shows how to use the BorderLayout layout manager. Although it is not very different from the GridLayout, it does have a slightly different syntax for adding components.

Key aspects of this example are

● a BorderLayout
● adding components to a BorderLayout.

A BorderLayout is divided into five areas, 'North', 'South', 'East', 'West' and 'Center'. Each of these areas can have a single component added to it, using a special form of the 'add' method:

```
add(area_name, object);
```

For example, to add the object 'text_label' to the top part of the layout, we would write:

```
add("North", text_label);
```

This class uses some of the components familiar from the previous examples and lays them out in the five areas:

```
/**
      BorderLayoutWindow.java
      demonstrates the BorderLayout layout manager
*/
import java.awt.*;
import java.awt.event.*;
public class BorderLayoutWindow extends Frame
{
      public BorderLayoutWindow()
      {
// set the layout of the window using a 'BorderLayout'. in fact
// this is the default layout manager for a 'Frame' object, so
// need not be explicitly stated. the parameters here set the
// horizontal and vertical gaps between the coponents
            setLayout(new BorderLayout(10,10));
// instantiate and display the components
// a text label
            Label text_label = new Label("My Java Radio",
                  Label.CENTER);
// two buttons
            Button on_button = new Button("On");
            Button off_button = new Button("Off");
// one check box
            Checkbox stereo_check = new Checkbox("Stereo");
// a text field (editable)
            TextField text_field = new TextField(20);
// add all the components to the window
            add("Center", text_field);
            add("North", text_label);
            add("West", on_button);
            add("East", off_button);
            add("South", stereo_check);
// add a window listener to close the window
            addWindowListener(new MainWindowListener());
      }
}
```

The test program is, by now, familiar:

```
/**
      ShowBorderWindow.java
      this class creates and displays a BorderLayoutWindow object
*/
public class ShowBorderWindow
{
      public static void main(String args[])
      {
// make a BorderLayoutWindow object and set its title
            BorderLayoutWindow window = new BorderLayoutWindow();
            window.setTitle("Border Layout Window");
```

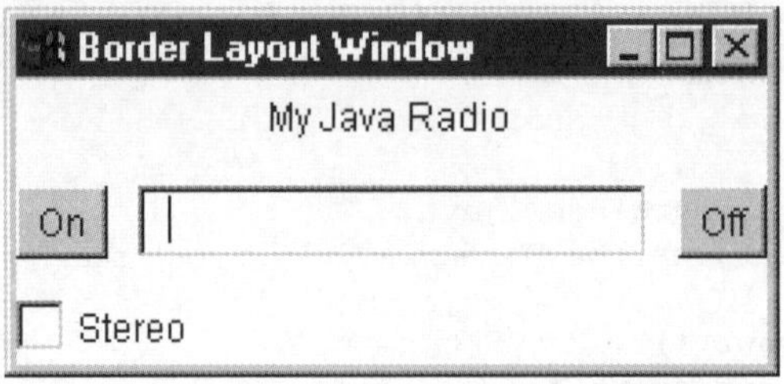

**Figure 8.5**   Five components in a BorderLayout.

```
// the 'pack' method (inherited by Frame from Window) sets the
// window size to the size of the components within the window
        window.pack();
// display the window
        window.show();
    }
}
```

Figure 8.5 shows the output from the border layout example.

## The GridBagLayout

The GridBagLayout can be used to gain a lot of control over the way that components are laid out on a general layout grid. This example gives some idea of how this
layout manager can be used but there are many more aspects to this layout than those
specifically shown here.

Key aspects of this example are

- the GridBagLayout
- GridBagConstraints objects
- setting constraints.

A GridBagLayout is similar to a GridLayout in that the components are laid out in a
grid. It differs in that a GridBagConstraints object can be used to add specific characteristics to the components in the layout. As well as declaring a layout manager,
then, we also declare a constraints object:

```
GridBagLayout layout = new GridBagLayout();
GridBagConstraints constraints = new GridBagConstraints();
setLayout(layout);
```

The GridBagConstraints class consists almost entirely of public static integers representing various characteristics of a component's layout, along with a number of
constants for setting their values. When we add components to the layout, we can
optionally add constraints to them by giving a constraints object as the second parameter to the 'add' method:

```
add(component, constraints);
```

The constraints object needs to be configured appropriately before we add the component using its public attributes and constants ('final' attributes). There are many available, so we will look at only a few examples here.

● *gridwidth*
This attribute specifies the width of a component in the layout. One value for this is 'REMAINDER' which causes the component to take up the rest of the current line, e.g.,

```
constraints.gridwidth = GridBagConstraints.REMAINDER;
add(text_label, constraints);
```

● *fill*
This attribute defines how a component fills the available space. We can set this to NONE, HORIZONTAL, VERTICAL or BOTH, e.g.,

```
constraints.fill = GridBagConstraints.HORIZONTAL;
add(on_button, constraints);
```

● *insets*
This attribute is an object of the Insets class that is used to represent the margins around a component. It has four public attributes that can be set: 'bottom', 'left', 'right' and 'top'. This example sets the right and left attributes:

```
constraints.insets.left = 10;
constraints.insets.right = 10;
add(stereo_check, constraints);
```

This is the complete class. It is only a partial demonstration of some of GridBagLayout's possibilities, rather than an attempt to create a useful layout:

```
/**
      GridBagWindow.java
      this class demonstrates a GridBagLayout and its
      associated GridBagConstraints
*/
import java.awt.*;
public class GridBagWindow extends Frame
{
// constructor
      public GridBagWindow()
      {
// declare a GridBagLayout and a constraints object
            GridBagLayout layout = new GridBagLayout();
            GridBagConstraints constraints = new
                  GridBagConstraints();
// set the layout of the window
            setLayout(layout);
// create the components:
// a text label
            Label text_label = new Label("My Java Radio  ");
```

```
// two buttons
            Button on_button = new Button("On");
            Button off_button = new Button("Off");
// two independent check boxes
            Checkbox stereo_check = new Checkbox("Stereo");
            Checkbox spatial_check = new Checkbox("Spatial");
// two checkboxes in a group (radio buttons)
            CheckboxGroup radio_buttons = new CheckboxGroup();
            Checkbox radio_1 = new Checkbox("radio 1",
                radio_buttons, true);
            Checkbox radio_2 = new Checkbox("radio 2");
            radio_2.setCheckboxGroup(radio_buttons);
// a text field (editable)
            TextField text_field = new TextField(30);
// add all the components to the window, some with constraints
// various settings can be applied to the constraints object. the
// REMAINDER value for a component's gridwidth specifies that the
// component (in this case the text label) will be the last one
// on its row
            constraints.gridwidth = GridBagConstraints.REMAINDER;
            add(text_label, constraints);
// no constraints for the text field
            add(text_field);
// setting the 'fill' to HORIZONTAL will enlarge the component to
// fill the horizontal space available, in this case the 'on'
// button
            constraints.fill = GridBagConstraints.HORIZONTAL;
            add(on_button, constraints);
// the 'off' button has no constraints
            add(off_button);
// the 'insets' object can be used to set the area around the
// component, in this case on the right and left of the 'stereo'
// check box
            constraints.insets.left = 10;
            constraints.insets.right = 10;
            add(stereo_check, constraints);
// these components have no constraints
            add(spatial_check);
            add(radio_1);
            add(radio_2);
// add the window listener to close the window
            addWindowListener(new MainWindowListener());
        }
    }
```

This is the test class:

```
/**
    ShowGridBagWindow.java
    this class creates and displays an object of the
    GridBagWindow class
*/
public class ShowGridBagWindow
{
    public static void main(String args[])
    {
```

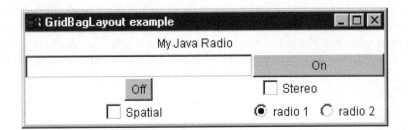

**Figure 8.6**   Some effects of using a GridBagLayout, applying GridBagConstraints to some components.

```
// create a GridBagWindow and set its title
        GridBagWindow window = new GridBagWindow();
        window.setTitle("GridBagLayout example");
// pack the window to the size of its components
        window.pack();
// show the window
        window.show();
    }
}
```

The layout result is shown in Figure 8.6:

## The CardLayout

Key aspects of this example are

- a CardLayout
- CardLayout methods
- button event listeners
- the 'this' keyword
- the 'getParent' method.

The next layout manager (CardLayout) is rather unusual in that it cycles through components individually, displaying only one at a time. In order to use it successfully, we need to introduce a little more processing into our methods, sending messages to component objects and to the layout manager itself. To do this both the layout manager and the components must be declared as attributes of the class. The example class consists of three buttons in a CardLayout:

```
private CardLayout layout;
private Button card1 = new Button("card1 : press for next card");
private Button card2 = new Button("card2 : press for next card");
private Button card3 = new Button("card3 : press for next card");
```

The CardLayout object, once created, can be sent messages. Its methods include:

```
first(Container)        // show the first 'card'
next(Container)         // show the next 'card'
previous(Container)     // show the previous 'card'
```

The 'Container' parameter in this case will be the main window object that contains the components. When we call 'first' in the constructor to begin at the first component, we need to pass the window itself as the parameter. We can do this by using the 'this' keyword, which gives us a reference to the object to which the method belongs.

```
layout.first(this);
```

## Adding to a CardLayout

When we add components to a CardLayout, the 'add' method is a little different. As well as passing the name of the object, we also have to pass an identifying string. Although in this example we do not actually use this string, it still has to be provided, e.g.,

```
add("card1", card1);
```

## Adding a button listener

The buttons in our previous examples did nothing when pressed. In this class, we need to respond to a button press by moving on to the next 'card' (in this case, another button). To do this we need to add a listener, which for button components will be an 'ActionListener'. Unlike the window listener, the button listeners will need to interact with other objects in the system. We could write our listener classes outside the window class (as we did for the window listener) but this can make life difficult when there needs to be a lot of communication between the components in the window and their listeners. The easiest way to make the objects in the window visible to the event listener is to use 'anonymous classes'. An anonymous class is one that is embedded inside another class. The syntax is a little strange, because we provide a set of method definitions for the appropriate event listener within the parameter list of the method that adds the listener to the object, like this:

```
component.addActionListener(new ActionListener()
{
    // provide the necessary method definitions here
});
```

The advantage of this is that the class is rather like a method, because it has access to all the private attributes of the class that it is inside. This is easier than creating an external listener class and having to pass it many parameters. Inside the button listener class we provide a definition for the 'actionPerformed' method. In this method, we call the 'next' method of the 'layout' object (the CardLayout attribute). In order to provide the 'Container' parameter, we have to use the 'getParent' method of the button. Using 'this' in this context will not be appropriate, since this code is inside the ActionListener object, not the main window object.

```
            card1.addActionListener(new ActionListener()
            {
// when the button is pressed...
                public void actionPerformed(ActionEvent e)
                {
                    layout.next(card1.getParent());
                }
            });
```

This is the complete class:

```
/**
        CardLayoutWindow.java
        this class is a simple demo of the CardLayout layout
        manager
*/
import java.awt.*;
import java.awt.event.*;
public class CardLayoutWindow extends Frame
{
// the layout manager is declared as an attribute so we can send
// it messages
        private CardLayout layout;
// declare the buttons as attributes so we can send them messages
        private Button card1 = new Button
                ("card1 : press for next card");
        private Button card2 = new Button
                ("card2 : press for next card");
        private Button card3 = new Button
                ("card3 : press for next card");
// constructor
        public CardLayoutWindow()
        {
// set the layout of the window
                layout = new CardLayout();
                setLayout(layout);
// add the components
                add("card1", card1);
                add("card2", card2);
                add("card3", card3);
// start with the first card
                layout.first(this);
// add a window listener (adapter) to close the window
                addWindowListener(new MainWindowListener());
// add a listener for each button so when they are pressed,
// the next 'card' is displayed
                card1.addActionListener(new ActionListener()
                {
// when the first button is pressed...
                    public void actionPerformed(ActionEvent e)
                    {
                        layout.next(card1.getParent());
                    }
                });
                card2.addActionListener(new ActionListener()
                {
```

```
// when the second button is pressed...
                public void actionPerformed(ActionEvent e)
                {
                        layout.next(card2.getParent());
                }
        });
        card3.addActionListener(new ActionListener()
        {
// when the third button is pressed...
                public void actionPerformed(ActionEvent e)
                {
                        layout.next(card3.getParent());
                }
        });
    }
}
```

The test class is similar to all our previous test code

```
/**
        ShowCardWindow.java
        creates and displays a CardLayoutWindow
*/
public class ShowCardWindow
{
        public static void main(String args[])
        {
// create a CardLayoutWindow and set its title
                CardLayoutWindow window = new CardLayoutWindow();
                window.setTitle("CardLayout example");
// pack the window to the size of its components
                window.pack();
// show the window
                window.show();
        }
}
```

Figure 8.7 shows how our card layout looks after the first button has been pressed:

**Figure 8.7**    A Button acting as one of the cards in a CardLayout.

# Writing programs with the AWT

Now we have looked at the main components, layout managers and event handlers in the AWT, we can bring them together to write a working program. In order to do this, we also need to interact with some of the components, not just by responding to events such as buttons being pressed but by sending messages to components. For example we can send a message to a 'Label' object to change to the text that it is displaying with the 'setText' method. In the next example, a number of labels are used with dynamically changing contents. The program is based on a non-graphical example in *Java Gently* by Judy Bishop that plays a game of Rock, Paper Scissors. In this game, the player chooses one of these three objects, and the computer chooses another. If they both choose the same object, then the game is a draw. Otherwise, they score as follows:

| | |
|---|---|
| rock v paper: | paper wraps rock, so paper wins |
| paper v scissors: | scissors cut paper, so scissors win |
| scissors v rock: | rock blunts scissors, so rock wins |

Key aspects of this example are

- the 'Random' class
- sending messages to component objects.

## The Random class

One of the classes in this program is the AutoPlayer. This class is simply a random number generating object that represent the computer's choice. Unlike previous random number generation where we have used Math.random this class uses the Java Random class, which provides a much easier way of generating random integers. You may recall that Math.random generates a random double between zero and one, which is not always very convenient. We had to do some further arithmetic, for example to generate the appropriate numbers for the Dice class. The Random class (in 'java.util') provides some other random number generating methods, including nextInt which generates a random integer across the full range of the data type. In this program, we need to generate a number of 0, 1 or 2 to represent rock, paper or scissors. Since an integer may be negative, we first need to check if the random integer is less than zero and, if it is, remove its sign. Then we use the remainder operator to get the remainder from dividing by three:

```
/**
        AutoPlayer.java
        this class generates random numbers to enable an
        automatic player for the Rock, Paper, Scissors game.
        instead of using Math.random it uses the rather more
        sophisticated 'Random' class
*/
import java.util.Random;
public class AutoPlayer
{
// an object of the 'Random' class to generate random numbers
        private Random selector = new Random();
        private int choice;
// return a random integer in the range 0 - 2
        int getChoice()
        {
// get a random integer
                int random_integer = selector.nextInt();
```

```
            // ensure that it is positive
                    if(random_integer < 0)
                    {
                            random_integer = -random_integer;
                    }
            // use the remainder of dividing by 3 to give a value of 0, 1 or 2
                    choice = random_integer % 3;
                    return choice;
            }
    }
```

## The component objects and other attributes

To send messages to components they must be visible to methods of the class, so should be declared as private attributes. In addition, a number of integer values are declared as attributes to record information such as the choices made and the current scores. A further attribute is an object of the AutoPlayer class.

Allowing the player to select from the three objects is a good example of using grouped check boxes (radio buttons), because they show the current choice and allow only one box to be checked at any one time. They are initialised so that the default choice is 'rock':

```
    rock = new Checkbox("Rock", user_choice, true);
    paper = new Checkbox("Paper", user_choice, false);
    scissors = new Checkbox("Scissors", user_choice, false);
```

A number of text labels are created with extra spaces to allow for data to be displayed in them later. For example, the 'computer_played' label is blank when the program starts but will be changed to 'rock', 'paper' or 'scissors' during the game. To ensure there is space for this text, the label is initialised with a long empty string:

```
    computer_played = new Label("                        ");
```

## Sending messages to components and responding to events

The game allows the check box to be set by the player, then gets the computer's choice from the AutoPlayer object when the play button is pressed. To respond to this button press, an ActionListener is added, similar to those used for the CardLayout example.

```
    play_button.addActionListener(new ActionListener()
    {
        public void actionPerformed(ActionEvent e)
        {
            // etc.
```

When the button is pressed, some messages have to be passed to various components in the window. For example, the 'computer_played' label is sent the 'setText' message appropriate to the value of the choice made, such as 'rock':

```
    computer_played.setText("Rock");
```

Another component method is 'getState' used to find out the state of the check boxes. A CheckBox will return 'true' if it is checked:

```
if(rock.getState())
// etc..
```

Some data conversion also needs to be done to match the types of parameters expected by some methods. For example, we need to convert the numeric values of the scores to strings to show them in label components, because the 'setText' method expects a string parameter, not an int. We can use the Integer class version of 'toString' to convert ints to strings:

```
computer_scores.setText(Integer.toString(computer_score));
```

This is the complete RockPaperScissors class. It contains some very clumsy code to work out what is happening but it is intended to be readable rather than efficient.

```java
/**
    RockPaperScissors.java
    this program uses AWT components as the interface to a
    simple 'rock, paper, scissors' game. the idea came from a
    program in Judy Bishops' book 'Java Gently' (Addison Wesley
    1997/1998).
*/
import java.awt.*;
import java.awt.event.*;
// the 'Frame' class provides a basic window with a title bar
public class RockPaperScissors extends Frame
{
// various game attributes
    private int player_choice;
    private int computer_choice;
    private int player_score = 0;
    private int computer_score = 0;
    private int games_played = 0;
    private int winner_id;
// declare the components of the window
    private CheckboxGroup user_choice;
    private Checkbox rock;
    private Checkbox paper;
    private Checkbox scissors;
    private Label computer_played_label;
    private Label computer_played;
    private Label player_scores_label;
    private Label player_scores;
    private Label computer_scores_label;
    private Label computer_scores;
    private Label game_counter_label;
    private Label game_counter;
    private Button play_button;
// declare an 'AutoPlayer' object to generate the computer's choice
    private AutoPlayer computer;
// the constructor
    public RockPaperScissors()
    {
```

```java
// use the FlowLayout layout manager to arrange the components on
// the screen
        setLayout(new FlowLayout(FlowLayout.LEFT));
// create the CheckBoxGroup and its CheckBoxes for the user's
// choice
        user_choice = new CheckboxGroup();
// the default choice will be 'Rock'
        rock = new Checkbox("Rock", user_choice, true);
        paper = new Checkbox("Paper", user_choice, false);
        scissors = new Checkbox("Scissors", user_choice, false);
// create the text labels for the computer choice, scores and
// game count
        computer_played_label = new Label("Computer plays: ");
        computer_played = new Label("                    ");
        player_scores_label = new Label("Player's score is: ");
        player_scores = new Label("0      ");
        computer_scores_label = new Label("Computer's score is");
        computer_scores = new Label("0      ");
        game_counter_label = new Label("Games played = ");
        game_counter = new Label("0     ");
// add the check boxes to the frame
        add(rock);
        add(paper);
        add(scissors);
// add all the text labels
        add(computer_played_label);
        add(computer_played);
        add(player_scores_label);
        add(player_scores);
        add(computer_scores_label);
        add(computer_scores);
        add(game_counter_label);
        add(game_counter);
// create and add the 'play' button
        play_button = new Button("Computer play");
        add(play_button);
// create the AutoPlayer object
        computer = new AutoPlayer();
// add a window listener (adapter) to close the window
        addWindowListener(new MainWindowListener());
// add an action listener for the 'play'  button
        play_button.addActionListener(new ActionListener()
        {
            public void actionPerformed(ActionEvent e)
            {
// if we change our choice, erase the previous computer choice to
// avoid confusion
                computer_played.setText("              ");
// check which Checkbox is selected (true) to find the player's
// choice
                if(rock.getState())
                {
                    player_choice = 0;
                }
                if(paper.getState())
                {
```

```
                player_choice = 1;
        }
        if(scissors.getState())
        {
                player_choice = 2;
        }
// get the computer's choice
        computer_choice = computer.getChoice();
// display the computer's choice
        switch(computer_choice)
        {
                case 0 : computer_played.setText("Rock");
                        break;
                case 1 : computer_played.setText("Paper");
                        break;
                case 2 : computer_played.setText("Scissors");
        }
// add to the games played counter and display it
        games_played++;
        game_counter.setText(Integer.toString(games_played);
// work out the winner of this game. set winner_id to 0 (draw)
// if the player wins, this is set to 1, if the computer wins it
// is set to 2. a clumsy algorithm, but hopefully easy to follow
        winner_id = 0;
        switch(computer_choice)
        {
// if computer chooses rock
                case 0 :
// player with paper wins
                        if(player_choice == 1)
                        {
                                winner_id = 1;
                                player_score++;
                        }
// but player with scissors loses
                        if(player_choice == 2)
                        {
                                winner_id = 2;
                                computer_score++;
                        }
                        break;
// if computer chooses paper
                case 1 :
// player with scissors wins
                        if(player_choice == 2)
                        {
                                player_score++;
                                winner_id = 1;
                        }
// but player with rock loses
                        if(player_choice == 0)
                        {
                                computer_score++;
                                winner_id = 2;
                        }
                        break;
```

```
// if computer chooses scissors
                case 2 :
// player with rock wins
                        if(player_choice == 0)
                        {
                                player_score++;
                                winner_id = 1;
                        }
// but player with paper loses
                        if(player_choice == 1)
                        {
                                computer_score++;
                                winner_id = 2;
                        }
                        break;
                }
// if it is not a draw, redisplay the scores
                        if(winner_id != 0)
                        {
computer_scores.setText(Integer.toString(computer_score));
player_scores.setText(Integer.toString(player_score));
                        }
                }
        });
    }
}
```

This class contains the 'main' methods to create a game object and start playing

```
/**
        PlayRPS.java
        this class starts playing a game of Rock, Paper, Scissors
*/
public class PlayRPS
{
        public static void main(String args[])
        {
// call the constructor and set the window title
                RockPaperScissors game = new RockPaperScissors();
                game.setTitle("Rock, paper, scissors game");
// set the initial size of the window
                game.setBounds(0, 0, 250, 200);
// display the window
                game.show();
        }
}
```

Figure 8.8 shows the rock, paper, scissors game in progress.

# Separating the 'model' from the 'view'

The next example provides another working program that introduces an important design issue in programs with a graphical interface, namely the separation of 'model'

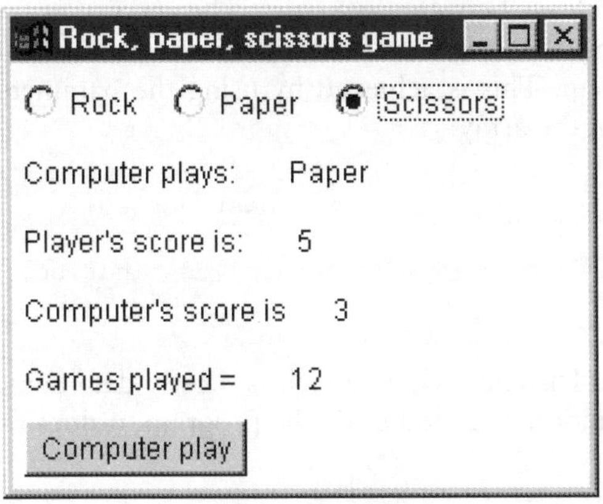

**Figure 8.8**    AWT components in the rock, paper, scissors game: grouped check boxes, labels and a button.

and 'view'. In the previous program, the code was almost entirely embedded in the visual components of the interface, but in larger programs we need to separate out the underlying program from its interface. This way we can develop programs and interfaces separately and make them more independent and maintainable. This example represents a table of mileages between major cities of the type often seen presented as a grid in road atlases. In this version, 'Choice' components are used to select two cities, and the distance between them is displayed using a label. The important point is that the table itself is a separate class with its own methods, not part of the graphical window class. The interface sends message to the underlying 'model' object and gets the necessary data for display.

## The model class: Distances

The Distances class is the underlying model that contains data about the distances between cities. Like RockPaperScissors it is written for readability rather than efficiency. It uses a two-dimensional array of integers to hold information about the distances between cities. A two-dimensional array can be thought of as having both rows and columns and is declared by using two sets of square brackets rather than one:

```
private int distance_table[][];
```

There are ten cities in the mileage table, so they can be represented by integers in the range zero to nine. The array is therefore created with both dimensions of size ten:

```
distance_table = new int[10][10];
```

The mileage data is manually put into the array in the constructor, not a very scaleable solution and rather clumsily expressed (each distance appears twice) but hopefully understandable. A more flexible file based system would obviously be appropriate if developing this application further.

To find out the mileage between two cities, The getDistance method is passed two integers representing the origin and destination of the journey and returns the mileage between them. This is achieved by using the parameter values to access a particular element in the array:

```
int getDistance(int origin, int destination)
{
        return distance_table[origin][destination];
}
```

This is the complete Distances class, which is mostly data being put into the array. Because this is the underlying model for the program, it does not contain any AWT interface classes

```
/**
        Distances.java
        this class encapsulates a table of distances between cities,
        stored in a two-dimensional array
*/
package javabook.chapter8;
public class Distances
{
// declare an two-dimensional array of integers
    private int distance_table[][];
// the constructor creates the array and fills it with data
    public Distances()
    {
// create a 10 by 10 array
        distance_table = new int[10][10];
// where the two indexes are the same, the distance is zero
// because the origin and destination are the same city
        for(int i = 0; i < 10; i++)
        {
                distance_table[i][i] = 0;
        }
// the other entries will be valid distances (reading these from
// file would be a useful improvement, as would not entering each
// distance twice!)
        distance_table[0][1] = 171;        // Birmingham -> Brighton
        distance_table[0][2] = 88;         // Birmingham -> Bristol
        distance_table[0][3] = 113;        // Birmingham -> Cambridge
        distance_table[0][4] = 198;        // Birmingham -> Carlisle
        distance_table[0][5] = 206;        // Birmingham -> Dover
        distance_table[0][6] = 162;        // Birmingham -> Exeter
        distance_table[0][7] = 115;        // Birmingham -> Leeds
        distance_table[0][8] = 120;        // Birmingham -> London
        distance_table[0][9] = 134;        // Birmingham -> Southampton
        distance_table[1][0] = 171;        // Brighton -> Birmingham
        distance_table[1][2] = 170;        // Brighton -> Bristol
        distance_table[1][3] = 121;        // Brighton -> Cambridge
        distance_table[1][4] = 377;        // Brighton -> Carlisle
        distance_table[1][5] = 78;         // Brighton -> Dover
        distance_table[1][6] = 173;        // Brighton -> Exeter
        distance_table[1][7] = 263;        // Brighton -> Leeds
```

```
distance_table[1][8] = 60;      // Brighton -> London
distance_table[1][9] = 64;      // Brighton -> Southampton
distance_table[2][0] = 88;      // Bristol -> Birmingham
distance_table[2][1] = 170;     // Bristol -> Brighton
distance_table[2][3] = 171;     // Bristol -> Cambridge
distance_table[2][4] = 282;     // Bristol -> Carlisle
distance_table[2][5] = 210;     // Bristol -> Dover
distance_table[2][6] = 84;      // Bristol -> Exeter
distance_table[2][7] = 220;     // Bristol -> Leeds
distance_table[2][8] = 120;     // Bristol -> London
distance_table[2][9] = 78;      // Bristol -> Southampton
distance_table[3][0] = 113;     // Cambridge -> Birmingham
distance_table[3][1] = 121;     // Cambridge -> Brighton
distance_table[3][2] = 171;     // Cambridge -> Bristol
distance_table[3][4] = 260;     // Cambridge -> Carlisle
distance_table[3][5] = 122;     // Cambridge -> Dover
distance_table[3][6] = 251;     // Cambridge -> Exeter
distance_table[3][7] = 149;     // Cambridge -> Leeds
distance_table[3][8] = 60;      // Cambridge -> London
distance_table[3][9] = 131;     // Cambridge -> Southampton
distance_table[4][0] = 198;     // Carlisle -> Birmingham
distance_table[4][1] = 377;     // Carlisle -> Brighton
distance_table[4][2] = 282;     // Carlisle -> Bristol
distance_table[4][3] = 260;     // Carlisle -> Cambridge
distance_table[4][5] = 398;     // Carlisle -> Dover
distance_table[4][6] = 355;     // Carlisle -> Exeter
distance_table[4][7] = 123;     // Carlisle -> Leeds
distance_table[4][8] = 313;     // Carlisle -> London
distance_table[4][9] = 340;     // Carlisle -> Southampton
distance_table[5][0] = 206;     // Dover -> Birmingham
distance_table[5][1] = 78;      // Dover -> Brighton
distance_table[5][2] = 210;     // Dover -> Bristol
distance_table[5][3] = 122;     // Dover -> Cambridge
distance_table[5][4] = 398;     // Dover -> Carlisle
distance_table[5][6] = 249;     // Dover -> Exeter
distance_table[5][7] = 271;     // Dover -> Leeds
distance_table[5][8] = 80;      // Dover -> London
distance_table[5][9] = 156;     // Dover -> Southampton
distance_table[6][0] = 162;     // Exeter -> Birmingham
distance_table[6][1] = 173;     // Exeter -> Brighton
distance_table[6][2] = 84;      // Exeter -> Bristol
distance_table[6][3] = 251;     // Exeter -> Cambridge
distance_table[6][4] = 355;     // Exeter -> Carlisle
distance_table[6][5] = 249;     // Exeter -> Dover
distance_table[6][7] = 294;     // Exeter -> Leeds
distance_table[6][8] = 200;     // Exeter -> London
distance_table[6][9] = 110;     // Exeter -> Southampton
distance_table[7][0] = 115;     // Leeds -> Birmingham
distance_table[7][1] = 263;     // Leeds -> Brighton
distance_table[7][2] = 220;     // Leeds -> Bristol
distance_table[7][3] = 149;     // Leeds -> Cambridge
distance_table[7][4] = 123;     // Leeds -> Carlisle
distance_table[7][5] = 271;     // Leeds -> Dover
distance_table[7][6] = 294;     // Leeds -> Exeter
distance_table[7][8] = 199;     // Leeds -> London
distance_table[7][9] = 234;     // Leeds -> Southampton
```

```
        distance_table[8][0] = 120;      // London -> Birmingham
        distance_table[8][1] = 60;       // London -> Brighton
        distance_table[8][2] = 120;      // London -> Bristol
        distance_table[8][3] = 60;       // London -> Cambridge
        distance_table[8][4] = 313;      // London -> Carlisle
        distance_table[8][5] = 80;       // London -> Dover
        distance_table[8][6] = 200;      // London -> Exeter
        distance_table[8][7] = 199;      // London -> Leeds
        distance_table[8][9] = 80;       // London -> Southampton
        distance_table[9][0] = 134;      // Southampton -> Birmingham
        distance_table[9][1] = 64;       // Southampton -> Brighton
        distance_table[9][2] = 78;       // Southampton -> Bristol
        distance_table[9][3] = 131;      // Southampton -> Cambridge
        distance_table[9][4] = 340;      // Southampton -> Carlisle
        distance_table[9][5] = 156;      // Southampton -> Dover
        distance_table[9][6] = 110;      // Southampton -> Exeter
        distance_table[9][7] = 234;      // Southampton -> Leeds
        distance_table[9][8] = 80;       // Southampton -> London
    }
// given integers to represent cities in the table, this method
// returns the mileage between them
    int getDistance(int origin, int destination)
    {
        return distance_table[origin][destination];
    }
}
```

## The View class: MileageTable

The MileageTable class provides the graphical user interface to the system, using two Choice objects, one for the name of the city of origin and one for the destination:

```
private Choice from_city;
private Choice to_city;
```

Strings can be added to a Choice object using the addItem method, for example:

```
from_city.addItem("Birmingham");
```

In this way, ten city names are added to both choices.

Like the rock, paper, scissors game, pressing a button starts a calculation process using an ActionListener. To find the mileage, the chosen city values need to be returned from the two choice objects. This is achieved using the getSelectedIndex method, which returns the index of the selected string. Since this starts at value zero for the first element, this matches our Distances table. Therefore we can use the values retrieved from the choice objects directly as parameters to the getDistance method of the distances object:

```
int origin = from_city.getSelectedIndex();
int destination = to_city.getSelectedIndex();
int distance = table.getDistance(origin, destination);
```

Once again, some conversion of numbers to strings is required to display the results in a Label:

```
result_label.setText(Integer.toString(distance) + " miles");
```

This is the complete MileageTable class:

```
/**
    MileageTable.java
    this program uses AWT components as the interface to a
    mileage table of the 'Distances' class
*/
import javabook.chapter8.Distances;
import java.awt.*;
import java.awt.event.*;
// the 'Frame' class provides a basic window with a title bar
public class MileageTable extends Frame
{
// declare the components of the window:
// declare two Choices to select the origin and destination of
// the journey
    private Choice from_city;
    private Choice to_city;
// declare text labels
    private Label from_label;
    private Label to_label;
    private Label distance_label;
    private Label result_label;
// declare a button to produce a result
    private Button calculate_button;
// declare a 'Distances' object
    private Distances table;
// the constructor
    public MileageTable()
    {
// use the FlowLayout layout manager to arrange the components on
// the screen
        setLayout(new FlowLayout());
// create the two 'Choice' objects
        from_city = new Choice();
        to_city = new Choice();
// add the city names to the 'from' choice
        from_city.addItem("Birmingham");
        from_city.addItem("Brighton");
        from_city.addItem("Bristol");
        from_city.addItem("Cambridge");
        from_city.addItem("Carlisle");
        from_city.addItem("Dover");
        from_city.addItem("Exeter");
        from_city.addItem("Leeds");
        from_city.addItem("London");
        from_city.addItem("Southampton");
// add the city names to the 'to' choice
        to_city.addItem("Birmingham");
        to_city.addItem("Brighton");
```

```
              to_city.addItem("Bristol");
              to_city.addItem("Cambridge")
              to_city.addItem("Carlisle");
              to_city.addItem("Dover");
              to_city.addItem("Exeter");
              to_city.addItem("Leeds");
              to_city.addItem("London");
              to_city.addItem("Southampton");
// create the text labels for the choices
              from_label = new Label("From:");
              to_label = new Label("To:");
// add these components to the frame
              add(from_label);
              add(from_city);
              add(to_label);
              add(to_city);
// create and add the 'calculate' button
              calculate_button = new Button("Calculate Distance");
              add(calculate_button);
// create and add the text label for the result
              distance_label = new Label
                  ("The distance between the cities is");
              add(distance_label);
// create and add a text label to display the result. the extra
// spaces ensure that when longer results are put into the label
// the text is not truncated
              result_label = new Label("0 miles     ");
              add(result_label);
// create the table object that contains the distance data
              table = new Distances();
// add a window listener to close the window
              addWindowListener(new MainWindowListener());
// add a listener for the 'calculate' button so when it is
// pressed the mileage between the currently selected cities is
// displayed
              calculate_button.addActionListener(new ActionListener()
              {
// when the button is pressed...
                  public void actionPerformed(ActionEvent e)
                  {
// get the index numbers of the currently selected cities from
// each 'Choice' object
                      int origin = from_city.getSelectedIndex();
                      int destination = to_city.getSelectedIndex();
// use these as parameters to 'getDistance' to return the
// distance between these two cities
                      int distance = table.getDistance(origin,
                      destination);
// since 'setText' requires a String parameter, the Integer class
// method 'toString(int)' is used to convert the int to a string
                      result_label.setText(Integer.toString(distance)
                      + " miles");
                  }
              });
      }
}
```

The RoadAtlas class tests the mileage table.

```
/**
      RoadAtlas.java
      creates an object of the MileageTable class
*/
public class RoadAtlas
{
// create an object
      public static void main(String args[])
      {
// create a 'MileageTable' object and set the window title
            MileageTable table = new MileageTable();
            table.setTitle("Mileage table between major cities");
// set the initial size of the window
            table.setBounds(100, 100, 500, 150);
// display the window
            table.show();
      }
}
```

Figure 8.9 shows the mileage table giving the distance between London and Southampton.

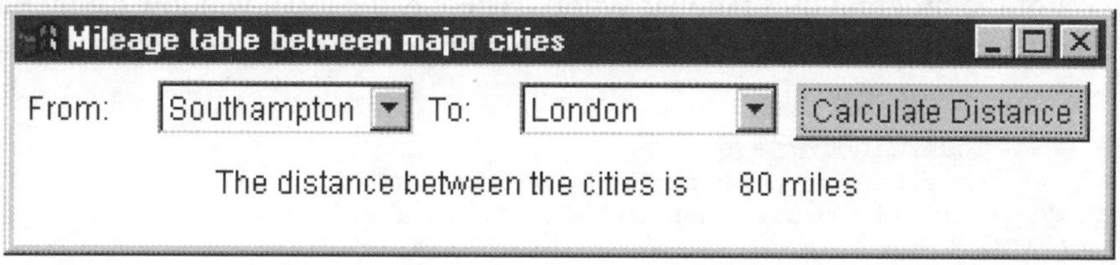

**Figure 8.9**   The mileage table application in use.

# Manually positioning components in a  window

All of the examples we have seen so far have used layout managers to position and size the components in the window. However, it is possible to manually add components to a window without a layout manager. The final example in this chapter gives a basic introduction to this approach.

Key aspects of this example are

- removing the default layout manager
- applying 'setBounds' to component objects.

This program is a very simple class that consists of a window with two buttons and a text label. One of the buttons is labelled with a − sign and the other with a +. The label contains an integer and starts at zero. When the + button is pressed, the number on the label increases by one, and when the − button is pressed it decreases by one but will not go below zero.

## Turning off the layout manager

As we have indicated before, a Frame object will have a default layout manager of the BorderLayout class. To add components to the window ourselves, we must turn this off by passing null to the setLayout method:

```
setLayout(null);
```

This allows us to add components without a layout manager.

## Positioning and sizing components

All components have a setBounds method. In fact we have already used this method with our windows, since class Window inherits from Container which in turn inherits from Component. Once components have been added to the window, we can set their position, width and height using this method. In the example, the buttons and text box are initialised in this way:

```
down_button.setBounds(10, 30, 50, 50);
up_button.setBounds(130, 30, 50, 50);
count.setBounds(80, 30, 40, 50);
```

The rest of the program uses familiar syntax. There is the usual window listener and button listeners to respond to the buttons being pressed. This is the complete class:

```
/**
    CountWindow.java
    this class shows how components can be
    manually positioned within the window frame
*/
import java.awt.*;
import java.awt.event.*;
public class CountWindow extends Frame
{
// declare the components as attributes to receive messages and
// send events
    private Button down_button;
    private Button up_button;
    private Label count;
// integer to record the counter value
    private int counter = 0;
// constructor
    public CountWindow()
    {
// turn off the default layout manager
        setLayout(null);
// create the components
        down_button = new Button(" - ");
        up_button = new Button(" + ");
        count = new Label("0  ");
// add them to the window
        add(down_button);
        add(up_button);
        add(count);
```

```
// manually position and size them
            down_button.setBounds(10, 30, 50, 50);
            up_button.setBounds(130, 30, 50, 50);
            count.setBounds(80, 30, 40, 50);
// add a window listener to close the window
            addWindowListener(new MainWindowListener());
// add a button listener to decrement the counter when the '-'
// button is pressed
            down_button.addActionListener(new ActionListener()
            {
                public void actionPerformed(ActionEvent e)
                {
// if the value is greater than zero, decrement it
                    if(counter > 0)
                    {
                        counter--;;
// update the label
                    count.setText(Integer.toString(counter));
                    }
                }
            });
// add a button listener to increment the counter when the '+'
// button is pressed
            up_button.addActionListener(new ActionListener()
            {
                public void actionPerformed(ActionEvent e)
                {
// increment the value
                    counter++;
// update the label
                    count.setText(Integer.toString(counter));
                }
            });
        }
}
```

The test class is ShowCountWindow:

```
/**
    ShowCountWindow.java
    this class tests 'CountWindow'
*/
public class ShowCountWindow
{
    public static void main(String args[])
    {
// call the constructor and set the window title
            CountWindow counter = new CountWindow();
            counter.setTitle("Counter Window");
// set the initial size of the window
            counter.setBounds(0, 0, 200, 100);
// display the window
            counter.show();
    }
}
```

Figure 8.10 shows the window in action.

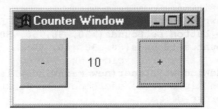

**Figure 8.10**   Components manually positioned within a window.

## Summary

In this chapter we have looked at a number of aspects of using the Abstract Windowing Toolkit (AWT) to create graphical user interfaces. These have included

- Components: the objects that we interact with such as buttons and check boxes.
- Containers: we have inherited from the 'Frame' class to contain the components within a window.
- Events: we have seen that the objects in a graphical user interface respond to events. We can provide program behaviour associated with these events by adding 'listeners'. Listeners may be added by implementing all the methods of an 'interface', but an alternative approach is to inherit from an 'adapter' class and only provide implementations for the methods we are interested in. Listeners can be separate classes or 'anonymous' classes.
- Layout managers: we have used a number of different layout managers to control the appearance of the components inside the frame.
- Model and view: we have seen that programs can consist of two levels, the model which is the underlying program logic, and the view which is the appearance and event handling in the GUI. It is always wise to separate these, rather than embedding all the program logic inside view classes.

We have looked at a great deal of syntax in this chapter, but perhaps the key elements are:

1. Writing a class that will display a window by inheriting from Frame, e.g.,

    ```
    public class FirstWindow extends Frame
    ```

2. Adding listeners to handle events, e.g.,

    ```
    addWindowListener(new MainWindowListener());
    ```

3. Setting the layout of a window, with setLayout, e.g.,

    ```
    setLayout(new FlowLayout());
    ```

4. Adding components with variations on the 'add' method, e.g.,

    ```
    add(text_label);
    ```

5. Sending messages to components, e.g.,

    ```
    computer_played.setText("rock");
    ```

In the next chapter we will continue to look at the AWT, exploring some other aspects including graphics, text styles and images, and look at handling events from menus and mice. We will also introduce a small element of file handling.

**EXERCISES**

**1** The FlowLayoutWindow uses the default version of the constructor that takes no parameters. Modify it to use the following constructor:

```
public FlowLayout(int align, int hgap, int vgap)
```

the align parameter can be FlowLayout.LEFT, FlowLayout.RIGHT or FlowLayout.CENTER. The other parameters (hgap and vgap) allow you to set the horizontal and vertical gaps between components. Experiment with these values to change the appearance of the window.

**2** The screen dump of Figure 8.11 shows a window containing labels, a text field and a text area, arranged in a right justified FlowLayout. Write a class to produce a similar output, then modify it so that no scroll bars appear in the text area.

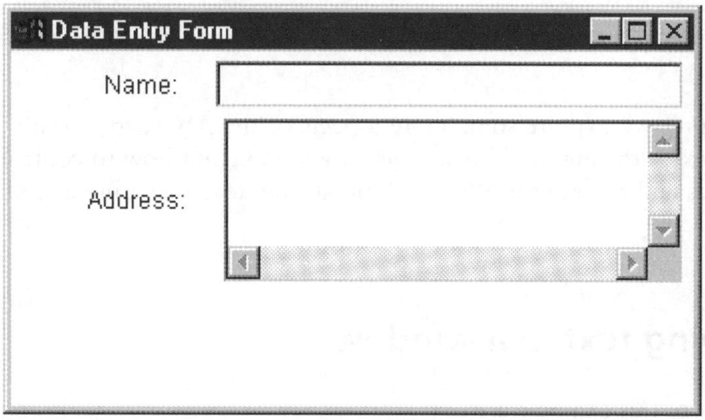

**Figure 8.11**   Text handling components in a FlowLayout.

**3** Modify the card layout example so that it starts at the last card rather than the first, and moves to the previous card when the button is pressed, rather than the next.

**4** Add four buttons and a label to a BorderLayout, with the label in the middle. When a button is pressed the label should display the text 'North', 'South', 'East' or 'West', depending on which of the four buttons has been pressed

**5** Write a RandomInteger class that returns a random integer when given a range, i.e., it has a method similar to:

```
getInteger(int lowest, int highest);
```

Implement this class using the Random class, then use it to rewrite the Dice class from Chapter four, replacing the existing algorithm based on Math.random.

**6** Modify the MileageTable so that it shows the distances in both miles and kilometres. One mile = 1.6093 kilometres.

**7** Modify RockPaperScissors so that the components are manually positioned in the window rather than using a layout manager.

# 9

# Of mice and menus

'The best laid schemes o' mice an' men gang aft a-gley' – Robert Burns (*To a Mouse*).

In this chapter we explore some more aspects of the AWT, specifically how to put graphical text, drawings and images into a window, and how to control a program using menus and the mouse. We also look at how text files can be read into a Java program.

## Displaying text in a window

Key aspects of this example are

- the 'paint' method
- the Graphics class
- displaying text with drawString.

When we are using the AWT to create a graphical user interface, any text that we want to display is graphical rather than character based. Therefore we use a different technique from that used with simple text-based applications. Text can be displayed inside a window using the drawString method of the Graphics class, one of many methods available for graphics output. Although it is possible to get a Graphics object reference using a method of 'Component', one is also automatically supplied as a parameter to the 'paint' method of 'Frame'. 'paint' is a method that is called automatically whenever the window needs to be redrawn by the system, for example, when the window first appears, or when it is minimised and then maximised again. We can provide our own version of 'paint' that uses the Graphics parameter object to display text in the window:

```
public void paint(Graphics g)
{
      g.drawString("This is graphical text in a window", 10, 50);
}
```

Note that there are three parameters to drawString, the text to be displayed, the x position of the text and the y position of the text, with the origin (where both x and

184

y are zero) in the top left-hand corner of the frame. It is important that the text is positioned far enough from the top of the frame to be visible, rather than being hidden under the title bar. This is the class, with a test 'main' in the same file (note that we import the MainWindowListener class from the javabook.chapter8 package).

```
/**
      TextView.java
      this class shows how text can be displayed in a window
*/
import java.awt.*;
import java.awt.event.*;
import javabook.chapter8.MainWindowListener;
// the 'Frame' class provides a basic window with a title bar
public class TextView extends Frame
{
// constructor
      public TextView()
      {
// add a window listener
            addWindowListener(new MainWindowListener());
      }
// in the 'paint' method, we write text onto the window
      public void paint(Graphics g)
      {
            g.drawString("This is graphical text in a window",
                  10, 50);
      }
// create an object
      public static void main(String args[])
      {
// call the constructor and add a window title
            TextView text_view = new TextView();
            text_view.setTitle("Text output window");
// set the initial size of the window
            text_view.setBounds(0, 0, 200, 100);
// display the window
            text_view.show();
      }
}
```

Figure 9.1 shows the window produced by this class.

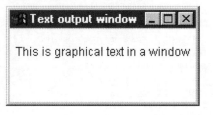

**Figure 9.1**   The output from the TextView class.

## Fonts and files

The default text font was used in our first example, but this can be changed using Font objects. We can also read text from file, to avoid large quantities of text being hard coded into a class. The next example uses file input as the source of its displayed text, with Font objects used to format its appearance.

Key aspects of this example are

- Font objects
- reading from file
- FileStreamReader and BufferedReader objects.

### Font objects

To change the text font, we can create a Font object. The constructor takes three parameters: the name of the font, the character style and the size. The possible font names are 'Serif', 'SansSerif', 'Monospaced', 'Dialog' and 'DialogInput'. The possible styles are 'Font.BOLD', 'Font.ITALIC' and 'Font.PLAIN'. BOLD and ITALIC can be combined (i.e., 'Font.BOLD + Font.ITALIC'). This example creates a bold sans serif font of size 20:

```
Font title_font = new Font("SansSerif", Font.BOLD, 20);
```

Once a font has been created, it can be passed to the 'setFont' method of the Graphics object, called 'g' in this example:

```
g.setFont(title_font);
```

Any subsequent text output with 'drawString' will then use this font.

### Reading from a text file

Our first example class put a small amount of text on the screen by hard-coding it as the parameter to drawString, but this is not a very flexible or scaleable approach. If we need to put a lot of text in a window, or want to change it, then it is better to store the text in a file and read it into the window for display. In this example, we assume that the following text file exists on disk, called 'PoemText.txt'

```
A Planet, derived from HeavenlyBody
the_earth, this object, this finite state
machine hasAir, hasWater, isBlue,
universal behaviours; orbit, rotate.

A generic container for dynamically bound
Life polymorphic of every class,
specialises, copies, generalises,
objects responding to messages passed.
```

```
Adam and Eve were our metadata,
Eve part of Adam, the rib aggregation.
We inherited the earth, and the method of the serpent
was knowledge, anApple (its instantiation)

Humanity's metaclass knows our numbers,
counting the transient human race.
A kind of Life, a part of persistence,
the cosmic object database.

Instantiated by the Big Constructor,
destroyed, deleted, memory reclaimed.
Falling from scope, garbage collected
among billions of stars, uncounted, unnamed.
```

File handling in Java is a big topic, so this example only touches on one aspect, namely reading in a pre-existing text file. To do this effectively, we use two classes from the 'java.io' package, namely FileReader (which is specifically designed to read data from text files) and BufferedReader (which works with a FileReader to provide simple methods for retrieving the file data). In the example class, we include references to objects of these classes as private attributes:

```
private FileReader poem_file;
private BufferedReader poem_reader;
```

In the 'paint' method, we create a FileReader object, passing the name of the file as its parameter:

```
poem_file = new FileReader("PoemText.txt");
```

The FileReader object is passed to the constructor of the BufferedReader, which is the object that we then send messages to:

```
poem_reader = new BufferedReader(poem_file);
```

This section of code must catch the possible 'FileNotFoundException', and stop processing if it occurs. Therefore a Boolean attribute ('file_opened') is used to indicate whether or not the exception is thrown. By using the condition 'if(file_opened)' we can ensure that we only attempt to read from the file if it has been opened successfully.

After two Font objects have been created and a title has been displayed (this is not read from file but provided as a parameter to a drawString message) the poem is read from the file one line at a time. We can read a single line of text with the readLine method of the BufferedReader class. This returns a String object containing the text:

```
text_line = poem_reader.readLine();
```

We continue reading lines in a while loop that is controlled by BufferedReader's 'ready' method. This returns a Boolean value, so when we have reached the end of file it will return 'false' and terminate the loop

```
while(poem_reader.ready())
{
      // etc..
```

This part of the code must catch a possible IOException, so is enclosed in a 'try' block. This is the complete class, including a test 'main':

```
/**
    FilePoemView.java
    this class shows how text can be read from a file and
    formatted in a window using some of Java's font settings
*/
import java.awt.*;
import java.awt.event.*;
import java.io.*;
import javabook.chapter8.MainWindowListener;
// the 'Frame' class provides a basic window with a title bar
public class FilePoemView extends Frame
{
// references to the FileReader and BufferedReader objects that
// we use to read strings from a text file
    private FileReader poem_file;
    private BufferedReader poem_reader;
// this attribute will tell us if we have opened the file
// successfully
    private boolean file_opened = false;
// constructor
    public FilePoemView()
    {
// add a window listener
        addWindowListener(new MainWindowListener());
    }
// in the 'paint' method, we write text onto the window by
// reading it from a file
    public void paint(Graphics g)
    {
// open the file (if possible) and create a BufferedReader from it
        try
        {
            poem_file = new FileReader("PoemText.txt");
            poem_reader = new BufferedReader(poem_file);
            file_opened = true;
        }
        catch(FileNotFoundException e)
        {
            g.drawString("unable to find file", 5, 35);
        }
// if the file was successfully opened, we can read from it
        if(file_opened)
        {
// two different font objects are created. the title font is
// sans serif bold, 20 point
            Font title_font = new Font("SansSerif", Font.BOLD,
                20);
// the font for the main text is serif italic, 15 point
            Font text_font = new Font("Serif", Font.ITALIC, 15);
```

```
// set the font using the 'setFont' method of the Graphics object
            g.setFont(title_font);
// draw the title on the window, indented by 10 and 40 down from
// the title bar (this is the position of the base of the text,
// not the top)
            g.drawString("It's An Object-Oriented[6] World", 10,
                40
// change the font for the main text
            g.setFont(text_font);
// write the lines of the poem. note that the vertical position
// of the lines is incremented using the 'y_value' variable, in
// this example it is initialised at 60 and incremented by 15 for
// each line.
            int y_value = 60;
// a String reference to get each line from the BufferedReader
            String text_line;
            try
            {
// 'ready' will return 'true' if there is more data to be read
                while(poem_reader.ready())
                {
// return a line of text as a String using the 'readLine' method
                    text_line = poem_reader.readLine();
// display the line and increment the y position by 15
                    g.drawString(text_line, 5, y_value);
                    y_value += 15;
                }
            }
            catch(IOException e)
            {
                g.drawString("no line available", 5, 35);
            }
        }
    }
// create an object
    public static void main(String args[])
    {
// call the constructor
        FilePoemView poem = new FilePoemView();
// set the initial size of the window
        poem.setBounds(0, 0, 500, 430);
// display the window
        poem.show();
    }
}
```

Figure 9.2 shows the text in the window, with the title in sans serif bold font and the main text in smaller serif italic. Note that the window has not been given a title so the title bar is blank.

# Displaying images

As well as text, other graphical output can be displayed in a window, including images loaded from file. Java can display either .GIF (Graphics Interchange Format)

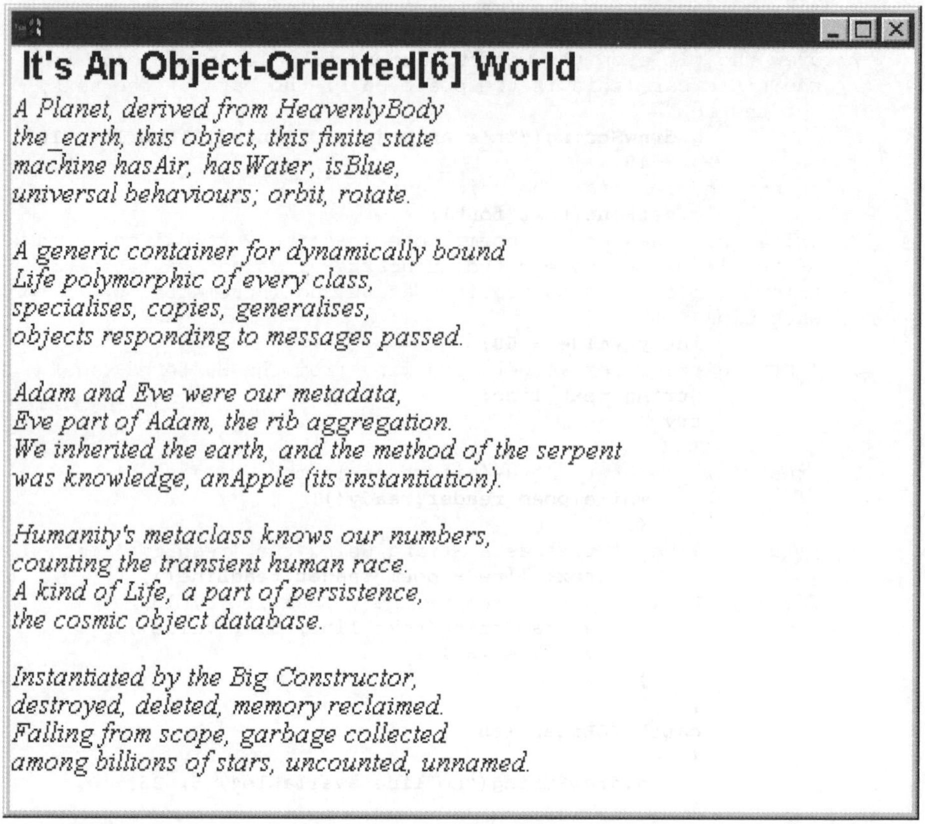

**Figure 9.2**    The output from the FilePoemView class.

or .JPG (JPEG – Joint Photographic Experts Group) files. In general terms, GIF files are used for line drawings and other images of up to 256 colours, whereas JPG files are sometimes better for photographs, though their quality depends on the extent of the compression used on the original image.

Key aspects of this example are

- displaying Image objects
- loading images with a Toolkit object
- the drawImage method
- using the 'this' keyword to provide an ImageObserver parameter.

Like the previous example this class relies on the existence of a suitable file, in this case an image of the Letts Educational logo that is freely available as a GIF file from the Letts website (www.lettsed.co.uk).

## Toolkit and Image objects

In order to load and manipulate images, some platform-specific processing is required behind the scenes. The class that handles this for us is the Toolkit (as in

Abstract Windowing Toolkit), which has a factory method to return an appropriate Toolkit object for our environment. The factory method is getDefaultToolkit:

```
Toolkit kit = Toolkit.getDefaultToolkit();
```

Once we have a Toolkit, we can use its getImage method to give us an Image object (from a given file name) that can be used to display images.

```
Image image = kit.getImage("lettsed.gif");
```

An Image can be displayed in a Frame using the drawImage method. The simplest version of drawImage takes the image object as its first parameter, its top-left corner coordinates as the second and third parameters and finally an ImageObserver object. ImageObserver is an interface that is implemented by Component, an implementation inherited by Frame. Therefore we can pass our Frame object as the final parameter. To get a reference to the current object (i.e., the one whose method we are currently in) we use the 'this' keyword:

```
g.drawImage(image, 50, 50, this);
```

This is the complete class including the test 'main':

```
/**
      PictureView.java
      this class shows how an image can be displayed in a window
*/
import java.awt.*;
import java.awt.event.*;
import javabook.chapter8.MainWindowListener;
// the 'Frame' class provides a basic window with a title bar
public class PictureView extends Frame
{
// constructor
      public PictureView()
      {
// add a window listener
            this.addWindowListener(new MainWindowListener());
      }
// in the 'paint' method, we display the image in the window
      public void paint(Graphics g)
      {
// the Toolkit class provide some simple image loading methods.
// it has a factory method to return a Toolkit object
            Toolkit kit = Toolkit.getDefaultToolkit();
// 'getImage' returns an Image object
            Image image = kit.getImage("lettsed.gif");
// the simplest version of 'drawImage' takes the image,
// its top left corner coordinates and an ImageObserver (this)
// as parameters
            g.drawImage(image, 50, 50, this);
      }
```

**Figure 9.3**   The output from the PictureView class that displays a GIF file in the main window.

```
// create an object
    public static void main(String args[])
    {
// call the constructor and set the window title
        PictureView pic = new PictureView();
        pic.setTitle("Picture Window");
// set the initial size of the window
        pic.setBounds(0, 0, 420, 280);
// display the window
        pic.show();
    }
}
```

Figure 9.3 shows the GIF file being displayed in the window.

## Adding panels to frames

All the AWT examples we have seen so far have comprised a window with a single drawing/writing/component space. However, this is not always flexible enough for building interfaces, and sometimes we need to divide up the window into separate areas that can have different roles. The next example gives some indication of how this can be done by adding separate panel objects to the window. A panel, like a frame, is a container that can be used for components and/or graphical output.

Key aspects of this example are

- subclassing Panel
- adding panels to a frame.

We can define any number of subclasses of Panel to manage different components or display graphical output. In this example, two separate subclasses (BookPanel and LogoPanel) are defined, though in fact they are identical except that they load different image files. LogoPanel loads the lettsed.gif file we have already seen. BookPanel loads another file available from the Letts website, book2.gif (the cover of *Object-Oriented Programming with C++*). Of course you can substitute other graphics files (in GIF or JPG format) if you have any available.

In practice, we would probably do something rather more interesting with the panels than just showing images, for example adding components to one of them to control events on the other. One example of this is to use components in one panel to manage a CardLayout in another panel.

Once the subclasses of Panel are defined, the main Frame constructor simply adds objects of these panels. The layout manager is disabled in this example, so setBounds is used to size the panels. Because the two panel classes are very simple and closely tied to the MultiPanel class they are put into the same source file, MultiPanel.java. This means that they cannot be declared public, since only one public class can appear in the file.

```java
/**
    MultiPanel.java
    this program shows how different images can be displayed on
    different panels, both within a window
*/
import java.awt.*;
import java.awt.event.*;
import javabook.chapter8.MainWindowListener;
class BookPanel extends Panel
{
    public void paint(Graphics g)
    {
// get a Toolkit
        Toolkit kit = Toolkit.getDefaultToolkit();
// get an Image
        Image image = kit.getImage("book2.gif");
// display the Image
        g.drawImage(image, 0, 0, this);
    }
}
class LogoPanel extends Panel
{
    public void paint(Graphics g)
    {
// get a Toolkit
        Toolkit kit = Toolkit.getDefaultToolkit();
// get an Image
        Image image = kit.getImage("lettsed.gif");
// display the Image
        g.drawImage(image, 0, 0, this);
    }
}
```

```
// the 'Frame' class provides a basic window with a title bar
public class MultiPanel extends Frame
{
        private BookPanel book_panel;
        private LogoPanel logo_panel;
// constructor
        public MultiPanel()
        {
// remove the default layout manager
                setLayout(null);
// cerate the Panel objects
                book_panel = new BookPanel();
                logo_panel = new LogoPanel();
                book_panel.setBounds(0, 0, 400, 240);
                logo_panel.setBounds(0, 240, 400, 400);
                add(book_panel);
                add(logo_panel);
// add a window listener
                addWindowListener(new MainWindowListener());
        }
// create an object
        public static void main(String args[])
        {
// call the constructor and set the window title
                MultiPanel page = new MultiPanel();
                page.setTitle("Multiple Image Panes");
// set the initial size of the window
                page.setBounds(0, 0, 500, 430);
// display the window
                page.show();
        }
}
```

Figure 9.4 shows the output from the program.

## A simple drawing program

The last example in this chapter is a larger set of classes that create a simple drawing window. Lines or rectangles can be drawn on the screen in different colours by selecting from menus and clicking and dragging with the mouse. The application classes in the system are:

- DrawingArea: a subclass of Canvas, a class that provides a general background for graphical output.
- DrawWindow: the main Frame window within which the DrawingArea appears.
- MenuListener: a class that implements the ActionListener interface to handle menu choices.
- DrawMouseListener: a listener class that handles mouse events.

Figure 9.5 shows these classes in a UML diagram with inheritance, aggregation and 'implements' relationships shown, along with the associations between the drawing window and its listeners (not all components are shown).

**Figure 9.4**    A window with two panels, each displaying a different image.

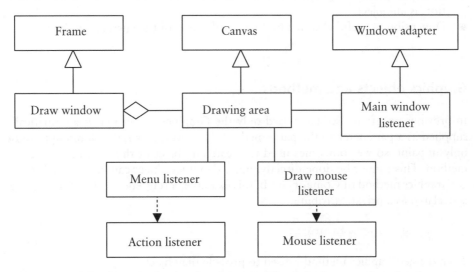

**Figure 9.5**    The classes in the drawing program. (The dashed arrows show 'implements' relationships)

Key aspects of this example are

- graphics methods
- mouse event listeners
- adding a menu to a window
- menu event listeners.

## A graphical drawing area

To draw graphical images, we need an appropriate class to provide an object on which to draw. To create a drawing area within the main window, we create a subclass of Canvas, which is a subclass of Component intended for just this kind of purpose:

```
class DrawingArea extends Canvas
{
// etc..
```

## Classes used for drawing

To draw shapes on the canvas we can use a number of objects. In this example we use:

- Graphics: a class that has many drawing methods, some of which we have already seen (e.g., drawString).
- Color: a class that allows us to change the current drawing colour.
- Point: not itself a graphical class, but one that makes it easy to store a screen location as an object.
- Dimension: a useful class for finding out the area of the current window.

## Graphics objects and methods

In previous programs, we have used only the Graphics object that is automatically supplied as a parameter to the paint method. However, it is rather limiting to draw only in paint, so we sometimes need to create an object of the class in some other method. This cannot be done directly, but a Graphics object can be returned by the getGraphics method of Component. In this example, a reference to a Graphics object is declared as a private attribute:

```
private Graphics graphics;
```

Then the getGraphics method is used to provide the object

```
graphics = getGraphics();
```

Once a Graphics object is available, there are many different methods for drawing with it. Ones used here are setColor(Color), drawLine and drawRect. In addition, we must dispose of the Graphics object when we have finished with it (in a similar way to disposing of a closing window in our window listener class) using the dispose method:

```
graphics.dispose();
```

## Color objects

The Color class provides objects that can be passed to the setColor method of Graphics to set the current drawing colour. This can be set using any of a number of constants ('final' public attributes) defined in the class, though the DrawingArea class does not directly set the colour of its own Color object since a parameter is passed to it via its own setColor method.

```
public void setColor(Color col)
{
      colour = col;
}
```

## Point and Dimension classes

These classes provide a way of storing and accessing information about the position and size of objects. The Point class has public x and y attributes that are easily accessed to store the position (in this example) of mouse clicks, passed to this class via parameters to setStart and setEnd, representing the start and end points of different shapes. This is the setStart method where start_point is a Point attribute that can store this position until it is required for drawing.

```
public void setStart(Point start)
{
      start_point = start;
}
```

Along with start_point, another Point attribute called 'end_point' is used to draw shapes, for example, in the method that draws a line between two points represented by four integers:

```
graphics.drawLine(start_point.x, start_point.y, end_point.x,
end_point.y);
```

A Dimension object can be used to find the size of a Component, since one is returned from the getSize method. Its public attributes 'width' and 'height' can then be retrieved. In the example program, these values are used to draw a rectangle within the window frame:

```
Dimension d = getSize();
int width = d.width - 5;
int height = d.height - 5;
g.drawRect(2, 2, width, height);
```

The rest of the code in DrawingArea is concerned with performing different actions depending on the state of various Boolean attributes. These are set by methods of the class called from outside. This is the complete class:

```
class DrawingArea extends Canvas
{
// a reference to a Graphics object
        private Graphics graphics;
// these boolean variables are used when drawing different shapes
// so we know if we are waiting for the mouse button to be released
// to complete a shape
        private boolean line_draw = false;
        private boolean rectangle_draw = false;
// the 'Point' objects are used to store the mouse positions that
// define an object's size and position
        private Point start_point;
        private Point end_point;
// this attribute holds the current colour value
        private Color colour;
// set the start position of a shape
        public void setStart(Point start)
        {
                start_point = start;
        }
// set the end position of a shape
        public void setEnd(Point end)
        {
// the 'getGraphics' method returns the current graphics object
// being used by this component (i.e. this 'Canvas' subclass).we
// cannot simply instantiate a 'Graphics' object because it is
// an abstract class
                graphics = getGraphics();
// set the current colour
                graphics.setColor(colour);
                end_point = end;
// draw a line
                if(line_draw)
                {
// 'drawLine' needs the start and end co-ordinates as parameters
                        graphics.drawLine(start_point.x, start_point.y,
                        end_point.x, end_point.y);
                        line_draw = false;
                }
// draw a rectangle
                if(rectangle_draw)
                {
// 'drawRect' needs the co-ordinates of the start point along
// with the width and height of the rectangle as parameters.
// therefore a bit of arithmetic is called for to calculate the
// width and height as the difference between the first and
```

```
// second mouse positions. to keep the sums simple, this
// algorithm does not work unless the second position is lower
// down and to the right of the first
                    int rwidth = end_point.x - start_point.x;
                    int rheight = end_point.y - start_point.y;
                    graphics.drawRect(start_point.x, start_point.y,
                    rwidth, rheight);
                    rectangle_draw = false;
            }
// having drawn the shape, dispose of the graphics object
            graphics.dispose();
        }
// the 'paint' method draws the screen
        public void paint(Graphics g)
        {
// draw a rectangle round the initial window area
            Dimension d = getSize();
            int width = d.width - 5;
            int height = d.height - 5;
            g.drawRect(2, 2, width, height);
        }
        public void drawLine()
        {
            line_draw = true;
        }
        public void drawRectangle()
        {
            rectangle_draw = true;
        }
        public void drawOval()
        {
            // not yet implemented
        }
        public void setColor(Color col)
        {
// set the drawing colour to that provided by this method's
// parameter
            colour = col;
        }
    }
```

## Adding a menu to a Frame

To control events on our drawing area, we will put it inside a window that has menus
and captures mouse events. To add a menu to a Frame, we use three classes: MenuItem,
MenuBar and Menu. A MenuItem is one selection from a menu, and is created using a
constructor that takes the text label of the item as its parameter. For example, there is
a menu for selecting the current drawing colour in the system that consists of three
menu items, declared as private attributes so that they can be used with event listeners:

```
private MenuItem red = new MenuItem("Red");
private MenuItem blue = new MenuItem("Blue");
private MenuItem green = new MenuItem("Green");
```

There is also a set of items for the menu that chooses which shape to draw. These menu items have to be added to Menu objects, so these are also created. Like menu items, their constructor takes their text label as a parameter:

```
Menu drawing_menu = new Menu("Drawing Menu");
Menu colour_menu = new Menu("Colour menu");
```

To add a MenuItem to a particular menu, we use the 'add' method of the Menu object, for example:

```
colour_menu.add(red);
```

This adds the MenuItem 'red' to the 'colour_menu'. All the other menu items are added to the appropriate menu in this way. Once a menu is complete, it has to be placed in a menu bar that must be added to the Frame. We can create a MenuBar with a simple constructor:

```
MenuBar menu_bar = new MenuBar();
```

The menus can be added to the menu bar, using MenuBar's 'add' method

```
menu_bar.add(drawing_menu);
menu_bar.add(colour_menu);
```

When the menu bar is complete, it can be added to the Frame using the 'setMenuBar' method

```
setMenuBar(menu_bar);
```

The menus will now automatically appear when selected. Figure 9.6 shows the drawing menu.

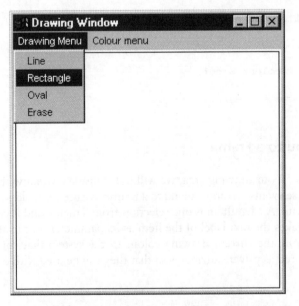

**Figure 9.6**   The drawing menu of the DrawWindow class.

However, nothing will actually happen unless we add an appropriate listener object to each of the MenuItems. As we did for Button objects in the last chapter, we must add an 'ActionListener' to the MenuItems. However, the implementation here is a little more complex. When adding listeners for buttons, we used 'anonymous classes' to enable easy access to the attributes of the class. In this example we see an alternative strategy, which is to keep the listener as a separate class as we did previously for the window listeners. This is helpful in terms of keeping our classes manageable, but adds the problem of visibility. If the listener is not inside the class, then it cannot directly access the attributes of the class, so we need to pass any appropriate objects as parameters to our listener. Since ActionListeners do not by default take parameters, we need to implement the ActionListener interface to create our own class that will take a parameter to its constructor. This parameter is an object of class DrawingArea, the class that will receive messages about what to draw:

```
class MenuListener implements ActionListener
{
      private DrawingArea drawing;
      public MenuListener(DrawingArea draw)
      {
            drawing = draw;
      }
//etc.
```

By writing this constructor, we now have a means of passing a reference to our drawing area to the event handlers for the menu items. When we add the ActionListeners to the MenuItems we use a MenuListener as the parameter along with the reference to the drawing area object, as in this example where an action listener is added to the 'red' menu item:

```
red.addActionListener(new MenuListener(drawing_area));
```

The MenuListener responds to different menu choices by getting the text label of the menu choice from the getActionCommand method of the event object:

```
String command = e.getActionCommand();
```

The string returned from this method can then be used in selection statements to choose the appropriate course of action, e.g.,

```
if(command == "Line")
{
      drawing.drawLine();
}
```

Most of the actions of the MenuListener class are to send messages to the DrawingArea object. When it sets the colour, it uses constants from the Color class, e.g.,

```
drawing.setColor(Color.red);
```

There are thirteen of these constants, namely black, blue, cyan, darkGray, gray, green, lightGray, magenta, orange, pink, red, white and yellow.

The class also uses the 'repaint' method to clear the window. 'repaint' actually calls the 'paint' method, so only clears the screen because we have not provided an alternative version of 'paint' to do anything else.

This is the complete 'MenuListener' class:

```
class MenuListener implements ActionListener
{
        private DrawingArea drawing;
        public MenuListener(DrawingArea draw)
        {
                drawing = draw;
        }
        public void actionPerformed(ActionEvent e)
        {
                String command = e.getActionCommand();
                if(command == "Line")
                {
                        drawing.drawLine();
                }
                if(command == "Rectangle")
                {
                        drawing.drawRectangle();
                }
                if(command == "Erase")
                {
                        drawing.repaint();
                }
                if(command == "Red")
                {
                        drawing.setColor(Color.red);
                }
                if(command == "Blue")
                {
                        drawing.setColor(Color.blue);
                }
        }
}
```

## Mouse listeners

As well as responding to choices made through menus, we also need to be able to respond to the mouse when it is drawing on the window. Therefore we need to add a class to implement the MouseListener interface. In this example, we provide implementations for 'mousePressed' (to get the start position of a shape) and 'mouseReleased' (to get the end position of a shape). The event object provides some useful methods, such as 'getX' and 'getY', that give us the position of the mouse when the event occurs. Also 'getSource', which gives us a reference to the object that received the mouse event. We can cast this to the appropriate DrawingArea class:

```
DrawingArea draw = (DrawingArea)event.getSource();
```

Then we are able to send messages to the DrawingArea object from the mouse listener methods.

Like the Window listener classes, there is an adapter class that we could extend instead of having to provide the three empty methods required by the interface class. This is the complete DrawMouseListener class:

```
class DrawMouseListener implements MouseListener
{
        public void mouseEntered(MouseEvent event) {}
        public void mouseExited(MouseEvent event) {}
        public void mouseClicked(MouseEvent event) {}
        public void mousePressed(MouseEvent event)
        {
                Point start_point = new Point(event.getX(),
                        event.getY());
                DrawingArea draw = (DrawingArea)event.getSource();
                draw.setStart(start_point);
        }
        public void mouseReleased(MouseEvent event)
        {
                Point end_point = new Point(event.getX(),
                        event.getY());
                DrawingArea draw = (DrawingArea)event.getSource();
                draw.setEnd(end_point);
        }
}
```

These three classes support the functionality of the 'DrawWindow' class, which provides the main window with its menus. Most of the code in this class is concerned with adding menus and event listeners to the window, as well as the DrawingArea object. All the run time processing actually takes place in the other objects. This is the only public class in the system, since the others exist purely to service its requirements and have little use in other applications.

```
/**
        DrawWindow.java
        a simple mouse driven drawing program
*/
import java.awt.*;
import java.awt.event.*;
import javabook.chapter8.MainWindowListener;
public class DrawWindow extends Frame
{
// decare the menu items
        private MenuItem line_choice = new MenuItem("Line");
        private MenuItem rectangle_choice = new
                MenuItem("Rectangle");
        private MenuItem oval_choice = new MenuItem("Oval");
        private MenuItem erase = new MenuItem("Erase");
        private MenuItem red = new MenuItem("Red");
        private MenuItem blue = new MenuItem("Blue");
        private MenuItem green = new MenuItem("Green");
// instantiate a new DrawingArea object (derived from 'Canvas')
        private DrawingArea drawing_area;
```

```
// the DrawWindow constructor
    public DrawWindow()
    {
// set up the menu bar
        MenuBar menu_bar = new MenuBar();
// set up two menus
        Menu drawing_menu = new Menu("Drawing Menu");
        Menu colour_menu = new Menu("Colour menu");
// add the options to the drawing menu
        drawing_menu.add(line_choice);
        drawing_menu.add(rectangle_choice);
        drawing_menu.add(oval_choice);
        drawing_menu.add(erase);
// add the options to the colour menu
        colour_menu.add(red);
        colour_menu.add(blue);
        colour_menu.add(green);
// add the menus to the menu bar
        menu_bar.add(drawing_menu);
        menu_bar.add(colour_menu);
// add the menu bar to the window
        setMenuBar(menu_bar);
// create the drawing area
        drawing_area = new DrawingArea();
// add the action listeners to the menu items
        line_choice.addActionListener(new
            MenuListener(drawing_area));
        rectangle_choice.addActionListener(new
            MenuListener(drawing_area));
        erase.addActionListener(new MenuListener(drawing_area));
        red.addActionListener(new MenuListener(drawing_area));
        blue.addActionListener(new MenuListener(drawing_area));
// add a mouse listener to the drawing area
        drawing_area.addMouseListener(new DrawMouseListener());
// add the drawing canvas
        add(drawing_area);
// add a listener to close the window
        addWindowListener(new MainWindowListener());
    }
// the main method starts the program running
    public static void main(String args[])
    {
        DrawWindow window = new DrawWindow();
        window.setTitle("Drawing Window");
        window.setBounds(100,100,300, 300);
        window.show();
    }
}
```

Figure 9.7 shows the drawing window in action.

As it stands, the program is still very crude and incomplete, but it demonstrates the basic principles of handling graphics, menus and mice in Java.

**Figure 9.7** Some lines and rectangles in the mouse-driven drawing application.

## Summary

In this chapter we have explored some features of the AWT that allow us to draw in a window, and to manage events from menus and mice. We have also learned how to read text from a file. To do this we have used:

- Graphics: a class that has many methods for drawing
- menu event listeners: classes that respond to menu choices
- mouse event listeners: classes that respond to mouse events
- classes for handling input file streams containing text.

Some of the key elements of syntax covered in this chapter were

1. Methods of the 'Graphics' class. These included output methods like 'drawString', 'drawRect' and 'drawImage' as well as 'setFont'. We saw that a Graphics object is provided as a parameter to the 'paint' method, but can also be retrieved from a Component object using 'getGraphics' e.g.,

    ```
    Graphics g = getGraphics();
    ```

    A Graphics object is also used in conjunction with the 'Toolkit' class to load and display images.

2. Reading text files. The 'InputStreamReader' class can be used to open a text file for input. This object can then be passed to the constructor of a 'Buffered Reader' object which has a simple 'readLine' method for reading in a line of text from a file:

    ```
    text_line = poem_reader.readLine();
    ```

3. Handling menus. Menus consist of MenuItem objects added to a Menu object. This in turn is added to a MenuBar that can be added to a Frame. To respond to a menu choice, we must implement the ActionListener interface to listen to menu choices. The menu choice selected can be detected within the listener class by the getActionCommand method:

```
public void actionPerformed(ActionEvent e)
{
        String command = e.getActionCommand();
```

4. Handling mouse events: to handle mouse events we implement the MouseListener interface, where we can respond to events such as the mouse button being pressed. Methods of the mouse event give us useful information, for example the position of the mouse:

```
Point start_point = new Point(event.getX(), event.getY());
```

## EXERCISES

**1** Modify the FilePoemView class so that it reads the poem title from the file. This will also require modification of the PoemText.txt data file.

**2** Create a class that writes a text file. You can do this by creating an object of the 'FileWriter' class. Use the following constructor:

```
public FileWriter(String filename) throws IOException
```

You can send data to the file using the 'write' method, followed by 'flush'. No data will actually appear in the file until after the flush method has been called:

```
public void write(String str)
public void flush()throws IOException
```

You can either 'hard-code' the text for test purposes or enter it at the keyboard.

**3** Write a class that can read your text file and display its contents in a window. Experiment with Font objects to change its appearance.

**4** Modify your file reading class so that the name of the file to be read can be passed as a parameter to main. Add in the ability to count the number of words in the file and display the total in the window. You can adapt the WordCounter class from Chapter five, since BufferedReader has a similar read method to System.in. Test your class with a number of different text files.

**5** Modify the classes in the MultiPanel example so that one panel shows a different image and the other shows some text loaded from a file.

**6** Write two subclasses of Panel that contain some of the Component objects from the previous chapter (e.g., Buttons, Labels, etc.). Use different layout managers for the two panels, including one CardLayout. Use the components on the other panel to cycle through the cards on the card layout.

**7** The DrawingArea class is incomplete. Implement the 'oval' menu option using the Graphics method:

```
void drawOval(int x, int y, int width, int height);
```

Implement the 'green' colour choice using Color.green. Add new options to the menus to change the colour to other constants from the Color class and draw a rounded rectangle using:

```
drawRoundRect(int x, int y, int width, int height, int arcwidth,
int archeight)
```

**Part 5**

# Java and the web

# 10

# Interfaces and threads

'Nothing in the world is single, all things by a law divine in one another's being mingle'
– Shelley (*Love's Philosophy*).

We have already seen that interfaces are used in Java to define a set of methods that can be implemented by other classes. Our AWT programs used various event listener interfaces, and we provided some method implementations to, for example, close the main window and respond to a mouse button press. In this chapter we will investigate how to write our own interfaces, as well as implementing another Java interface called 'Runnable'.

One of the unusual features of Java is that it allows us to write programs with multiple threads. Many programming languages run with a single thread of control, meaning that the program can do only one thing at a time. A multithreaded language allows programs to do more than one thing at the same time, to perform multiple tasks concurrently. In practice, of course, most computers can still only perform one task at a time, but it can appear as if they are performing different tasks simultaneously by swapping between them at high speed. As a traditional mainframe computer can have many terminals connected to it at the same time, a single Java program can have many threads running at once.

In this chapter we will begin by looking at the syntax for writing and using interfaces. Then we will look at threads, first creating and running a single thread of control and then looking at how programs can be multithreaded to perform more than one task simultaneously. Multithreaded programs can be written using either inheritance (inheriting from class Thread) or by implementing the Runnable interface. Our final example will draw interfaces and threads together by creating multithreaded objects that implement this interface.

## Writing interfaces

It is actually very simple to write an interface class, since it is almost exactly the same as writing an ordinary class except that we use the keyword 'interface' instead of 'class', and the methods have no definition.

Key aspects of this example are

● writing an interface
● implementing an interface
● creating objects using interface references.

The interface we are going to use for this example is called 'Displayable', and declares a single method called 'display'. The interface declaration is simply the keyword 'interface' followed by the interface name and the declaration of the method:

```
/**
     Displayable.java
     an example of a programmer-defined interface
     that other classes can implement
*/
import java.awt.*;
public interface Displayable
{
     void display(Component c);
}
```

The idea of this interface is that any class that implements it can display itself on a Component object (or any derived class of Component such as Frame) passed as a parameter. An interface makes no other assumptions about the class, which can have many other methods not related to implementing the display method. However, in our example we will provide only the necessary method to implement the interface. We will write two different classes, both implementing 'Displayable'. The first is TextDisplay, a class that displays a line of text (passed to its constructor) when its display method is called. It uses the getGraphics method to get a Graphics object from the Component parameter to the display method, then displays the text using drawString:

```
/**
     TextDisplay.java
     this class implements the 'Displayable' interface by
     displaying a string of text on a 'Component' object
*/
import java.awt.*;
public class TextDisplay implements Displayable
{
// a String reference to store the text
     private String text;
// the constructor is passed the text to be displayed
     public TextDisplay(String text_in)
     {
          text = text_in;
     }
// implement the 'display' method
     public void display(Component c)
     {
// get a Graphics object from the Component parameter
          Graphics g = c.getGraphics();
```

```
// display the text
          g.drawString(text, 100, 50);
// dispose of the Graphics resource
          g.dispose();
      }
  }
```

The other class is called 'PictureDisplay', and displays an image on the Component passed to its display method. Using syntax familiar from the previous chapter, it uses a Toolkit object to load an image and then displays it using the Graphics drawImage method:

```
/**
       PictureDisplay.java
       this class implements the 'Displayable' interface
       by showing an image
*/
import java.awt.*;
public class PictureDisplay implements Displayable
{
// an 'Image' reference to display an image file
     private Image picture;
// implement the 'display' method
     public void display(Component c)
     {
// use a Toolkit object to get the Image
          Toolkit kit = Toolkit.getDefaultToolkit();
          picture = kit.getImage("lettsed.gif");
// get a Graphics object from the Component parameter
          Graphics g = c.getGraphics ();
// use the Graphics and Component objects as parameters to
// 'drawImage'
          g.drawImage(picture, 0, 100, c);
// dispose of the Graphics resource
          g.dispose();
     }
}
```

## Creating objects with interface references

When we looked at inheritance, we saw that it was possible to use a reference to a superclass to create objects of subclasses. In Chapter seven, references of the 'IDCardBase' class were used to create objects of the StaffID2 and VisitorID2 classes. We can do something very similar with interface references, so we can for example create a PictureDisplay object using a Displayable reference:

```
Displayable pic = new PictureDisplay();
```

We can then send the display message via the reference to the object (where 'this' is a Component object):

```
pic.display(this);
```

The TestInterface class uses references of the Displayable interface to create objects of the TextDisplay and PictureDisplay classes and send them both a display message. Since it inherits from Frame, it can be passed as the Component parameter to the method:

```
/**
    TestInterface.java
    this class tests objects of classes that implement
    the 'Displayable' interface
*/
import java.awt.*;
import java.awt.event.*;
import javabook.chapter8.MainWindowListener;
// 'Displayable' objects need to be passed some kind of Component
// as a parameter. in this example, it is a subclass of 'Frame'
public class TestInterface extends Frame
{
// the constructor adds a window listener
    public TestInterface()
    {
        addWindowListener(new MainWindowListener());
    }
// 'paint' displays 'Displayable' objects
    public void paint(Graphics g)
    {
// create a 'PictureDisplay' object
        Displayable pic = new PictureDisplay();
// call its 'display' method, passing the Frame as the parameter
        pic.display(this);
// create a 'TextDisplay' object
        Displayable text = new TextDisplay("Letts Educational");
// call its 'display' method
        text.display(this);
    }
// in 'main' create a 'TestInterface' object and show it
    public static void main(String args[])
    {
        TestInterface ti = new TestInterface();
        ti.setTitle("Testing the \"Displayable\" interface");
        ti.setBounds(0,0,400,300);
        ti.show();
    }
}
```

Figure 10.1 shows the output from this class, with both objects displaying within the window frame.

## Interfaces v. inheritance

Given that we could achieve a very similar result with both interfaces and inheritance, what is the advantage of using an interface? In fact there are some important differences.

**Figure 10.1**   TextDisplay and PictureDisplay objects implementing the Displayable interface.

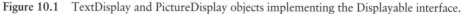

- A class can only inherit from one superclass, but can implement more than one interface.
- A class can both extend a superclass and implement one or more interfaces.
- Implementing an interface does not imply any close relationship between classes, unlike inheritance.

When we want to create a collection of closely related classes that share some behaviours, then we should use inheritance. However, if we only want a collection of objects to be able to perform some common tasks, such as being displayed, or writing themselves to a file, then using an interface is a better strategy. Since Java does not allow multiple inheritance (where classes can have more than one superclass) there are occasions when using an interface is the only possible strategy.

## Threads

It is important to understand something about threads in Java, not because we will necessarily want to run multithreaded programs but because applets (which we look at in the next chapter) use threads to run themselves. Although there are many important aspects of threads not covered in this chapter, we will look at some of their fundamental characteristics and methods.

Key aspects of this example are

- extending the Thread class
- the Thread constructor
- the 'getName', 'run', 'sleep' and 'start' methods of Thread.

## Creating and running a thread object

The first thread example is a class that uses a single thread of control. Running a program with a single thread object does not look very different from a program with no declared threads, but this example introduces some important syntax. In the program, a thread describes the journey of a tortoise. One way to use threads in a Java program is to create a class that inherits from the Thread class and can therefore use its public methods. In this case, class Tortoise inherits from (extends) Thread. It calls the superclass constructor to set the name of the thread, which can be returned using the getName method. The method of Thread that Tortoise overrides is called 'run', and this describes what happens when a particular thread is running. In this case, not a lot actually happens, except that the tortoise slowly travels ten metres. The journey is slowed using the thread method 'sleep' that stops the thread executing for a given number of milliseconds. 'sleep' demands that it is used with an exception handler for InterruptedException, hence the 'try/catch' block in the code. When the 'run' method finishes, the thread dies (hopefully the tortoise lives on of course). This example is not graphical so the output is displayed using 'System.out'.

```java
/**
    Tortoise.java
    a class that inherits from 'Thread'
*/
public class Tortoise extends Thread
{
// set the name of the thread in the constructor
    public Tortoise(String name)
    {
        super(name);
    }
// override the 'run' method to provide the behaviour of the
// thread
    public void run()
    {
// local variable to store a random waiting time
        int sleepy_time;
// loop ten times (the tortoise travels ten metres)
        for(int i = 0; i < 10; i++)
        {
// use 'getName' to display the name of the thread
            System.out.println(getName() + " has gone " +
                i + " metres");
// generate a random delay
            sleepy_time = (int)(Math.random() * 1000);
// 'sleep' for the specified time
            try
            {
                sleep(sleepy_time);
            }
            catch(InterruptedException e)
            {
                System.out.println("Interrupted");
            }
        }
```

```
                System.out.println(getName() + " has finished!");
        }
    }
```

The WalkingTortoise class makes a tortoise and sets it off using the 'start' method of Thread. 'start' indirectly calls the 'run' method.

```
/**
        WalkingTortoise.java
        a class that tests the Tortoise thread class
*/
public class WalkingTortoise
{
        public static void main(String args[])
        {
// create a 'Tortoise' object
                Tortoise racing_tortoise = new Tortoise("Tortoise");
// use its 'start' method to make its thread run
                racing_tortoise.start();
        }
}
```

Running this class produces (rather slowly!) the following output:

```
Tortoise has gone 0 metres
Tortoise has gone 1 metres
Tortoise has gone 2 metres
Tortoise has gone 3 metres
Tortoise has gone 4 metres
Tortoise has gone 5 metres
Tortoise has gone 6 metres
Tortoise has gone 7 metres
Tortoise has gone 8 metres
Tortoise has gone 9 metres
Tortoise has finished!
```

# Multithreading

Using the syntax described above, we can create an object of a class derived from Thread and set it running. It is a simple step to move to a program that has more than one thread, i.e., that is multithreaded.

The key aspect of this example is declaring multiple thread objects. The main reason for starting with a tortoise in the first example was to use it as a basis for this program, 'the tortoise and the hare' (Figure 10.2).

You will no doubt be familiar with the fable about the race between the tortoise and the hare, where the hare was so overconfident of victory that he fell asleep half way through the race and lost as a result. This program simulates that race by sending the hare thread to sleep for rather a long time. The Hare class extends Thread, and contains a very crude 'run' method that slows the journey of the hare with a very long sleep between the top of the hill and the finish line.

**Figure 10.2**   The tortoise and the hare run their race concurrently but with different behaviours, rather like separate threads.

```
/**
    Hare.java
    a subclass of Thread
*/
public class Hare extends Thread
{
// the constructor sets the name of the thread
    public Hare(String name)
    {
        super(name);
    }
// the 'run' method displays the journey of the hare
    public void run()
    {
        System.out.println(getName() + " has started racing");
// a short time to get to the oak tree..
        try
        {
            sleep(1000);
        }
        catch(InterruptedException e)
        {
            System.out.println("Interrupted");
        }
        System.out.println(getName() +
            " has passed the oak tree");
// a short time to get to the top of the hill
        try
        {
            sleep(1000);
        }
        catch(InterruptedException e)
        {
            System.out.println("Interrupted");
        }
        System.out.println(getName() +
        " is at the top of the hill (and has fallen asleep)");
// falls asleep for a long time
        try
        {
            sleep(20000);
        }
```

```
                catch(InterruptedException e)
                {
                        System.out.println("Interrupted");
                }
// gets to the end (after the tortoise, probably)
                System.out.println(getName() + " has finished!");
        }
}
```

The tortoise takes longer as a rule to get between landmarks, but does not fall asleep on the final stretch so gets to the end quicker overall. This is a different class from the previous Tortoise, so is called 'RacingTortoise':

```
/**
        RacingTortoise.java
        a subclass of Thread
*/
public class RacingTortoise extends Thread
{
        public RacingTortoise(String name)
        {
                super(name);
        }
// 'run' displays the journey of the tortoise
        public void run()
        {
// slow but steady progress to the oak tree
                System.out.println(getName() +
                        " has started racing");
                try
                {
                        sleep(5000);
                }
                catch(InterruptedException e)
                {
                        System.out.println("Interrupted");
                }
                System.out.println(getName() +
                        " has passed the oak tree");
// slow but steady progress to the top of the hill
                try
                {
                        sleep(5000);
                }
                catch(InterruptedException e)
                {
                        System.out.println("Interrupted");
                }
                System.out.println(getName() +
                        " is at the top of the hill");
// slow but steady progress to the chequered flag
                try
                {
                        sleep(5000);
                }
```

```
                catch(InterruptedException e)
                {
                        System.out.println("Interrupted");
                }
                System.out.println(getName() + " has finished!");
        }
}
```

In 'TheTortoiseAndTheHare', both animals start at (more or less) the same time, but the tortoise wins.

```
/**
        TheTortoiseAndTheHare.java
        demonstrates two threads running concurrently
*/
public class TheTortoiseAndTheHare
{
        public static void main(String args[])
        {
// create two separate thread objects (a tortoise and a hare)
                Hare racing_hare = new Hare("Hare");
                RacingTortoise racing_tortoise =
                        newRacingTortoise("Tortoise");
// start them both racing
                racing_hare.start();
                racing_tortoise.start();
        }
}
```

The story unfolds slowly at run time:

```
Tortoise has started racing
Hare has started racing
Hare has passed the oak tree
Hare is at the top of the hill (and has fallen asleep)
Tortoise has passed the oak tree
Tortoise is at the top of the hill
Tortoise has finished!
Hare has finished!
```

## Thread priority

We have seen from the previous example that a program can have more than one thread running at the same time. One issue that arises is what happens if two threads want to access the same program resources at the same time. Multithreading appears to be handling different tasks in parallel, but in fact the system is invisibly choosing between them so there is potential for conflict. Different Java implementations can have different ways of handling two threads competing for the same resource but the programmer also has some influence. Different threads can be provided with different priorities, ensuring that a high-priority thread can be guaranteed more access to processing time than a low-priority thread.

Key aspects of this example are

● the setPriority method
● the priority constants in the Thread class.

## Setting thread priority

In the next example program, we compare the priority of bees and a bear when accessing a honeycomb. Since a bear is much larger than a bee and impervious to stings, it has a higher priority for eating honeycomb.

The bees are a thread, and given the chance will spend all their time buzzing round the honeycomb. However, as we will see, the bees will be given a lower thread priority than the bear.

```java
/**
        Bees.java
        A simple thread class
*/
public class Bees extends Thread
{
        public Bees(String name)
        {
                super(name);
        }
// the bees buzz around their honey all the time, but can be
// interrupted by the bear who has a higher priority
        public void run()
        {
                for(int i = 0; i < 1000; i++)
                {
                        System.out.print("z");
                }
        }
}
```

The bear is also a thread but spends more time asleep than looking for honey, however, it does occasionally wake up and go looking for lunch.

```java
/**
        Bear.java
        a simple thread class
*/
public class Bear extends Thread
{
        public Bear(String name)
        {
                super(name);
        }
        public void run()
        {
// the bear sleeps at first
                try
                {
```

```
                        sleep(1000);
                }
                catch(InterruptedException e)
                {
                        System.out.println("Interrupted");
                }
// when it wakes up, it goes straight for the honey. because it
// has a higher priority than the bees, they have to stop until
// the bear has finished
                System.out.println("Mmmmmm, honey, yum yum!");
        }
}
```

In this class, the priorities of the bear and bee threads are set using the setPriority method. The bees have the lowest possible priority (MIN_PRIORITY), whereas the bear has the highest (MAX_PRIORITY). These constants are public final attributes of the Thread class, so are invoked using the class name (e.g., Thread.MAX_PRIORITY). In resource competition with the bear, the bees stand no chance.

```
/**
        BearBeesAndHoney.java
        this class sets the priority of running threads
*/
public class BearBeesAndHoney
{
        public static void main(String args[])
        {
// the bees have minimum priority
                Bees honey_bees = new Bees("Honey bees");
                honey_bees.setPriority(Thread.MIN_PRIORITY);
// the bear has maximum priority
                Bear hungry_bear = new Bear("Hungry bear");
                hungry_bear.setPriority(Thread.MAX_PRIORITY);
                honey_bees.start();
                hungry_bear.start();
        }
}
```

The output from this program is rather unpredictable, depending on the relative speed of the 'for' loop, suffice to say that at some point the bear should get its nose in the honey:

```
zzzzzzzzzzzzzzzzzzzzzzzzzzzzzzzzzzzzzzzzzzzzzzzzzzzzzzzzzzzzzzzzzzzz
zzzzzzzzzzzzzzzzzzzzzzzzzzzzzzzzzzzzzzzzzzzzzzzzzzzzzzzzzzzzzzzzzzzz
zzzzzzzzzzzzzzzzzzzzzzzzzzzzzzzzzzzzzzzzzzzzzzzzzzzzzzzzzzzzzzzzzzzz
zzzzzzzzzzzzzzzzzzzzzzzzzzzzzzzzzzzzzzzzzzzzzzzzzzzzzzzzzzzzzzzzzzzz
zzzzzzzzzzzzzzzzzzzzzzzzzzzzzzzzzzzzzzzzzzzzzzzzzzzzzzzzzzzzzzzzzzzz
zzzzzzzzzzzzzzzzzzzzzzzzzzzzzzzzzzzzzzzzzzzzzzzzzzzzzzzzzzzzzzzzzzzz
zzzzzzzzzzzzzzzzzzzzzzzzzzzzzzzzzzzzzzzzzzzzzzzzzzzzzzzzzzzzzzzzzzzz
zzzzzzzzzzzzzzzzzzzzzzzzzzzzzzzzzzzzzzzzzzzzzzzzzzzzzzzzzzzzzzzzzzzz
zzzzzzzzzzzzzzzzzzzzzzzzzzzzzzzzzzzzzzzzzzzzzzzzzzzzzzzzzzzzzzzzzzzz
zzzzzzzzzzzzzzzzzzzzzzzzzzzzzzzzzzzzzzzzzzzzzzzzzzzzzzzzzzzzzzzzzzzz
zzzzzzzzzzzzzzzzzzzzzzzzzzzzzzzzzzzzzzzzzzzzzzzzzzzzzzzzzzzzzzzzzzzz
zzzzzzzzzzzzzzzzzzzzzzzzzzzzzzzzzzzzzzzzzzzzzzzzzzzzzzzzzzzzzzzzzzzz
```

```
zzzzzzzzzzzzzzzzzzzzzzzzzzzzzzzzzzzzzzzzzzzzzzzzzzzzzzzzzzzzzzzzz
zzzzzzzzzzzzzzzzzzzzzzzzzzzzzzzzzzzzzzzzzzzzzzzzzzzzzzzzzzzzzzzzz
zzzzzzzzzzzzzzzzzzzzzzzzzzzzzMmmmmm, honey, yum yum!
zzzzzzzzzzzzzzzzzzzzzzzzzzzzzzzzzzzzzzzzzz
```

You may feel that you are unlikely to use threads except in the most complex of programs but, in fact, even the simplest Java applets use threads so it is useful to understand the concept in even an introductory text. However, rather than using inheritance as we have done here, applets use threads by implementing the 'Runnable' interface. In the next example, we will use the Runnable interface to create multithreaded objects.

## Implementing the Runnable interface

In the final example from this chapter, we will demonstrate multithreading by implementing the Runnable interface in a program that shows simple graphical images of several aircraft flying in different directions and at different speeds.

Key aspects of this example are

- the Runnable interface
- declaring Thread objects
- sending messages to a Thread object.

There are a number of differences between writing a class that inherits from Thread and one that implements the Runnable interface. First, it must include the 'implements' clause rather than extending Thread:

```
class Aeroplane implements Runnable
```

The class must also declare its own Thread object. In this example, the Aeroplane class has a Thread declared as a private attribute

```
private Thread thread;
```

This is then created in the constructor by passing the Runnable object as the parameter to the Thread constructor:

```
thread = new Thread(this);
```

When a class inherits from Thread, it inherits all the Thread methods such as 'start'. In contrast, the Runnable interface declares only a single 'run' method. Therefore all other thread methods are sent from this class to the Thread object, e.g.,

```
thread.start();
```

Similarly the class method 'sleep' is called using the Thread class:

```
Thread.sleep(1000/speed);
```

The rest of the code in the class relates to what an Aeroplane does while its thread is running, namely moving across the screen. The animation is very crude – an aeroplane is moved by drawing over its current image in the background colour to erase it, moving it along in the appropriate direction and then redrawing it in the foreground colour. The background colour can be returned from a component using the getBackground method:

```
background_colour = component.getBackground();
```

The four possible directions an aeroplane can travel in are north, south, east and west, so movement is limited to changing the current x or y values of the aeroplane's position:

```
switch(direction)
{
// East
    case 1 : x += 1;
            break;
// West
    case 2 : x -= 1;
            break;
// South
    case 3 : y += 1;
            break;
// North
    case 4 : y -= 1;
}
```

A similar 'switch' statement is used to draw the aeroplane's shape at the appropriate angle, though the code here is very crude. There are much more elegant ways to rotate an object's coordinates that you might like to explore. This is the complete Aeroplane class

```
/**
        Aeroplane.java
        a 'Runnable' class that uses a Thread
*/
import java.awt.*;
// the Runnable interface has a single 'run' method
public class Aeroplane implements Runnable
{
// attributes to record the position, direction and speed of the
// plane
        private int x;
        private int y;
        private int direction;
        private int speed;
// references to Graphics, Component and Color objects for
// drawing the plane
        private Graphics graphics;
        private Component component;
        private Color background_colour;
// a Thread in which to run
        private Thread thread;
```

```
// the constructor initialises the attributes and starts the
// thread running
    public Aeroplane(int start_x, int start_y, int
    direction_in, int speed_in, Component c)
    {
        x = start_x;
        y = start_y;
        direction = direction_in;
        speed = speed_in;
        component = c;
        graphics = component.getGraphics();
        background_colour = component.getBackground();
// create a new Thread for 'this' object
        thread = new Thread(this);
// start it running
        thread.start();
    }
// this method runs the thread
    public void run()
    {
// run the thread while the plane is within a given area of the
// window
        while(x > 0 && x < 500 && y > 0 && y < 400)
        {
            try
            {
// pause for a time relative to the speed of the plane
                Thread.sleep(1000 / speed);
// erase the current image by drawing over it in the background
// colour
                draw(background_colour);
// move the plane in the appropriate direction
                switch(direction)
                {
// East
                    case 1 : x += 1;
                            break;
// West
                    case 2 : x -= 1;
                            break;
// South
                    case 3 : y += 1;
                            break;
// North
                    case 4 : y -= 1;
                }
// redraw the plane in its new position
                draw(Color.black);
            }
            catch(InterruptedException e)
            {
                System.out.println("Interrupted");
            }
        }
        graphics.dispose();
    }
```

```
// draw the plane in a given colour
    public void draw(Color col)
    {
// set the drawing colour
        graphics.setColor(col);
// draw the plane in the current position. for each direction the
// shape will be different. there are much more elegant ways of
// doing this!
        switch(direction)
        {
            // East
            case 1 : graphics.drawLine(x, y, x + 10, y);
                graphics.drawLine(x, y-3, x, y+3);
                graphics.drawLine(x + 7, y - 7, x + 7, y + 7);
                break;
            // West
             case 2 : graphics.drawLine(x, y, x - 10, y);
                graphics.drawLine(x, y-3, x, y+3);
                graphics.drawLine(x - 7, y - 7, x - 7, y + 7);
                break;
            // South
            case 3 : graphics.drawLine(x, y, x, y + 10);
                graphics.drawLine(x-3, y, x + 3, y);
                graphics.drawLine(x - 7, y + 7, x + 7, y + 7);
                break;
            // North
            case 4 : graphics.drawLine(x, y, x, y - 10);
                graphics.drawLine(x-3, y, x + 3, y);
                graphics.drawLine(x - 7, y - 7, x + 7, y - 7);
        }
    }
}
```

The Aeroplane class represents an object with a single thread of control within it. We can write a multithreaded program by creating several of these objects. The Planes class creates four Aeroplane objects, initialising them to travel in four different directions and at four different speeds:

```
plane[0] = new Aeroplane(100, 100, 1, 2, this);
plane[1] = new Aeroplane(400, 150, 2, 1, this);
plane[2] = new Aeroplane(200, 50, 3, 4, this);
plane[3] = new Aeroplane(300, 350, 4, 3, this);
```

As soon as the constructor is called, each aeroplane starts its own thread. Notice that we create the objects in 'paint' rather than in the constructor. This is because the component ('this') passed to the Aeroplane constructor is not available until after the Planes constructor has executed. A boolean attribute called 'painted' is used to check if we are visiting the 'paint' method for the first time

```
if(!painted)
```

This is necessary because otherwise every time Paint is called (by resizing or minimising and maximising the window) we would create four new aeroplanes. The aeroplanes run their threads until they reach the approximate original boundaries of the window when they will stop. The window can, however, be closed at any time. This is the complete Planes class:

```
/**
    Planes.java
    a window that runs objects using multiple threads
*/
import java.awt.*;
import javabook.chapter8.MainWindowListener;
public class Planes extends Frame
{
// an array to contain four 'Aeroplane' objects
    private Aeroplane plane[] = new Aeroplane[4];
// attribute to check if 'paint' has been called
    private boolean painted = false;
// constructor
    public Planes()
    {
// add a window listener
        addWindowListener(new MainWindowListener());
// set the window background colour to green
        setBackground(Color.green);
    }
    public void paint(Graphics g)
    {
// only start the planes if this is the first time 'paint' is
// called i.e. when the window first appears
        if(!painted)
        {
// create four Aeroplane objects, each running in a different
// direction and at a different speed
                plane[0] = new Aeroplane(100, 100, 1, 2, this);
                plane[1] = new Aeroplane(400, 150, 2, 1, this);
                plane[2] = new Aeroplane(200, 50, 3, 4, this);
                plane[3] = new Aeroplane(300, 350, 4, 3, this);
// set 'painted' to 'true' so the aeroplanes are only created
// once
                painted = true;
        }
    }
// create a 'Planes' object
    public static void main(String args[])
    {
        Planes plane_window = new Planes();
        plane_window.setTitle("Bandits at One O' Clock!");
        plane_window.setBounds(0,0,500,400);
        plane_window.show();
    }
}
```

Figure 10. 3 shows the Planes window soon after the threads have begun to run.

There are many other aspects to programming using threads, including syntax for allowing threads to communicate with one another and work without getting in each

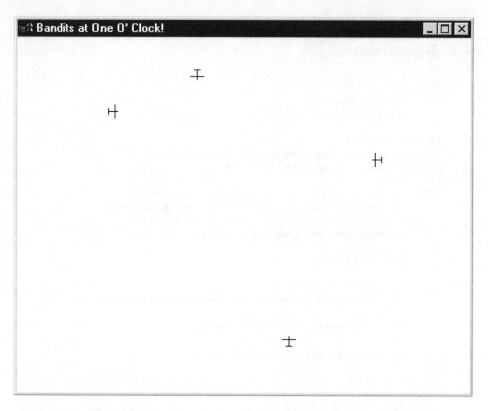

**Figure 10.3**   The Aeroplane objects in the window move concurrently in different directions and at different speeds.

other's way. However, these are beyond the scope of this book. Our use of threads is largely confined to their relevance to running applets, which we discuss in the next chapter.

## Summary

In this chapter we have revisited interfaces (first introduced in Chapter eight) and looked at threads. We have drawn these two aspects of Java together by implementing the Runnable interface with multithreaded objects. Five main aspects of Java programming were investigated:

1. writing an interface
2. inheriting from class Thread
3. multithreading
4. thread priority
5. implementing the Runnable interface.

In a number of these areas, new syntax has been introduced:

1. An interface is written in a similar way to a class, but using 'interface' rather than 'class', and the methods have no definitions, e.g.,

```
public interface Displayable
{
        void display(Component c);
}
```

2. Inheriting from Thread means that our classes can use the methods:

```
getName, run, sleep and start
```

We can set thread priority using final constants such as

```
Thread.MIN_PRIORITY
Thread.MAX_PRIORITY
```

3. Implementing Runnable means that our objects can be passed as parameters to the Thread constructor:

```
public class Aeroplane implements Runnable
{
//...
        private Thread thread;
//...
        thread = new Thread(this);
```

## EXERCISES

**1** Write an interface called 'Identifiable' that declares a method called 'className()' with a String return type. Implement the interface with modified versions of the StaffID2 and VisitorID2 classes from Chapter seven so that the method returns the name of the class. Test the interface by creating objects of the two classes using 'Identifiable' references.

**2** Write a class called 'Shape' that implements the Displayable interface by drawing some kind of graphical shape on the screen using a Graphics object.

**3** The race between the tortoise and the hare was rigged from the start. Write a class called 'RaceHorse' that inherits from Thread and jumps fences between randomly generated sleeps. After a horse has jumped five fences it passes the finishing line. Use the constructor to set the name of the horse. Create a Steeplechase class that starts a number of horses running (but don't bet real money on the winner).

**4** Fix the Steeplechase class so that your horse always wins by having maximum priority. Now you can bet real money.

**5** Modify the Aeroplane class so that it has methods to change its speed and direction at run time. Add another method to return the current position of the aeroplane. Write a new class called 'PlaneController' that shows a single aeroplane in a window. Add appropriate components to control the speed and direction of a plane while it is flying and display its current position.

**6** Modify Planes.java so that you control one of the four planes. Provide some kind of warning indicator that shows if your plane is flying too close to another plane (e.g., within about 20 pixels).

# 11

# Applets

'My apple trees will never get across and eat the cones under his pines, I tell him. He only says, 'Good fences make good neighbors.' ' – Robert Frost (*Mending Wall*)

An applet is a Java program that is specifically designed to run within a web browser. Unlike an application, a Java applet can be run on a remote computer via the internet, either as a complete program in its own right or as part of a larger client-server system. It was Java's applets that made such a big impact when it first appeared, with its 'write once, run anywhere' philosophy. Although it is never quite that simple in practice, there has certainly been an explosion of interest in writing applets for the world wide web. There are many aspects to distributed computing with Java, so this chapter covers only a very small part of Java's potential. However, the applet encapsulates the most important feature of web-based programming, the ability to distribute a program to remote clients using any platform with a single implementation. To achieve this, an applet relies on a number of factors:

- web browser software
- HTML (Hyper Text Mark-up Language) and the <APPLET> tag
- the Java virtual machine.

## Applets and web browser software

Web browser software is designed to retrieve information from remote sites on the world wide web (WWW) using uniform resource locators (URLs). A URL is basically the Internet address of a particular server, and typically is written in three parts.

1. http://    This stands for 'hyper text transfer protocol' and all URLs start this way. Indeed this part is often omitted
2. The server address, usually beginning www (world wide web), then followed by the name of the site, the type of site and finally the country. Each of these is separated by a period (full stop). Take, for example, the following URL:

    http://www.solent.ac.uk

   'solent' is the name of the server site, 'ac' means an academic institution and 'uk' is the country. United States URLs are an exception to this pattern in that no country is defined. Rather, all US companies simply have a '.com' address (e.g. www.sun.com), and US academic institutions are '.edu'. Other organisations have the suffix '.org'.

3. The location (directory) and name of the particular file at the site. For example:

```
http://www.solent.ac.uk/syseng/index.html
```

This looks for the file 'index.html' in the 'syseng' directory. The file name will generally end in 'html' because it will be a file written in HTML (see below). If no filename is specified, 'index.html' is often the server's default file name that the browser will attempt to load. If no index file is present then a directory listing will be displayed instead. Browsers can support Java applets by responding to a special 'tag' in an HTML page.

## HTML

Web browsers display screens of information written using HTML (HyperText Mark-up Language). The browser takes the basic information stored in the HTML file and formats it appropriately using codes (called 'tags') embedded into the text of the file. This is a very simple html file, showing tags for main headings (<H1>) and the body of the text (<BODY>). All HTML tags can be terminated by a forward slash followed by the tag name, e.g., </H1> and </BODY>:

```
<HTML>
<H1> This is the heading of my HTML page </H1>
<BODY>
Here is the text of my HTML page
</BODY>
</HTML>
```

Simple files can easily be written by hand, but for more complex pages it is better to use one of the many available HTML editing tools, often provided as extensions to existing word processors. From the point of view of Java, the most important aspect of an HTML page is that it can contain a tag that loads the byte code from a compiled Java class and runs it within the page. The minimum content for a Java tag looks like this:

```
<APPLET CODE = javaclass HEIGHT = n WIDTH = n>
</APPLET>
```

The 'javaclass' is the name of a compiled Java class, and HEIGHT and WIDTH values must be provided to set the size of the applet within the browser. The examples in this chapter use upper case for all HTML tags, but in fact they are not case-sensitive so lower case is equally valid.

## The Java virtual machine

We have seen in an earlier chapter that Java programs are compiled into a special 'byte code', and that this byte code is interpreted by a Java virtual machine at run time. Browsers can run Java programs by incorporating Java virtual machines into their software. The <APPLET> tag causes the virtual machine to be used to run the class code loaded from the same URL as the HTML page, or some other specified location.

Since the advent of HotJava, the first Java-aware web browser, all browsers have incorporated the ability to run Java applets. However, different versions of web browsers have supported different versions of the Java Virtual Machine, so we cannot guarantee that a given browser can run a particular applet. For example, a browser that supports only Java version 1.0 cannot run applets written using syntax specific to later versions.

## Writing a Java applet

Key aspects of this example are

- inheriting from the 'Applet' class
- using 'paint' with applets
- 'appletviewer' and browsers.

The code for Java applets looks rather different from code for a Java application. Applets must inherit from the Applet class, which is a subclass of Panel, like the Panel objects we put into a Frame in Chapter eight. An Applet is a Panel that can be displayed in a browser. Since Panel ultimately inherits from Component, applets have a number of methods familiar to us from previous examples, such as 'paint'. We must import the Applet class package:

```
import java.applet.Applet;
```

There are few classes in this package so we frequently need only to import the single class. The simplest method of applet to use is 'paint' (inherited from 'Component') which is adequate for displaying some graphical output on the main panel. This shows a very basic applet that uses 'paint' to display a string of text. You might usefully compare this with our first Java application that displayed a string of text using the operating system text output.

```
/**
      JavaApplet.java
      a simple Java Applet with text output
*/
import java.awt.Graphics;
import java.applet.Applet;
public class JavaApplet extends Applet
{
      public void paint (Graphics g)
      {
            g.drawString("Java Applet", 10, 20);
      }
}
```

This uses the drawString method in a Panel, so is familiar to us from previous classes.

An applet is compiled using 'javac' in the normal way, but is not run in the same way as an application because there is no 'main' method. Rather, it runs only as part of an HTML page such as this one:

```
<HTML>
<H1> My Java Applet running </H1>
<APPLET CODE = JavaApplet HEIGHT = 30 WIDTH = 300>
</APPLET>
</HTML>
```

To see the applet run, we can load this page into a suitable web browser (i.e. one that is Java 1.1. compatible) or alternatively use the 'appletviewer', a piece of software (supplied with the JDK) that allows you to test applets without using a web browser. Other Java programming environments have similar applet viewers. Figure 11.1 shows the output from this class when run using appletviewer.

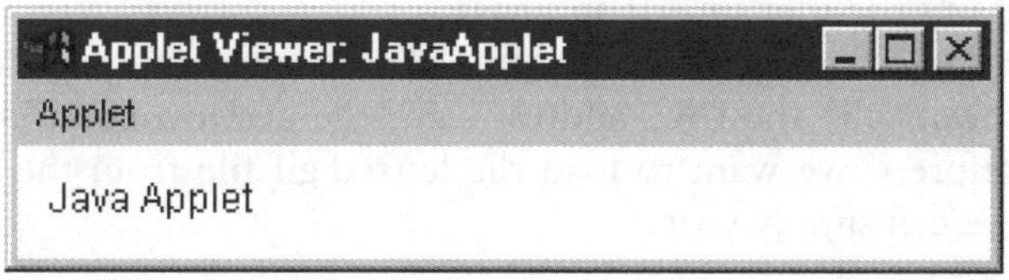

**Figure 11.1** An applet displaying a string of text in the 'appletviewer'.

You will notice that appletviewer ignores any contents of the HTML page except the applet itself. If we load the HTML page into a browser, we will see both the applet and the text on the page (Figure 11.2).

**Figure 11.2** An applet displaying a string of text in the Microsoft Internet Explorer web browser.

# Loading images in an applet

Because one of the key features of applets is to enable some interactive multimedia content on web pages, the loading of image files is a very important part of the behaviour of many applets. In the next example we will look at some aspects of loading images into applets.

Key features of this example are

- loading images with the 'getImage' method
- using a 'MediaTracker' to track the loading of images.

In Chapter nine we saw how to load images into applications from the local file system using a Toolkit object. However, because applets will load images from remote sites rather than local files they have a special method for loading image files, namely:

```
getImage(URL url, string filename);
```
or
```
getImage(URL url);
```

if the URL contains the filename of an image.

If we are loading an image from the same place as the html page, then we do not need to state specifically the URL address since the getDocumentBase method will return it. Therefore if we want to load the lettsed.gif file from the location of the original page, we can simply write:

```
image = getImage(getDocumentBase(), "lettsed.gif");
```

assuming that 'image' is a reference to an 'Image' object.

## Using a MediaTracker to handle image loading

If we simply load and display an image, then it appears as a sequence of fragments on the screen as it loads, particularly if it is being loaded from a remote site. This can look rather chaotic, so sometimes we may want to make sure an image is fully loaded before displaying it. Java provides a class called MediaTracker that allows us to track the progress of an image as it is loaded, and wait until loading is complete before calling 'paint' to display it. The MediaTracker constructor takes a Component as its parameter, which will generally be 'this'. In this example media_tracker is a reference to a MediaTracker object:

```
media_tracker = new MediaTracker(this);
```

Among the methods of the class is addImage, which registers a particular image with the tracker and also provides an integer identification number. This is useful if we are tracking more than one image:

```
media_tracker.addImage(image, image_id);
```

Once an image has been registered with the media tracker, we can use the waitForID method to wait until that particular image has been loaded before displaying it. We pass the identification number of the image to this method so it is aware which image to wait for. Because it throws an InterruptedException, we put the method into a 'try' block:

```
try
{
      media_tracker.waitForID(image_id);
}
catch(InterruptedException e)
{}
```

The following applet uses the getImage method and a MediaTracker to load and display an image on the applet panel so that the image appears complete rather than in sections. You might try commenting out the MediaTracker code before recompiling and running the applet again to see the effect. Notice that we are providing an implementation for a method of Applet called 'init'. The main role of init is to initialise the state of the applet, so it is in effect the equivalent of the constructors we have been using in our applications. We always use init rather than a constructor in applet classes:

```
/**
      WebImage.java
      this class loads a single image and displays it.
      it checks that the image has been fully loaded using
      a 'MediaTracker' object
*/
import java.applet.*;
import java.awt.*;
public class WebImage extends Applet
{
// 'Image' attribute to reference a loaded image file
      private Image image;
// a 'MediaTracker' to track the loading of the image
      private MediaTracker media_tracker;
// an id number for the image. although in this example it is not
// really used, we can use id numbers to track the loading of
// multiple images
      private int image_id = 1;
// the 'init' method loads the image file
      public void init()
      {
// load the 'lettsed.gif' image from the same source as the html
// page
            image = getImage(getDocumentBase(), "lettsed.gif");
// instantiate the media tracker object
            media_tracker = new MediaTracker(this);
// register the image with the media tracker
            media_tracker.addImage(image, image_id);
// the 'waitForID' method forces the applet to wait until the
// specified image is loaded before continuing execution.
// it uses the image id number as its parameter.
```

```
// the 'try' block is required for the exception.
        try
        {
                media_tracker.waitForID(image_id);
        }
        catch(InterruptedException e)
        {}
}
public void paint(Graphics g)
{
// the simplest version of 'drawImage' takes the image,
// its top left corner coordinates and an ImageObserver as
// parameters
        g.drawImage(image, 0, 0, this);
}
}
```

This html file loads the WebImage applet:

```
<HTML>
<HEAD>
<TITLE>Letts Educational logo applet</TITLE>
</HEAD>
<BODY>
<H1>This is the Letts Educational logo</H1>
<BR>
<APPLET CODE = WebImage HEIGHT = 180 WIDTH = 335>
</APPLET>
<P>visit the web site at <I>www.lettsed.co.uk</I>
</BODY>
</HTML>
```

Figure 11.3 shows this applet running in the appletviewer, which shows only the applet and not the text in the HTML page.

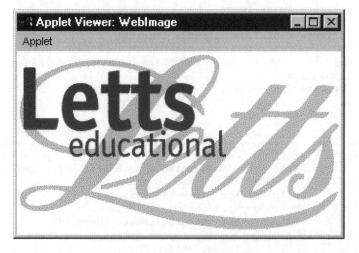

**Figure 11.3**    The WebImage applet loads an Image file.

Of course, simply using applets to display static text and/or images is not very productive since the same effect could more easily be achieved using standard HTML pages. Java comes into its own when it is used to run applications on the web, using an HTML page as an environment for active programs using the AWT components, graphics and animated images. However, writing more complex applets is not always straightforward due to the security features built into Java and web browser software. Writing a useful Java applet that will actually run on a web page on a remote computer can be difficult.

## Running applets

For simple classes like our first two examples, it makes no difference whether you run them under appletviewer or a web browser. However, once we write more complex classes there are many important differences in the things that can be done in an applet because of the security aspects of web browsers. The appletviewer is purely for testing local applet code, so there are no security implications in letting it run applets. A browser running an applet from some remote server is, however, in a rather different position, and puts many more limitations on what an applet can do and how it can be written. One significant effect of this is that we can easily convert our applications to run as applets under the applet viewer, but sometimes we need to make much more significant modifications to make them run successfully on a remote browser.

# Applets and applications

There are many similarities between applets and applications but there are also some important differences.

*The 'init' method*
One of the most important changes is the 'init' method. Rather than setting up the interface to an applet in the constructor, as we frequently did for our application examples based on Frames, we use the 'init' method for all initialisation processes.

*No 'main' method*
Loading a web page containing an applet will start the applet running, calling the 'init' method. There is no 'main' method in an applet.

*Event listeners*
Rather than having separate event listener classes, we need to make the applets themselves into event listeners by letting them implement the necessary interfaces.

*The default layout manager*
The default layout manager for applications running within frame windows is BorderLayout. In contrast, an applet's default layout manager is FlowLayout. This is one reason why it is better explicitly to set the layout manager, even if it is the

default. That way we do not have unexpected changes when converting an application to an applet or vice versa.

*Menus*

In our drawing program in Chapter nine, we created MenuItems that were put into Menus that were in turn put into MenuBars. A MenuBar can be added to a Frame, but not a Panel, so we cannot directly transfer applications with frame-based menus to applets.

## Converting an application to an applet

Key aspects of this example are

- implementing ActionListener with an applet class
- adding components in the 'init' method
- removing window listeners
- checking event sources in the 'actionPerformed' method.

In many cases, the conversion of a program from an application to an applet is relatively straightforward. Indeed, we could have written our applications in a different way to make them more easily convertible. However, the constraints on applets mean that sometimes the architecture of their classes is not ideal, so they do not always encourage good practice!

As an example to highlight the differences between our applications and applets we will convert the mileage table example from Chapter eight into an applet. In the previous version, we had four classes:

1. 'Distances' – the underlying data about distances between cities.
2. 'MileageTable' – the GUI that handled user i/o and retrieved information from the Distances object.
3. 'MainWindowListener' – the listener that allowed the window to be closed.
4. 'RoadAtlas' – the test program that created the MileageTable object.

The Distances class, since it does not involve any user interaction, remains unchanged, except that to keep things as simple as possible on the web site, the Distances class appears in the same package as the main applet class. This means that it no longer requires a specific package name. The RoadAtlas class is no longer required, since its role was to invoke a frame based object which we no longer have, though it is possible to test an applet by running it inside a frame since an applet is basically a Panel. The window listener is also redundant since without a frame there is no window to be closed. The MileageTable class remains much as before but does need some modification.

First, we need to ensure that we have access to the Distances class, but we assume here that they reside in the same package (as they do on the Letts web site) so we do not need an import statement. Second, we need to change it so that instead of inheriting from Frame it inherits from Applet and implements the ActionListener interface. This is because the separate or anonymous classes we have used before to listen for events are not easily run in browsers.

```
import chapter8.Distances;
public class MileageTableApplet
     extends Applet implements ActionListener
{
     // etc.
```

Instead of using the constructor to add all the components to the window, initialise them and add the button listener, this is done in the 'init' method:

```
public void init()
{
     setLayout(new FlowLayout());
     // etc.
```

We also need to make some changes to the listeners. We remove the MainWindowListener since the class no longer has a window, and we also change the way the button listener is added. Before, we used an anonymous class but in the applet version we simply add the applet itself to the button, since the applet implements the ActionListener interface:

```
calculate_button.addActionListener(this);
```

Of course, we must also provide an implementation for this interface, which requires an actionPerformed method to be defined. Because the class has only one of these methods, regardless of how many events it might have to respond to, we have to check the nature of the event using the getSource method that we first saw in Chapter eight. In this example there is in fact only one possible source, the calculate_button object:

```
public void actionPerformed(ActionEvent e)
{
     if(e.getSource() == calculate_button)
     {
          etc.
```

Otherwise, the actual processes that take place in the class are the same as before. This is the complete applet:

```
/**
     MileageTableApplet.java
     this Applet uses AWT components as the interface to a
     mileage table of the 'Distances' class
*/
import java.awt.*;
import java.awt.event.*;
import java.applet.Applet;
public class MileageTableApplet
extends Applet implements ActionListener
{
// declare the components of the window
// declare two Choices to select the origin and destination of
// the journey
     private Choice from_city;
     private Choice to_city;
```

```
// declare text labels
    private Label from_label;
    private Label to_label;
    private Label distance_label;
    private Label result_label;
// declare a button to produce a result
    private Button calculate_button;
// declare a 'Distances' object
    private Distances table;
// 'init' performs tasks similar to the constructor in the
// MileageTable application
    public void init()
    {
// use the FlowLayout layout manager to arrange the components on
// the screen
            setLayout(new FlowLayout());
// create the two 'Choice' objects
            from_city = new Choice();
            to_city = new Choice();
// add the city names to the 'from' choice
            from_city.addItem("Birmingham");
            from_city.addItem("Brighton");
            from_city.addItem("Bristol");
            from_city.addItem("Cambridge");
            from_city.addItem("Carlisle");
            from_city.addItem("Dover");
            from_city.addItem("Exeter")
            from_city.addItem("Leeds");
            from_city.addItem("London");
            from_city.addItem("Southampton");
// add the city names to the 'to' choice
            to_city.addItem("Birmingham");
            to_city.addItem("Brighton");
            to_city.addItem("Bristol");
            to_city.addItem("Cambridge");
            to_city.addItem("Carlisle");
            to_city.addItem("Dover");
            to_city.addItem("Exeter");
            to_city.addItem("Leeds");
            to_city.addItem("London");
            to_city.addItem("Southampton");
// create the text labels for the choices
            from_label = new Label("From:");
            to_label = new Label("To:");
// add these components to the frame
            add(from_label);
            add(from_city);
            add(to_label);
            add(to_city);
// create and add the 'calculate' button
            calculate_button = new Button("Calculate Distance");
            add(calculate_button);
// create and add the text label for the result
            distance_label = new Label
("The distance between the cities is");
            add(distance_label);
```

```
// create and add a text label to display the result. the extra
// spaces ensure that when longer results are put into the label
// the text is not truncated
            result_label = new Label("0 miles    ");
            add(result_label);
// create the table object that contains the distance data
            table = new Distances();
// add a listener for the 'calculate' button so when it is
// pressed, the mileage between the currently selected cities is
// displayed
            calculate_button.addActionListener(this);
        }
// when the button is pressed...
        public void actionPerformed(ActionEvent e)
        {
            if(e.getSource() == calculate_button)
            {
// get the index numbers of the currently selected cities from
// each 'Choice' object
                int origin = from_city.getSelectedIndex();
                int destination = to_city.getSelectedIndex();
// use these as parameters to 'getDistance' to return the
// distance between these two cities
                int distance = table.getDistance(origin,
                destination);
// since 'setText' requires a String parameter, the Integer class
// method 'toString(int)' is used to convert the int to a string
                result_label.setText(Integer.toString(distance)
                + " miles");
            }
        }
}
```

This HTML page will run the MileageTableApplet:

```
<HTML>
<TITLE> Mileage Table Applet </TITLE>
<BODY>
<H1> Distances between major cities </H1>
<APPLET CODE = MileageTableApplet HEIGHT = 100 WIDTH = 500>
</APPLET>
</HTML>
```

Figure 11.4 shows MileageTableApplet running in the applet viewer.

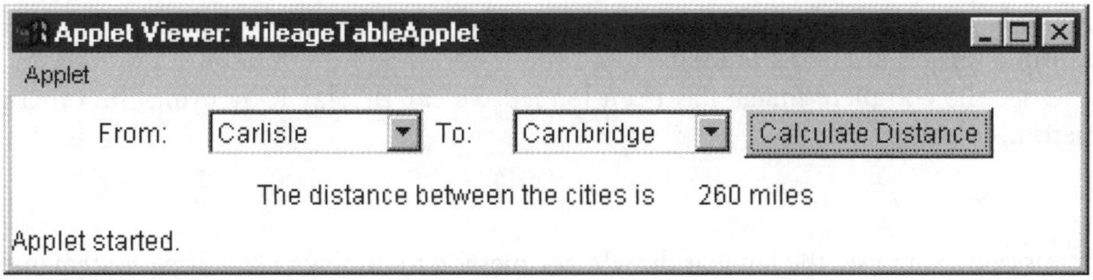

Figure 11.4   The mileage table application converted to an applet running in the appletviewer.

# An applet with components and images

In this example, we combine images with components that control which image is on screen at any one time. The applet comprises two buttons, two areas of text and one specialised subclass of Panel to contain an image, arranged within a BorderLayout with the image in the centre.

Key aspects of this example are

- subclassing Panel
- the 'waitForAll' method of the MediaTracker class
- adding components to an applet.

## The ImagePanel class

In Chapter nine we saw that it was possible to load an image onto a panel, and earlier in this chapter we saw how images could be loaded into an applet using the getImage method. We also saw how a MediaTracker object can help us to wait until an image is fully loaded before displaying it. In this example, we encapsulate the process of waiting for an image to load and then displaying it on a panel inside a class called ImagePanel. This class has two methods: setImage, which loads an image from an Image reference supplied as a parameter and its own version of 'paint', which displays the loaded image on the panel. The class inherits from Panel:

```
public class ImagePanel extends Panel
```

The ImagePanel class uses a MediaTracker to wait for the image to load before displaying it. Our previous MediaTracker example set the identification number of the image and then used the waitForID method to wait for that particular image to load. This example is slightly different in that it uses waitForAll, which waits for all registered images to be loaded before continuing. Like waitForID this throws an InterruptedException so we have to add a try/catch block to the code:

```
try
{
        tracker.waitForAll()
}
catch(InterruptedException e)
{}
```

In both our examples we have been loading only a single image, so both of these methods have the same effect. Clearly, however, they will have different uses if multiple images are being loaded.

Once the complete image has been loaded we can display it by using the repaint method to call paint:

```
repaint();
```

In this case, paint uses the familiar drawImage method to display the picture on the panel:

```
g.drawImage(image, 0,0, this);
```

This is the complete ImagePanel class:

```
/**
       ImagePanel.java
       this class encapsulates the process of loading an image
       onto a panel. its 'setImage' method will display an image
       passed as a parameter
*/
import java.awt.*;
// ImagePanel is a subclass of Panel
public class ImagePanel extends Panel
{
// a private attribute to reference the image
       private Image image;
// this method loads the image using the reference provided,
// waits for the image to load fully and then repaints the panel
       public void setImage(Image photo)
       {
// use the parameter to set the 'Image' attribute
              image = photo;
// create a MediaTracker to keep track of the loading process
              MediaTracker tracker = new MediaTracker(this);
// add the image to the tracker
              tracker.addImage(image, 0);
// wait for the image to load fully, catching the required
// exception
              try
              {
                     tracker.waitForAll();
              }
              catch(InterruptedException e)
              {}
// once the complete image is loaded, call 'paint' indirectly
// with the 'repaint' method
              repaint();
       }
       public void paint(Graphics g)
       {
// the simplest version of 'drawImage' takes the image,
// its top left corner coordinates and an ImageObserver as
// parameters
              g.drawImage(image, 0,0, this);
       }
}
```

## The ShipApplet class

This applet uses the ImagePanel class to create a 'slide show' of photographs of passenger liners in Southampton Docks. The image being displayed is controlled by 'forward' and 'back' buttons, and each photo has an associated caption displayed in a Label. These are held in arrays of strings. The data for the file names of the photographic images and the text for the captions have been hard coded into the class here, but a more flexible system would read this data from file to make it more easily changeable and extensible. The bulk of the class consists of an 'init' method that performs the following actions:

- The array of image file names is created and the file names added to it.
- The array of captions is created and the text added to it.
- The layout is set to a BorderLayout.
- The components are created and added to the layout.
- An action listener ('this') is added to the 'forward' button.
- An action listener ('this') is added to the 'back' button.

Whenever the 'forward' button is pressed, the action listener increments the current array index. It then changes the image by sending the next file name to the setImage method of the ImagePanel object and a setText message to the Label object that shows the captions. The back button does a very similar task, but decrements the array index number. Each listener will reset the index number to the other end of the array when it reaches its boundary so that the images can be continually cycled round in either direction. This is the complete ShipApplet class:

```
/**
        ShipApplet.java
        an applet that combines components and images
*/
import java.applet.Applet;
import java.awt.*;
import java.awt.event.*;
public class ShipApplet extends Applet implements ActionListener
{
// array to hold the file names of the images
        private String ships[];
// array to hold the strings displayed in text labels
        private String captions[];
// the ship count is used to cycle round the images
        private int ship_count = 7;
// the current array index starts at zero
        private int array_index = 0;
// components for the screen - an 'ImagePanel' (a subclass of
// 'Panel') two buttons and a label
        private ImagePanel image_panel;
        private Button next_button;
        private Button previous_button;
        private Label caption;
// an 'Image' reference for loading image files
        private Image photo;
// the 'init' method starts the applet
        public void init()
        {
// create the array of file names and add the data
                ships = new String[ship_count];
                ships[0] = new String("Canback.gif");
                ships[1] = new String("Oriana1.gif");
                ships[2] = new String("Oriana2.gif");
                ships[3] = new String("Queback.gif");
                ships[4] = new String("Queside.gif");
                ships[5] = new String("Brit.gif");
                ships[6] = new String("Star.gif");
// create the array of captions and add the data. larger captions
```

```
// might be better loaded from file
            captions = new String[ship_count];
            captions[0] = new String
   ("The P&O liner \"Canberra\" docked at Ocean Terminal");
            captions[1] = new String
   ("The P&O liner \"Oriana\" photographed from the Hythe ferry");
            captions[2] = new String
   ("The \"Oriana\" heading down Southampton Water");
            captions[3] = new String
   ("The Cunard liner \"QE2\" at Ocean Terminal");
            captions[4] = new String
   ("The \"QE2\" leaving Southampton docks");
            captions[5] = new String
   ("The Ellinis liner \"Britanis\" in the Eastern Docks");
            captions[6] = new String
   ("The \"Northern Star\" at the cruise liner terminal, seen
            from Mayflower park");
// set the layout as a BorderLayout
            setLayout(new BorderLayout());
// create the 'ImagePanel' and add it to the centre
            image_panel = new ImagePanel();
            add("Center", image_panel);
// add the first image to the panel
            photo = getImage(getDocumentBase(), ships[0]);
            image_panel.setImage(photo);
// add the two buttons to the left and right borders
            next_button = new Button("Next >>");
            add("East", next_button);
            previous_button = new Button("<< Previous");
            add("West", previous_button);
// add a label as the heading. note that since we do not change
// this, it does not need to be sent messages so need not be
// declared as an attribute
            add("North", new Label("Liners in Southampton Docks",
                Label.CENTER));
// add the caption label to the bottom of the layout
            caption = new Label(captions[0]);
            add("South", caption);
// add 'this' applet as the action listener for the buttons
            next_button.addActionListener(this);
            previous_button.addActionListener(this);
      }
// implement the 'ActionListener' interface by adding an
// 'actionPerformed' method
      public void actionPerformed(ActionEvent e)
      {
// if the 'next_button' is pressed, increment the array index.
// if we are at the end of the array, start again at element zero
            if(e.getSource() == next_button)
            {
                if(array_index < 6)
                {
                    array_index++;
                }
                else
                {
                    array_index = 0;
                }
            }
```

```
// if the 'previous_button' is pressed, decrement the array
// index. if we are at element zero of the array, reset the index
// to the other end of the array (element 6)
            if(e.getSource() == previous_button)
            {
                if(array_index > 0)
                {
                    array_index-;;
                }
                else
                {
                    array_index = 6;
                }
            }
// change the image and the caption
            photo = getImage(getDocumentBase(),
                    ships[array_index]);
            image_panel.setImage(photo);
            caption.setText(captions[array_index]);
    }
}
```

This HTML page will run the applet.

```
<TITLE>
<HEAD>
Liners in Southampton Docks
</HEAD>
</TITLE>
<APPLET CODE = ShipApplet HEIGHT = 350 WIDTH = 560>
</APPLET>
```

Figure 11.5 shows the applet displaying one of the images.

## Animating applets

One of the characteristics of Java that made such an impression when it first appeared was its ability to add animations to web pages. Although there are now many other tools to do this, the fact that Java is a programming language with a rich syntax means that it can be used to create very sophisticated animations. The final example in this chapter is not by any means a sophisticated animation but it gives an idea of some aspects of syntax that might be used.

In Chapter ten we saw a crude animation of aircraft in flight to demonstrate multiple threads of control. The next example is rather similar in that it also uses the Runnable interface and a crude animation mechanism to make an object move across the screen, but in this case only a single thread is run.

Key aspects of this example are

- using Thread and Runnable methods in an animated applet
- coordinating 'run' and 'paint'
- overriding 'update'.

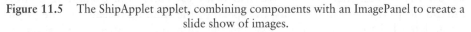

Figure 11.5   The ShipApplet applet, combining components with an ImagePanel to create a
slide show of images.

As indicated in the previous chapter, the main reason for discussing threads was to
prepare the ground for threads in applets. If we are going to write an applet that
provides a continuous process such as animation, we need some way of controlling
that process so that it does not take up resources when the web page is still open but
minimised. We do this by running the animation as a thread in an applet that implements the Runnable interface. The run method from the Runnable interface and the
start and stop methods of the Thread class work together to control the thread of
execution. The run method provides the continuous process that creates the animation, while the applet itself provides start and stop methods that are used to control
the thread. This thread is declared as a private attribute:

```
private Thread train_thread;
```

When the applet's web page is loaded its start method is called, which creates the
thread object. Once the Thread object has been created its own start method is called
which in turn calls the run method:

```
public void start()
{
// if the thread does not yet exist, create it and start it
// running
    if(train_thread == null)
    {
```

```
                    train_thread = new Thread(this);
                    train_thread.start();
            }
    }
```

The applet runs until either the window is closed or minimised. Either way, the stop method is called which stops the run method from executing. Directing the train_thread reference to null gives the garbage collector an indication that we have finished with the object. This can speed it up a bit but is not essential:

```
    public void stop()
    {
            if(train_thread != null)
            {
                    train_thread.stop();
                    train_thread = null;
            }
    }
```

The run method itself consists of an infinite loop ('while(true)') that will continue until the applet itself is closed. Inside this loop we change the position of the image of the train (by incrementing the integer train_position attribute) moving it to the right by one pixel each time. When it disappears off the right-hand side of the applet margin, we reset its position to the left margin again. To display the image, we use the repaint method, but we also delay each iteration by adding a short Thread.sleep. If we do not do this, the speed of the running thread and the physical update of the screen get out of synchronisation and the image leaps about all over the place.

The only other method of the class is 'update' (inherited by Applet from Component), which we override in order to prevent its normal behaviour of erasing the entire background of the applet before painting the image. By calling paint directly in this method, we can bypass the redrawing of the background and improve the smoothness of the animation. However, the price we pay is that the train can leave a trail behind it depending on the default background of the browser window.

```
    public void update(Graphics g)
    {
            paint(g);
    }
```

This is the complete applet:

```
/**
        RunawayTrain.java
        the 'RunawayTrain' applet includes implementation of the
        'Runnable' interface to allow a continuous animation
*/
import java.applet.Applet;
import java.awt.*;
public class RunawayTrain extends Applet implements Runnable
{
```

```
// a reference to the image of the train
      private Image train_image;
// this thread is used to run the train
      private Thread train_thread;
// this variable is used to check the train's progress across the
// screen. when the train reaches the right hand side it will
// restart from the left. it begins off screen to the left, hence
// the negative value
      private int train_position = -100;
// the 'init' method loads the image
    public void init()
    {
          train_image = getImage(getDocumentBase(), "loco.gif");
    }
// the 'start' method begins the execution of the thread
    public void start()
    {
// if the thread does not yet exist, create it and start it running
          if(train_thread == null)
          {
              train_thread = new Thread(this);
              train_thread.start();
          }
    }
// the 'stop' method stops the animation when the user leaves the
// web page or minimises the window
    public void stop()
    {
          if(train_thread != null)
          {
// use 'suspend' in Java 1.2
              train_thread.stop();
// give the garbage collector a hint
              train_thread = null;
          }
    }
// the 'run' method controls the running of the applet so it will
// keep going as long as we like
    public void run()
    {
// infinite loop
        while(true)
        {
// move the image along by one pixel, unless we are off the right
// margin of the applet, in which case start again from the left
              if(train_position < 500)
              {
                  train_position++;
              }
              else
              {
                  train_position = -100;
              }
// call the 'paint' method to draw the train in its new position
              repaint();
// we have to slow the process down a bit or 'run' and 'paint'
```

```
              // will get out of synch and the image will leap about all over
              // the place
                        try
                        {
                            Thread.sleep(10);
                        }
                        catch(InterruptedException e)
                        {}
                    }
              }
        // the default 'update' method always clears the background. by
        // overriding it with a method that simply calls 'paint' and does
        // not erase the background, we can reduce flicker
              public void update(Graphics g)
              {
                    paint(g);
              }
              public void paint(Graphics g)
              {
        // since 'Applet' is a descendant of 'ImageObserver' we can use
        // 'this' as the parameter to 'drawImage'.
                        g.drawImage(train_image, train_position, 0, this);
              }
        }
```

The applet runs in this HTML page:

```
<HTML>
<TITLE>Runaway train applet</TITLE>
<BODY>
<H2>Look out, it's a runaway train!!</H2>
<APPLET CODE = RunawayTrain HEIGHT = 50 WIDTH = 500>
</APPLET>
</BODY>
</HTML>
```

Figure 11.6 shows the runaway train speeding towards the margin of the applet (only to reappear again *ad infinitum*).

Figure 11.6    The RunawayTrain applet running (away).

## Developing animated applets

The RunawayTrain applet is rather basic, particularly since it uses only one image. Many animated applets are built by using a series of images to create effects such as rotation and zooming. To create successfully these kinds of animation more sophisticated techniques such as 'double buffering' (drawing an image off screen before displaying it) and updating specific parts of the screen can be used. We can also use MediaTrackers to handle multiple image loading. This chapter is intended only as an introduction to what can be done with applets and there are many books on the market that explore both applets and the wider aspects of distributed programming with Java in greater detail.

## Summary

In this chapter we have looked at applets and how they differ from applications. There are four key differences.

1. Applets run in web browsers or in the 'appletviewer', not in a frame, and have no 'main' method.
2. Applets are initialised using the 'init' method rather than the constructor.
3. Applets run more easily in browsers if they are their own event listeners.
4. Applets can use threads and the runnable interface to provide animations that can stop and start.

Much of the syntax used with applets in this chapter has been introduced in the context of applications in previous chapters. However, there are some important new elements:

1. Applets inherit from java.applet.Applet, e.g.,

```
import java.applet.Applet;
public class JavaApplet extends Applet
{
```

2. Applets have a special 'getImage' method for loading images from remote sites, e.g.,

```
image = getImage(getDocumentBase(), "lettsed.gif");
```

3. To wait until images have loaded completely before displaying them, we can use a MediaTracker, e.g.,

```
media_tracker = new MediaTracker(this);
media_tracker.addImage(image, image_id);
media_tracker.waitForAll();
```

When writing animated applets, we combine a Thread with implementing the Runnable interface, using thread and runnable methods to control the activity of the animated thread, e.g.,

```
train_thread.start();
train_thread.stop();
```

In the next and final chapter, we look at some further aspects of Java that you might like to explore, and consider what the future might hold for Java.

**EXERCISES**

1 Convert the rock, paper, scissors, application into an applet.

2 Create your own 'slide show' of images, reading the captions from a text file.

3 Write an 'Ohms law' applet using AWT components. Ohms law calculates the resistance of a circuit by dividing the voltage by the current. Your applet should allow the user to enter the voltage and the current into text fields, displaying the resistance when a button is pressed.

4 Write an animated 'bouncing ball' applet. Unlike the runaway train, which moves from left to right, the ball should move up and down. If you are feeling really ambitious it could be made to bounce along as well as up and down.

# 12

# Where do you want to go tomorrow?

'Your children are not your children … For their souls dwell in the house of tomorrow'
– Kahlil Gibran (*The Prophet*).

This chapter suggests a few directions you might want to go in now that you have covered the basics of Java programming. It also looks at where Java might be going in the future.

## Further Java features

In this book you have been introduced to the fundamental features of Java, but there is plenty more to explore. The following list is just a few suggestions of where you might want to go next.

### Graphical user interfaces

Although we have looked at the basics of the AWT there is plenty more to it that we have not covered. The interfaces we have used have been very basic and crude, simply adding components to a single window. Much more sophisticated interfaces are possible, particularly since the introduction of the Java Foundation Classes that provide a number of extensions to the basic AWT including 'Swing', a set of class libraries that provide greater control over GUI functionality and 'look and feel'.

### JDBC

Java's database connectivity API provides the programmer with the facilities to write Java programs that can provide interaction with databases. Database queries can be sent to the database from a Java program.

### Internet programming

There are many aspects to programming for the internet, of which applets are just the simplest and smallest part. Facilities such as RMI (remote method invocation),

CORBA (Common Object Request Broker Architecture) support and the Socket, ServerSocket and Servlet classes allow sophisticated distributed systems to be built using Java.

### Visual programming

Java Beans allow visual programming using components. These components can range from the simple AWT style components to mini applications. The Java Beans API allows beans to be reused, modified and managed to build applications entirely from predefined components.

### Files and persistence

This book introduced some very simple text-based file handling. But Java has a range of classes for handing files of various types. It also has 'serialization' facilities that can be used to make objects persistent (i.e., last beyond the lifetime of a single program).

## Tomorrow's Java

In its short history, Java has seen many changes. In its three main versions between 1995 and 1998 (1.0, 1.1 and 1.2) there was a steady expansion of its APIs and some significant revisions to some of its classes and their methods, particularly in the event-handling mechanisms that changed significantly between versions 1.0 and 1.1, principally to assist in the handling of Java Beans. It seems likely that Java will continue to build on what has now become a fairly stable core syntax. However, it is likely that future changes will occur in the AWT and its extensions. Patrick Naughton (who wrote the original AWT) made the point that it was only ever a 'quick fix' to allow a platform independent GUI to be built, and that it would need further development. It is expected that the current inheritance-based system will be replaced by one that uses more delegation and aggregation.

The best way to keep abreast of Java developments is to check the Java Internet sites regularly, and to read journals such as the 'Java Report'. The Letts web page for this book maintains a number of useful links to Java-related sites to help you in this endeavour. Whatever the future, no doubt it will be many years before the Java story is complete.

# Appendix: Answers to exercises

This appendix contains suggested answers to some of the exercises in the book. These are generally the first one or two exercises at the end of each chapter, covering the basic syntax and ideas that underpin the longer exercises that follow. Where exercises cover more than one area of Java (e.g. interfaces and threads) the introductory exercises from each area are provided. These programs (along with all the examples for the book) can be downloaded from the Letts website. Suggested answers to the other exercises are available in the lecturers' supplement. Contact the publisher for details.

## Chapter 3

### Exercise 1

```
/**
      C3Ex1.java
      model answer to chapter 3, exercise 1
      a simple Java application with screen output
*/
public class C3ex1
{
      public static void main(String args[])
      {
// display a message on the screen
            System.out.print("Java" + ' ');
            System.out.print("Application");
      }
}
```

### Exercise 2

When run with too many arguments, 'MainStrings' simply ignores the extra strings. However, if no parameters are provided, then the program fails, displaying a 'java.lang.ArrayIndexOutOfBounds exception' message.

## Exercise 3

```
/**
    C3ex3.java
    model answer to chapter 3, exercise 3
    this class demonstrates how the arguments to 'main'
    can be accessed as an array of Strings
*/
public class C3ex3
{
    public static void main(String[] args)
    {
        System.out.println(args[2]);
        System.out.println(args[1]);
        System.out.println(args[0]);
        System.out.println("The number of strings passed to
        'main' was " + args.length);
    }
}
```

# Chapter 4

## Exercise 1

```
/**
    Counter.java
    model answer to chapter 4, exercise 1
*/
package javabook.chapter4;
public class Counter
{
    private String colour = "White";
    private int current_square = 0;
    public void setColour(String colour_in)
    {
        colour = colour_in;
    }
    public String getColour()
    {
        return colour;
    }
    public void moveToSquare(int move_to)
    {
        current_square = move_to;
    }
        public int getCurrentSquare()
    {
        return current_square;
    }
}
```

## Exercise 2

The code in this exercise is somewhat tedious. This is rather deliberate, since it makes the point that without the ability to repeat code, programs are difficult to write. This therefore leads into the syntax for writing loops in Chapter 5.

```java
/**
    BoardGame.java
    model answer to chapter 4, exercise 2
*/
package javabook.chapter4;
public class BoardGame
{
    public static void main(String args[])
    {
// declare two Counters
        Counter counter1 = new Counter();
        Counter counter2 = new Counter();
        Dice dice = new Dice();
        dice.throwDice();
        int dice_throw = 0;
        dice_throw = dice.getDiceValue();
        counter1.moveToSquare(dice_throw);
        System.out.println("Counter 1 is on square " +
            counter1.getCurrentSquare());
        dice.throwDice();
        dice_throw = dice.getDiceValue();
        counter2.moveToSquare(dice_throw);
        System.out.println("Counter 2 is on square " +
        counter2.getCurrentSquare());
// second throw
        dice.throwDice();
        dice_throw = dice.getDiceValue();
        counter1.moveToSquare(dice_throw +
            counter1.getCurrentSquare());
        System.out.println("Counter 1 is on square " +
            counter1.getCurrentSquare());
        dice.throwDice();
        dice_throw = dice.getDiceValue();
        counter2.moveToSquare(dice_throw +
            counter2.getCurrentSquare());
        System.out.println("Counter 2 is on square " +
            counter2.getCurrentSquare());
// third throw
        dice.throwDice();
        dice_throw = dice.getDiceValue();
        counter1.moveToSquare(dice_throw +
            counter1.getCurrentSquare());
        System.out.println("Counter 1 is on square " +
            counter1.getCurrentSquare());
        dice.throwDice();
        dice_throw = dice.getDiceValue();
        counter2.moveToSquare(dice_throw +
            counter2.getCurrentSquare());
        System.out.println("Counter 2 is on square " +
            counter2.getCurrentSquare());
```

```
// fourth throw
        dice.throwDice();
        dice_throw = dice.getDiceValue();
        counter1.moveToSquare(dice_throw +
            counter1.getCurrentSquare());
        System.out.println("Counter 1 is on square " +
            counter1.getCurrentSquare());
        dice.throwDice();
        dice_throw = dice.getDiceValue();
        counter2.moveToSquare(dice_throw +
counter2.getCurrentSquare());
        System.out.println("Counter 2 is on square " +
counter2.getCurrentSquare());
    }
}
```

# Chapter 5

## Exercise 1

For this to work, the 'Coin' class must be in the package 'javabook.chapter4'. If your 'Coin' is in a different package, change the 'import' statement accordingly.

```
/**
    TenHeads.java
    model answer to chapter 5, exercise 1
    flips a coin until ten heads have appeared, displaying the
    number of times the coin was flipped at the end
*/
import javabook.chapter4.Coin;
public class TenHeads
{
    public static void main(String args[])
    {
        int flip_count = 0;
        int head_count = 0;
        Coin coin = new Coin();
        while(head_count < 10)
        {
            coin.flipCoin();
            if(coin.headsOrTails() == 'H')
            {
                head_count++;
            }
            flip_count++;
        }
        System.out.println("the coin was flipped " +
            flip_count + " times");
    }
}
```

# Chapter 6

## Exercise 1

There are a few changes to the SnakesAndLadders class required. In this case it has been renamed 'Snakes2' to avoid confusion between filenames. First, an extra attribute is added for the second counter:

```
public class Snakes2
{
      private int counter1 = 0;
      private int counter2 = 0;
      //etc.
```

Then in the 'playGame' method we update the positions of both counters. This code would be much shorter if we used an array of two integers – you might like to make this modification.

```
          public void playGame()
          {
                int next_square = 0;
// iterate until we reach the end (square 100)
                while(counter1 != 100 && counter2 != 100)
                {
// throw the dice
                        dice.throwDice();
// see what square it will take us to
                        next_square = counter1 + dice.getDiceValue();
// we only use the throw if it does not take us beyond square 100
// (i.e. we need an exact number to win)
                        if(next_square <= 100)
                        {
                                counter1 = next_square;
                        }
// if we have not finished, we check the board to see if we have
// to go up a ladder or down a snake
                        if(counter1 < 100)
                        {
// calling this method will change the value of 'counter' only if
// it goes up a ladder or down a snake
                                counter1 =
                                        board.checkForSnakesOrLadders(counter1);
                                System.out.println("Counter one on square " +
                                        counter1);
                        }
// throw the dice
                        dice.throwDice();
// see what square it will take us to
                        next_square = counter2 + dice.getDiceValue();
// we only use the throw if it does not take us beyond square 100
// (i.e. we need an exact number to win)
                        if(next_square <= 100)
                        {
                                counter2 = next_square;
                        }
```

```
// if we have not finished, we check the board to see if we have
// to go up a ladder or down a snake
                    if(counter2 < 100)
                    {
// calling this method will change the value of 'counter' only if
// it goes up a ladder or down a snake
                        counter2 =
                            board.checkForSnakesOrLadders(counter2);
                        System.out.println("Counter two on square " +
                            counter2);
                    }
            }
            if(counter1 == 100)
            {
                System.out.println("counter one wins!");
            }
            else
            {
                System.out.println("counter two wins!");
            }
        }
// 'main' creates a 'Snakes2' object and starts the game
        public static void main(String args[])
        {
            Snakes2 my_game = new Snakes2();
            my_game.playGame();
        }
}
```

# Chapter 7

## Exercise 2

This is the extra 'showStatistics' method

```
public void showStatistics()
{
    System.out.println("The vector capacity is " +
    card_list.capacity());
    if(card_list.isEmpty())
    {
        System.out.println("There are no cards in the container");
    }
    else
    {
        System.out.println("There are " + card_list.size() +
        " cards in the container");
    }
}
```

## Exercise 3

This 'StringSet' class includes a test 'main' that demonstrates that although the word 'Hello' is added twice, is only appears once in the object.

```
/**
        StringSet.java
        model answer to chapter 7, exercise 3
*/
import java.util.Vector;
public class StringSet
{
        private Vector string_set = new Vector(10);
        public void addString(String added)
        {
                if(!string_set.contains(added))
                {
                        string_set.addElement(added);
                }
        }
        public void showStrings()
        {
                System.out.println(string_set);
        }
        public static void main(String args[])
        {
                StringSet strings = new StringSet();
                strings.addString("Hello");
                strings.addString("there");
                strings.showStrings();
                strings.addString("Hello");
                strings.addString("banana");
                strings.showStrings();
        }
}
```

# Chapter 8

## Exercise 1

There are many different ways of creating the FlowLayout. This is just one example, that aligns the components to the left and puts 20 pixels between them in both directions.

```
setLayout(new FlowLayout(FlowLayout.LEFT, 20, 20));
```

## Exercise 2

This is the code for the window as it appears. To remove the scroll bars we have to use 'TextArea.SCROLLBARS_NONE' as the final parameter to the constructor

```
/**
        LayoutExercise.java
        model answer to chapter 8, exercise 2
*/
```

```
import java.awt.*;
public class LayoutExercise extends Frame
{
      public LayoutExercise()
      {
// set the layout manager
            setLayout(new FlowLayout(FlowLayout.RIGHT));
// create the components
            Label name_label = new Label("Name:");
            TextField text1 = new TextField(30);
            Label address_label = new Label("Address:");
            TextArea text2 = new TextArea(4, 30);
// add them to the frame
            add(name_label);
            add(text1);
            add(address_label);
            add(text2);
// add a window listener to close the window
            addWindowListener(new MainWindowListener());
      }
// test main method
      public static void main(String args[])
      {
            LayoutExercise layout = new LayoutExercise();
            layout.setTitle("Data Entry Form");
            layout.setBounds(100, 100, 350, 200);
            layout.show();
      }
}
```

# Chapter 9

## Exercise 1

The part of the class that writes the heading needs to be replaced with this code:

```
// a String reference to get each line from the BufferedReader
    String text_line;
// if the file successfully opened, we can read from it
    if(file_opened)
    {
// two different font objects are created. the title font is
// sans serif bold, 20 point
    Font title_font = new Font("SansSerif", Font.BOLD, 20);
// the font for the main text is serif italic, 15 point
    Font text_font = new Font("Serif", Font.ITALIC, 15);
// set the font using the 'setFont' method of the Graphics object
    g.setFont(title_font);
// read the title from the file and display it on the window,
// indented by 10 and 40 down from the title bar (this is the
// position of the base of the text, not the top)
            try
            {
// 'ready' will return 'true' if there is data to be read
                if(poem_reader.ready())
                {
```

```
// return a line of text as a String using the 'readLine' method
                        text_line = poem_reader.readLine();
// display the line
                        g.drawString(text_line, 10, 40);
                }
        }
        catch(IOException e)
        {
                g.drawString("no line available", 5, 35);
        }
        // etc. as before
```

## Exercise 2

This version of the file writer uses hard coded text. The '\n\r' is necessary to force a line feed and a carriage return in the file.

```
/**
        FileWrite.java
        Model answer to chapter 9, exercise 2
        write some text to a file
*/
import java.io.*;
public class FileWrite
{
        public static void main(String args[])
        {
                try
                {
// create a 'FileWriter' object associated with a file
                        FileWriter file = new FileWriter("text.txt");
// write three lines to the file
                        file.write("The cat\n\r");
                        file.write("sat on\n\r");
                        file.write("the mat\n\r");
// flush the FileWriter to send the data
                        file.flush();
                }
                catch(java.io.IOException e)
                {
                        System.out.println(e);
                }
        }
}
```

# Chapter 10

## Exercise 1

This is the 'Identifiable' interface:

```
/**
        Identifiable.java
        model answer to chapter 10, exercise 1
        the 'Identifiable' interface
*/
```

```
interface Identifiable
{
        public String className();
}
```

The 'StaffID2' class must implement this interface as well as extending 'IDCardBase'

```
public class StaffID2 extends IDCardBase implements Identifiable
```

It then provides its own implementation for the 'classname' method

```
public String className()
{
        return "StaffID2";
}
```

Likewise, 'VisitorID2' must implement 'Identifiable' and its method

```
public class VisitorID2 extends IDCardBase implements
Identifiable

public String className()
{
        return "VisitorID2";
}
```

This class tests the interface and the classes that implement it

```
/**
        TestIdentifiable.java
        testing the 'Identifiable' interface
*/
public class TestIdentifiable
{
        public static void main(String args[])
        {
                Identifiable i1 = new StaffID2("Mr.", 'A', "Java",
                        1, 1, 1998);
                Identifiable i2 = new VisitorID2("Mr.", 'X', "Ray");
                System.out.println(i1.className());
                System.out.println(i2.className());
        }
}
```

## Exercise 3

These classes are similar to the tortoise, hare and race classes in the chapter.

```
/**
        RaceHorse.java
        model answer to chapter 10, exercise 3
        a subclass of Thread
*/
```

```
public class RaceHorse extends Thread
{
// the constructor sets the name of the thread
      public RaceHorse(String name)
      {
            super(name);
      }
// the 'run' method displays the journey of the horse
      public void run()
      {
            System.out.println(getName() +
                  "has started the race");
            for(int i = 0; i < 5; i++)
            {
// a pause before the fence
                  try
                  {
                        sleep((long)Math.random() * 1000);
                  }
                  catch(InterruptedException e)
                  {
                        System.out.println("Interrupted");
                  }
                  System.out.println(getName() +
                        " is over fence " + i);
            }
// the finish line
            System.out.println(getName() + " has finished!");
      }
}

/**
      Steeplechase.java
      runs a race with several thread-based RaceHorse objects
*/
public class Steeplechase
{
      public static void main(String args[])
      {
            RaceHorse lightning = new RaceHorse("Lightning");
            RaceHorse thunder = new RaceHorse("Thunder");
            RaceHorse pegasus = new RaceHorse("Pegasus");
            lightning.start();
            thunder.start();
            pegasus.start();
      }
}
```

# Chapter 11

## Exercise 1

Only a few changes need to be made to the rock, paper, scissors class for it to work as a Applet (here called 'WebRockPaperScissors')

First, it needs to inherit from Applet and implement the 'ActionListener' interface

```
import java.applet.Applet;
public class WebRockPaperScissors extends Applet implements
ActionListener
{
      // etc.
```

The attributes are the same, but the constructor is replaced by an 'init' method:

```
public void init()
{
//etc.
```

In this method, we have to add the applet as the action listener to the 'play' button and provide an appropriate method to handle the event.

```
      play_button.addActionListener(this);
}
public void actionPerformed(ActionEvent e)
{
      if(e.getSource() == play_button)
      {
      // etc..
```

The rest of the class is basically the same as before.

# Glossary

**Applet** A Java program that runs remotely in a browser.

**Application** A Java program that runs locally under an operating system.

**Attribute** A property of an object. It may be a simple variable, a container or another object.

**AWT (Abstract Windowing Toolkit)** A set of classes that allow graphical user interfaces to be built in Java.

**Class** The definition of a particular type of object. The class defines the type of data that objects of that type can contain and the behaviours they can have.

**Event** An event occurs when an AWT component receives some message from the mouse or keyboard. A listener can be used to respond to these events. Graphical user interfaces are 'event driven' because they respond to events on their components such as a button being pressed.

**GIF (Graphics Information File)** A method for compressing images that can be displayed in applets. Applets can also display JPG files that use a different form of compression.

**HTML (Hyper Text Markup Language)** A syntax for creating pages that can be interpreted by browser software. The world wide web consists of HTML pages. From the point of view of Java, the most important aspect of an HTML page is the <APPLET> tag that allows an applet to be run.

**HTTP (Hyper Text Transfer Protocol)** The protocol used by HTML pages when displayed in a browser.

**JDK (Java Development Kit)** A collection of programs from Sun Microsystems that allows Java code to be developed and run. It includes the Java compiler ('javac') the Java Virtual Machine (JVM) the 'appletviewer' and the 'Javadoc' document generator (among other things).

**JVM (Java Virtual Machine)** The Java virtual machine runs Java programs that have been compiled into 'byte code' by the Java compiler. It is embedded inside Java-aware browsers so they can run applets in HTML pages.

**Listener** An object that responds to an event taking place in an AWT graphical user interface. Listeners respond to events such as mouse button clicks and window 'close' buttons being pressed.

**Method** A behaviour of an object. Sending a message to an object means using one of its public methods.

**Object** An instance of a class. An object can be sent messages and encapsulates data.

**Stream** A flow of data to or from a program. Input streams can come from the keyboard, files or over a network. Output streams can go to the screen, to files or be sent over a network.

**Thread** A thread of control that runs a single process. A Java program can have more than one thread running simultaneously.

**URL (Uniform Resource Locator)** Internet addresses are defined by IP (Internet protocol) numbers. Web servers also have text versions of their addresses (known as URLs) that are more easily remembered and used.

# Bibliography

These books and other materials were the primary sources for *Introductory Java*. However, there are so many Java books available that this should not be taken to mean that these are necessarily the best Java books, just the ones that I read that I found useful. There are many others equally good. *Java in a Nutshell* is mainly a reference book, listing all the Java classes and their methods with some commentary. Patrick Naughton's book (*The Java Handbook*) has the advantage of being written by the man who created the AWT, and includes a fascinating chapter on his experience of being a key member of the original Java team. James Gosling (who wrote much of the language) has also written a book.

*Java Gently* by Judy Bishop, Addison-Wesley, Harlow, 1997

*The Java Tutorial* by Mary Campione and Kathy Walrath, Addison-Wesley. As well as being published as a book, this tutorial is provided on Sun's web site at:

http://java.sun.com/docs/books/tutorial/index.html

There are many other materials available on this site.

*Principles of Object-Oriented Programming in Java 1.1* by James W. Cooper, Ventana, N.C., 1997

*Learn Java Now* by Stephen R. Davis, Microsoft Press, 1996

*Presenting Java* by John December, Sams.net, Indianapolis, 1995

*Java: How To Program* by Deitel and Deitel, Prentice Hall, 1996/7

*Java in a Nutshell* by David Flanagan, O'Reilly, Cambridge, 1996/7

*The Java Handbook* by Patrick Naughton, Osborne McGraw-Hill, Berkeley, 1996

*On To Java* by Patrick Winston and Sundar Narasimhan, Addison-Wesley, Reading, Mass. 1996

*I Ching, The Book of Change* by John Blofeld, Allen & Unwin, 1965

*Illustrating Computers* by Colin Day and Donald Alcock, Pan Books, 1982

In addition, the first and probably most important Java journal:

*Java Report*, SIGS Publications, New York

and this article:

'All That Java' by Jim Smith, *Personal Computer World*, February 1996 pp. 232–237
Of course there have been thousands of magazine articles about Java, but it was this one that got me interested in the first place.

# Index

KING ALFRED'S COLLEGE
LIBRARY